AN INDIGENOUS PEOPLES' HISTORY
OF THE UNITED STATES

PRAISE FOR
AN INDIGENOUS PEOPLES' HISTORY
OF THE UNITED STATES

"In this riveting book, Roxanne Dunbar-Ortiz decolonizes American history and illustrates definitively why the past is never very far from the present. Exploring the borderlands between action and narration—between what happened and what is said to have happened—Dunbar-Ortiz strips us of our forged innocence, shocks us into new awarenesses, and draws a straight line from the sins of our fathers—settler-colonialism, the doctrine of discovery, the myth of manifest destiny, white supremacy, theft, and systematic killing—to the contemporary condition of permanent war, invasion and occupation, mass incarceration, and the constant use and threat of state violence. Best of all, she points a way beyond amnesia, paralyzing guilt, or helplessness toward discovering our deepest humanity in a project of truth-telling and repair. *An Indigenous Peoples' History of the United States* will forever change the way we read history and understand our own responsibility to it."

—BILL AYERS

"Dunbar-Ortiz provides a historical analysis of the US colonial framework from the perspective of an Indigenous human rights advocate. Her assessment and conclusions are necessary tools for all Indigenous peoples seeking to address and remedy the legacy of US colonial domination that continues to subvert Indigenous human rights in today's globalized world."

—MILILANI B. TRASK, Native Hawai'ian international
law expert on Indigenous peoples' rights and former
Kia Aina (prime minister) of Ka La Hui Hawai'i

"Justice-seekers everywhere will celebrate Dunbar-Ortiz's unflinching commitment to truth—a truth that places settler-colonialism and genocide exactly where they belong: as foundational to the existence of the United States."

—WAZIYATAWIN, PhD, activist and author of
For Indigenous Minds Only: A Decolonization Handbook

"Roxanne Dunbar-Ortiz's *An Indigenous Peoples' History of the United States* is a fiercely honest, unwavering, and unprecedented statement, one that has never been attempted by any other historian or intellectual. The presentation of facts and arguments is clear and direct, unadorned by needless and pointless rhetoric, and there is an organic feel of intellectual solidity that provides weight and inspires trust. It is truly an Indigenous peoples' voice that gives Dunbar-Ortiz's book direction, purpose, and trustworthy intention. Without doubt, this crucially important book is required reading for everyone in the Americas!"

—SIMON J. ORTIZ, Regents Professor of English and
American Indian Studies, Arizona State University

AN
INDIGENOUS
PEOPLES'
HISTORY
OF THE
UNITED STATES

ROXANNE DUNBAR-ORTIZ

ReVisioning American History

BEACON PRESS BOSTON

BEACON PRESS
Boston, Massachusetts
www.beacon.org

Beacon Press books
are published under the auspices of
the Unitarian Universalist Association of Congregations.

18 17 16 15   8 7 6 5 4 3 2 1

Beacon Press's ReVisioning American History series consists of
accessibly written books by notable scholars that reconstruct
and reinterpret US history from diverse perspectives.

This book is printed on acid-free paper that meets the uncoated paper
ANSI/NISO specifications for permanence as revised in 1992.

Text design and composition by Wilsted & Taylor Publishing Services

Excerpts from Simon J. Ortiz's *from Sand Creek: Rising in This Heart
Which Is Our America* (Tucson: University of Arizona Press, 2000)
are reprinted here with permission.

LIBRARY OF CONGRESS CATALOGING-IN-PUBLICATION DATA
Dunbar-Ortiz, Roxanne.
An indigenous peoples' history of the United States / Roxanne Dunbar-Ortiz.
pages cm — (ReVisioning American history)
Includes bibliographical references and index.
ISBN 978-0-8070-5783-4 (paperback : alk. paper) —
ISBN 978-0-8070-0041-0 (ebook) 1. Indians of North America—Historiography.
2. Indians of North America—Colonization. 3. Indians, Treatment of—
United States—History. 4. United States—Colonization. 5. United States—
Race relations. 6. United States—Politics and government. I. Title.
E76.8.D86 2014
970.004'97— dc23   2013050262

TO

Howard Adams (1921–2001)

Vine Deloria Jr. (1933–2005)

Jack Forbes (1934–2011)

CONTENTS

AUTHOR'S NOTE

As a student of history, having completed a master's degree and PhD in the discipline, I am grateful for all I learned from my professors and from the thousands of texts I studied. But I did not gain the perspective presented in this book from those professors or studies. This came from outside the academy.

My mother was part Indian, most likely Cherokee, born in Joplin, Missouri. Unenrolled and orphaned, having lost her mother to tuberculosis at age four and with an Irish father who was itinerant and alcoholic, she grew up neglected and often homeless along with a younger brother. Picked up by authorities on the streets of Harrah, Oklahoma, the town to which their father had relocated the family, she was placed in foster homes where she was abused, expected to be a servant, and would run away. When she was sixteen, she met and married my father, of Scots-Irish settler heritage, eighteen, and a high school dropout who worked as a cowboy on a sprawling cattle ranch in the Osage Nation. I was the last of their four children. As a sharecropper family in Canadian County, Oklahoma, we moved from one cabin to another. I grew up in the midst of rural Native communities in the former treaty territory of the Southern Cheyenne and Arapaho Nations that had been allotted and opened to settlers in the late nineteenth century. Nearby was the federal Indian boarding school at Concho. Strict segregation ruled among the Black, white, and Indian towns, churches, and schools in Oklahoma, and I had little interchange with Native people. My mother was ashamed of being part Indian. She died of alcoholism.

In California during the 1960s, I was active in the civil rights, anti-apartheid, anti–Vietnam War, and women's liberation movements, and ultimately, the pan-Indian movement that some labeled

Red Power. I was recruited to work on Native issues in 1970 by the remarkable Tuscarora traditionalist organizer Mad Bear Anderson, who insisted that I must embrace my Native heritage, however fragile it might be. Although hesitant at first, following the Wounded Knee siege of 1973 I began to work—locally, around the country, and internationally—with the American Indian Movement and the International Indian Treaty Council. I also began serving as an expert witness in court cases, including that of the Wounded Knee defendants, bringing me into discussions with Lakota Sioux elders and activists. Based in San Francisco during that volatile and historic period, I completed my doctorate in history in 1974 and then took a position teaching in a new Native American studies program. My dissertation was on the history of land tenure in New Mexico, and during 1978–1981 I was visiting director of Native American studies at the University of New Mexico. There I worked collaboratively with the All Indian Pueblo Council, Mescalero Apache Nation, Navajo Nation, and the Dinébe'iiná Náhiiłna be Agha'diit'ahii (DNA) People's Legal Services, as well as with Native students, faculty, and communities, in developing a research institute and a seminar training program in economic development.

I have lived with this book for six years, starting over a dozen times before I settled on a narrative thread. Invited to write this ReVisioning American History series title, I was given parameters: it was to be intellectually rigorous but relatively brief and written accessibly so it would engage multiple audiences. I had grave misgivings after having agreed to this ambitious project. Although it was to be a history of the United States as experienced by the Indigenous inhabitants, how could I possibly do justice to that varied experience over a span of two centuries? How could I make it comprehensible to the general reader who would likely have little knowledge of Native American history on the one hand, but might consciously or unconsciously have a set narrative of US history on the other? Since I was convinced of the inherent importance of the project, I persisted, reading or rereading books and articles by North American Indigenous scholars, novelists, and poets, as well as unpublished dissertations, speeches, and testimonies, truly an extraordinary body of work.

I've come to realize that a new periodization of US history is needed that traces the Indigenous experience as opposed to the following standard division: Colonial, Revolutionary, Jacksonian, Civil War and Reconstruction, Industrial Revolution and Gilded Age, Overseas Imperialism, Progressivism, World War I, Depression, New Deal, World War II, Cold War, and Vietnam War, followed by contemporary decades. I altered this periodization to better reflect Indigenous experience but not as radically as needs to be done. This is an issue much discussed in current Native American scholarship.

I also wanted to set aside the rhetoric of race, not because race and racism are unimportant but to emphasize that Native peoples were colonized and deposed of their territories as distinct peoples—hundreds of nations—not as a racial or ethnic group. "Colonization," "dispossession," "settler colonialism," "genocide"—these are the terms that drill to the core of US history, to the very source of the country's existence.

The charge of genocide, once unacceptable by establishment academic and political classes when applied to the United States, has gained currency as evidence of it has mounted, but it is too often accompanied by an assumption of disappearance. So I realized it was crucial to make the reality and significance of Indigenous peoples' survival clear throughout the book. Indigenous survival as peoples is due to centuries of resistance and storytelling passed through the generations, and I sought to demonstrate that this survival is dynamic, not passive. Surviving genocide, by whatever means, *is* resistance: non-Indians must know this in order to more accurately understand the history of the United States.

My hope is that this book will be a springboard to dialogue about history, the present reality of Indigenous peoples' experience, and the meaning and future of the United States itself.

A note on terminology: I use "Indigenous," "Indian," and "Native" interchangeably in the text. Indigenous individuals and peoples in North America on the whole do not consider "Indian" a slur. Of course, all citizens of Native nations much prefer that their nations' names in their own language be used, such as Diné (Navajo), Haudenosaunee (Iroquois), Tsalagi (Cherokee), and Anishinaabe (Ojibway,

Chippewa). I have used some of the correct names combined with more familiar usages, such as "Sioux" and "Navajo." Except in material that is quoted, I don't use the term "tribe." "Community," "people," and "nation" are used instead and interchangeably. I also refrain from using "America" and "American" when referring only to the United States and its citizens. Those blatantly imperialistic terms annoy people in the rest of the Western Hemisphere, who are, after all, also Americans. I use "United States" as a noun and "US" as an adjective to refer to the country and "US Americans" for its citizens.

THIS LAND

We are here to educate, not forgive.
We are here to enlighten, not accuse.

—Willie Johns, Brighton Seminole Reservation, Florida

Under the crust of that portion of Earth called the United States of America—"from California . . . to the Gulf Stream waters"—are interred the bones, villages, fields, and sacred objects of American Indians.[1] They cry out for their stories to be heard through their descendants who carry the memories of how the country was founded and how it came to be as it is today.

It should not have happened that the great civilizations of the Western Hemisphere, the very *evidence* of the Western Hemisphere, were wantonly destroyed, the gradual progress of humanity interrupted and set upon a path of greed and destruction.[2] Choices were made that forged that path toward destruction of life itself—the moment in which we now live and die as our planet shrivels, overheated. To learn and know this history is both a necessity and a responsibility to the ancestors and descendants of all parties.

What historian David Chang has written about the land that became Oklahoma applies to the whole United States: "Nation, race, and class converged in land."[3] Everything in US history is about the land—who oversaw and cultivated it, fished its waters, maintained its wildlife; who invaded and stole it; how it became a commodity ("real estate") broken into pieces to be bought and sold on the market.

US policies and actions related to Indigenous peoples, though

1

often termed "racist" or "discriminatory," are rarely depicted as what they are: classic cases of imperialism and a particular form of colonialism—settler colonialism. As anthropologist Patrick Wolfe writes, "The question of genocide is never far from discussions of settler colonialism. Land is life—or, at least, land is necessary for life."[4]

The history of the United States is a history of settler colonialism—the founding of a state based on the ideology of white supremacy, the widespread practice of African slavery, and a policy of genocide and land theft. Those who seek history with an upbeat ending, a history of redemption and reconciliation, may look around and observe that such a conclusion is not visible, not even in utopian dreams of a better society.

Writing US history from an Indigenous peoples' perspective requires rethinking the consensual national narrative. That narrative is wrong or deficient, not in its facts, dates, or details but rather in its essence. Inherent in the myth we've been taught is an embrace of settler colonialism and genocide. The myth persists, not for a lack of free speech or poverty of information but rather for an absence of motivation to ask questions that challenge the core of the scripted narrative of the origin story. How might acknowledging the reality of US history work to transform society? That is the central question this book pursues.

Teaching Native American studies, I always begin with a simple exercise. I ask students to quickly draw a rough outline of the United States at the time it gained independence from Britain. Invariably most draw the approximate present shape of the United States from the Atlantic to the Pacific—the continental territory not fully appropriated until a century after independence. What became independent in 1783 were the thirteen British colonies hugging the Atlantic shore. When called on this, students are embarrassed because they know better. I assure them that they are not alone. I call this a Rorschach test of unconscious "manifest destiny," embedded in the minds of nearly everyone in the United States and around the world. This test reflects the seeming inevitability of US extent and power, its destiny, with an implication that the continent had previously been *terra nullius,* a land without people.

Woody Guthrie's "This Land Is Your Land" celebrates that the land belongs to everyone, reflecting the unconscious manifest destiny we live with. But the extension of the United States from sea to shining sea was the intention and design of the country's founders. "Free" land was the magnet that attracted European settlers. Many were slave owners who desired limitless land for lucrative cash crops. After the war for independence but preceding the writing of the US Constitution, the Continental Congress produced the Northwest Ordinance. This was the first law of the incipient republic, revealing the motive for those desiring independence. It was the blueprint for gobbling up the British-protected Indian Territory ("Ohio Country") on the other side of the Appalachians and Alleghenies. Britain had made settlement there illegal with the Proclamation of 1763.

In 1801, President Jefferson aptly described the new settler-state's intentions for horizontal and vertical continental expansion, stating: "However our present interests may restrain us within our own limits, it is impossible not to look forward to distant times, when our rapid multiplication will expand itself beyond those limits and cover the whole northern, if not the southern continent, with a people speaking the same language, governed in similar form by similar laws." This vision of manifest destiny found form a few years later in the Monroe Doctrine, signaling the intention of annexing or dominating former Spanish colonial territories in the Americas and the Pacific, which would be put into practice during the rest of the century.

Origin narratives form the vital core of a people's unifying identity and of the values that guide them. In the United States, the founding and development of the Anglo-American settler-state involves a narrative about Puritan settlers who had a covenant with God to take the land. That part of the origin story is supported and reinforced by the Columbus myth and the "Doctrine of Discovery." According to a series of late-fifteenth-century papal bulls, European nations acquired title to the lands they "discovered" and the Indigenous inhabitants lost their natural right to that land after Europeans arrived and claimed it.[5] As law professor Robert A. Williams observes about the Doctrine of Discovery:

Responding to the requirements of a paradoxical age of Renaissance and Inquisition, the West's first modern discourses of conquest articulated a vision of all humankind united under a rule of law discoverable solely by human reason. Unfortunately for the American Indian, the West's first tentative steps towards this noble vision of a Law of Nations contained a mandate for Europe's subjugation of all peoples whose radical divergence from European-derived norms of right conduct signified their need for conquest and remediation.[6]

The Columbus myth suggests that from US independence onward, colonial settlers saw themselves as part of a world system of colonization. "Columbia," the poetic, Latinate name used in reference to the United States from its founding throughout the nineteenth century, was based on the name of Christopher Columbus. The "Land of Columbus" was—and still is—represented by the image of a woman in sculptures and paintings, by institutions such as Columbia University, and by countless place names, including that of the national capital, the District of Columbia.[7] The 1798 hymn "Hail, Columbia" was the early national anthem and is now used whenever the vice president of the United States makes a public appearance, and Columbus Day is still a federal holiday despite Columbus never having set foot on the continent claimed by the United States.

Traditionally, historians of the United States hoping to have successful careers in academia and to author lucrative school textbooks became protectors of this origin myth. With the cultural upheavals in the academic world during the 1960s, engendered by the civil rights movement and student activism, historians came to call for objectivity and fairness in revising interpretations of US history. They warned against moralizing, urging instead a dispassionate and culturally relative approach. Historian Bernard Sheehan, in an influential essay, called for a "cultural conflict" understanding of Native–Euro-American relations in the early United States, writing that this approach "diffuses the locus of guilt."[8] In striving for "balance," however, historians spouted platitudes: "There were good and bad people on both sides." "American culture is an amalgamation of all its ethnic groups." "A frontier is a zone of interaction between cultures, not merely advancing European settlements."

Later, trendy postmodernist studies insisted on Indigenous "agency" under the guise of individual and collective empowerment, making the casualties of colonialism responsible for their own demise. Perhaps worst of all, some claimed (and still claim) that the colonizer and colonized experienced an "encounter" and engaged in "dialogue," thereby masking reality with justifications and rationalizations—in short, apologies for one-sided robbery and murder. In focusing on "cultural change" and "conflict between cultures," these studies avoid fundamental questions about the formation of the United States and its implications for the present and future. This approach to history allows one to safely put aside present responsibility for continued harm done by that past and the questions of reparations, restitution, and reordering society.[9]

Multiculturalism became the cutting edge of post-civil-rights-movement US history revisionism. For this scheme to work—and affirm US historical progress—Indigenous nations and communities had to be left out of the picture. As territorially and treaty-based peoples in North America, they did not fit the grid of multiculturalism but were included by transforming them into an inchoate oppressed racial group, while colonized Mexican Americans and Puerto Ricans were dissolved into another such group, variously called "Hispanic" or "Latino." The multicultural approach emphasized the "contributions" of individuals from oppressed groups to the country's assumed greatness. Indigenous peoples were thus credited with corn, beans, buckskin, log cabins, parkas, maple syrup, canoes, hundreds of place names, Thanksgiving, and even the concepts of democracy and federalism. But this idea of the gift-giving Indian helping to establish and enrich the development of the United States is an insidious smoke screen meant to obscure the fact that the very existence of the country is a result of the looting of an entire continent and its resources. The fundamental unresolved issues of Indigenous lands, treaties, and sovereignty could not but scuttle the premises of multiculturalism.

With multiculturalism, manifest destiny won the day. As an example, in 1994, Prentice Hall (part of Pearson Education) published a new college-level US history textbook, authored by four members of a new generation of revisionist historians. These radical social historians are all brilliant scholars with posts in prestigious universities. The book's title reflects the intent of its authors and publisher: *Out of Many: A History of the American People*. The origin story of a supposedly unitary nation, albeit now multicultural, remained intact. The original cover design featured a multicolored woven fabric—this image meant to stand in place of the discredited "melting pot." Inside, facing the title page, was a photograph of a Navajo woman, dressed formally in velvet and adorned with heavy sterling silver and turquoise jewelry. With a traditional Navajo dwelling, a hogan, in the background, the woman was shown kneeling in front of a traditional loom, weaving a nearly finished rug. The design? The Stars and Stripes! The authors, upon hearing my objection and explanation that Navajo weavers make their livings off commissioned work that includes the desired design, responded: "But it's a real photograph." To the authors' credit, in the second edition they replaced the cover photograph and removed the Navajo picture inside, although the narrative text remains unchanged.

Awareness of the settler-colonialist context of US history writing is essential if one is to avoid the laziness of the default position and the trap of a mythological unconscious belief in manifest destiny. The form of colonialism that the Indigenous peoples of North America have experienced was modern from the beginning: the expansion of European corporations, backed by government armies, into foreign areas, with subsequent expropriation of lands and resources. Settler colonialism is a genocidal policy. Native nations and communities, while struggling to maintain fundamental values and collectivity, have from the beginning resisted modern colonialism using both defensive and offensive techniques, including the modern forms of armed resistance of national liberation movements and what now is called terrorism. In every instance they have fought for survival as peoples. The objective of US colonialist authorities was to terminate their existence as peoples—not as random individuals. This is the very definition of modern genocide as contrasted with premodern instances of extreme violence that did not have the goal of extinction. The United States as a socioeconomic and political entity is a result of this centuries-long and ongoing colonial process.

Today's Indigenous nations and communities are societies formed by their resistance to colonialism, through which they have carried their practices and histories. It is breathtaking, but no miracle, that they have survived as peoples.

To say that the United States is a colonialist settler-state is not to make an accusation but rather to face historical reality, without which consideration not much in US history makes sense, unless Indigenous peoples are erased. But Indigenous nations, through resistance, have survived and bear witness to this history. In the era of worldwide decolonization in the second half of the twentieth century, the former colonial powers and their intellectual apologists mounted a counterforce, often called neocolonialism, from which multiculturalism and postmodernism emerged. Although much revisionist US history reflects neocolonialist strategy—an attempt to accommodate new realities in order to retain the dominance— neocolonialist methods signal victory for the colonized. Such approaches pry off a lid long kept tightly fastened. One result has been the presence of significant numbers of Indigenous scholars in US universities who are changing the terms of analysis. The main challenge for scholars in revising US history in the context of colonialism is not lack of information, nor is it one of methodology. Certainly difficulties with documentation are no more problematic than they are in any other area of research. Rather, the source of the problems has been the refusal or inability of US historians to comprehend the nature of their own history, US history. The fundamental problem is the absence of the colonial framework.

Through economic penetration of Indigenous societies, the European and Euro-American colonial powers created economic dependency and imbalance of trade, then incorporated the Indigenous nations into spheres of influence and controlled them indirectly or as protectorates, with indispensable use of Christian missionaries and alcohol. In the case of US settler colonialism, land was the primary commodity. With such obvious indicators of colonialism at work, why should so many interpretations of US political-economic development be convoluted and obscure, avoiding the obvious? To some extent, the twentieth-century emergence of the field of "US

West" or "Borderlands" history has been forced into an incomplete and flawed settler-colonialist framework. The father of that field of history, Frederick Jackson Turner, confessed as much in 1901: "Our colonial system did not start with the Spanish War [1898]; the U.S. had had a colonial history and policy from the beginning of the Republic; but they have been hidden under the phraseology of 'interstate migration' and 'territorial organization.'"[10]

Settler colonialism, as an institution or system, requires violence or the threat of violence to attain its goals. People do not hand over their land, resources, children, and futures without a fight, and that fight is met with violence. In employing the force necessary to accomplish its expansionist goals, a colonizing regime institutionalizes violence. The notion that settler-indigenous conflict is an inevitable product of cultural differences and misunderstandings, or that violence was committed equally by the colonized and the colonizer, blurs the nature of the historical processes. Euro-American colonialism, an aspect of the capitalist economic globalization, had from its beginnings a genocidal tendency.

The term "genocide" was coined following the Shoah, or Holocaust, and its prohibition was enshrined in the United Nations convention adopted in 1948: the UN Convention on the Prevention and Punishment of the Crime of Genocide. The convention is not retroactive but is applicable to US-Indigenous relations since 1988, when the US Senate ratified it. The terms of the genocide convention are also useful tools for historical analysis of the effects of colonialism in any era. In the convention, any one of five acts is considered genocide if "committed with intent to destroy, in whole or in part, a national, ethnical, racial or religious group":

> killing members of the group;
> causing serious bodily or mental harm to members of the group;
> deliberately inflicting on the group conditions of life
>   calculated to bring about its physical destruction in whole
>   or in part;
> imposing measures intended to prevent births within the
>   group;
> forcibly transferring children of the group to another group.[11]

In the 1990s, the term "ethnic cleansing" became a useful descriptive term for genocide.

US history, as well as inherited Indigenous trauma, cannot be understood without dealing with the genocide that the United States committed against Indigenous peoples. From the colonial period through the founding of the United States and continuing in the twentieth century, this has entailed torture, terror, sexual abuse, massacres, systematic military occupations, removals of Indigenous peoples from their ancestral territories, and removals of Indigenous children to military-like boarding schools. The absence of even the slightest note of regret or tragedy in the annual celebration of the US independence betrays a deep disconnect in the consciousness of US Americans.

Settler colonialism is inherently genocidal in terms of the genocide convention. In the case of the British North American colonies and the United States, not only extermination and removal were practiced but also the disappearing of the prior existence of Indigenous peoples—and this continues to be perpetuated in local histories. Anishinaabe (Ojibwe) historian Jean O'Brien names this practice of writing Indians out of existence "firsting and lasting." All over the continent, local histories, monuments, and signage narrate the story of first settlement: the founder(s), the first school, first dwelling, first everything, as if there had never been occupants who thrived in those places before Euro-Americans. On the other hand, the national narrative tells of "last" Indians or last tribes, such as "the last of the Mohicans," "Ishi, the last Indian," and *End of the Trail*, as a famous sculpture by James Earle Fraser is titled.[12]

Documented policies of genocide on the part of US administrations can be identified in at least four distinct periods: the Jacksonian era of forced removal; the California gold rush in Northern California; the post–Civil War era of the so-called Indian wars in the Great Plains; and the 1950s termination period, all of which are discussed in the following chapters. Cases of genocide carried out as policy may be found in historical documents as well as in the oral histories of Indigenous communities. An example from 1873 is typical, with General William T. Sherman writing, "We must act with vindictive earnestness against the Sioux, even to their extermination, men, women and children . . . during an assault, the soldiers can not pause to distinguish between male and female, or even discriminate as to age."[13] As Patrick Wolfe has noted, the peculiarity of settler colonialism is that the goal is elimination of Indigenous populations in order to make land available to settlers. That project is not limited to government policy, but rather involves all kinds of agencies, voluntary militias, and the settlers themselves acting on their own.[14]

In the wake of the US 1950s termination and relocation policies, a pan-Indigenous movement arose in tandem with the powerful African American civil rights movement and the broad-based social justice and antiwar movements of the 1960s. The Indigenous rights movement succeeded in reversing the US termination policy. However, repression, armed attacks, and legislative attempts to undo treaty rights began again in the late 1970s, giving rise to the international Indigenous movement, which greatly broadened the support for Indigenous sovereignty and territorial rights in the United States.

The early twenty-first century has seen increased exploitation of energy resources begetting new pressures on Indigenous lands. Exploitation by the largest corporations, often in collusion with politicians at local, state, and federal levels, and even within some Indigenous governments, could spell a final demise for Indigenous land bases and resources. Strengthening Indigenous sovereignty and self-determination to prevent that result will take general public outrage and demand, which in turn will require that the general population, those descended from settlers and immigrants, know their history and assume responsibility. Resistance to these powerful corporate forces continues to have profound implications for US socioeconomic and political development and the future.

There are more than five hundred federally recognized Indigenous communities and nations, comprising nearly three million people in the United States. These are the descendants of the fifteen million original inhabitants of the land, the majority of whom were farmers who lived in towns. The US establishment of a system of

Indian reservations stemmed from a long British colonial practice in the Americas. In the era of US treaty-making from independence to 1871, the concept of the reservation was one of the Indigenous nation reserving a narrowed land base from a much larger one in exchange for US government protection from settlers and the provision of social services. In the late nineteenth century, as Indigenous resistance was weakened, the concept of the reservation changed to one of land being carved out of the public domain of the United States as a benevolent gesture, a "gift" to the Indigenous peoples. Rhetoric changed so that reservations were said to have been "given" or "created" for Indians. With this shift, Indian reservations came to be seen as enclaves within state' boundaries. Despite the political and economic reality, the impression to many was that Indigenous people were taking a free ride on public domain.

Beyond the land bases within the limits of the 310 federally recognized reservations—among 554 Indigenous groups—Indigenous land, water, and resource rights extend to all federally acknowledged Indigenous communities within the borders of the United States. This is the case whether "within the original or subsequently acquired territory thereof, and whether within or without the limits of a state," and includes all allotments as well as rights-of-way running to and from them.[15] Not all the federally recognized Indigenous nations have land bases beyond government buildings, and the lands of some Native nations, including those of the Sioux in the Dakotas and Minnesota and the Ojibwes in Minnesota, have been parceled into multiple reservations, while some fifty Indigenous nations that had been removed to Oklahoma were entirely allotted—divided by the federal government into individual Native-owned parcels. Attorney Walter R. Echo-Hawk writes:

> In 1881, Indian landholdings in the United States had plummeted to 156 million acres. By 1934, only about 50 million acres remained (an area the size of Idaho and Washington) as a result of the General Allotment Act of 1887. During World War II, the government took 500,000 more acres for military use. Over one hundred tribes, bands, and Rancherias

relinquished their lands under various acts of Congress during the termination era of the 1950s. By 1955, the indigenous land base had shrunk to just 2.3 percent of its original size.[16]

As a result of federal land sales, seizures, and allotments, most reservations are severely fragmented. Each parcel of tribal, trust, and privately held land is a separate enclave under multiple laws and jurisdictions. The Diné (Navajo) Nation has the largest contemporary contiguous land base among Native nations: nearly sixteen million acres, or nearly twenty-five thousand square miles, the size of West Virginia. Each of twelve other reservations is larger than Rhode Island, which comprises nearly eight hundred thousand acres, or twelve hundred square miles, and each of nine other reservations is larger than Delaware, which covers nearly a million and a half acres, or two thousand square miles. Other reservations have land bases of fewer than thirty-two thousand acres, or fifty square miles.[17] A number of independent nation-states with seats in the United Nations have less territory and smaller populations than some Indigenous nations of North America.

Following World War II, the United States was at war with much of the world, just as it was at war with the Indigenous peoples of North America in the nineteenth century. This was total war, demanding that the enemy surrender unconditionally or face annihilation. Perhaps it was inevitable that the earlier wars against Indigenous peoples, if not acknowledged and repudiated, ultimately would include the world. According to the origin narrative, the United States was born of rebellion against oppression—against empire—and thus is the product of the first anticolonial revolution for national liberation. The narrative flows from that fallacy: the broadening and deepening of democracy; the Civil War and the ensuing "second revolution," which ended slavery; the twentieth-century mission to save Europe from itself—twice; and the ultimately triumphant fight against the scourge of communism, with the United States inheriting the difficult and burdensome task of keeping order in the world. It's a narrative of progress. The 1960s social revolutions, ignited by the African American liberation movement, complicated the origin narrative, but its structure and periodization have been left intact. After the 1960s, historians incorporated women, African Americans, and immigrants as contributors to the commonweal. Indeed, the revised narrative produced the "nation of immigrants" framework, which obscures the US practice of colonization, merging settler colonialism with immigration to metropolitan centers during and after the industrial revolution. Native peoples, to the extent that they were included at all, were renamed "First Americans" and thus themselves cast as distant immigrants.

The provincialism and national chauvinism of US history production make it difficult for effective revisions to gain authority. Scholars, both Indigenous and a few non-Indigenous, who attempt to rectify the distortions, are labeled advocates, and their findings are rejected for publication on that basis. Indigenous scholars look to research and thinking that has emerged in the rest of the European-colonized world. To understand the historical and current experiences of Indigenous peoples in the United States, these thinkers and writers draw upon and creatively apply the historical materialism of Marxism, the liberation theology of Latin America, Frantz Fanon's psychosocial analyses of the effects of colonialism on the colonizer and the colonized, and other approaches, including development theory and postmodern theory. While not abandoning insights gained from those sources, due to the "exceptional" nature of US colonialism among nineteenth-century colonial powers, Indigenous scholars and activists are engaged in exploring new approaches.

This book claims to be a history of the United States from an Indigenous peoples' perspective but there is no such thing as a collective Indigenous peoples' perspective, just as there is no monolithic Asian or European or African peoples' perspective. This is not a history of the vast civilizations and communities that thrived and survived between the Gulf of Mexico and Canada and between the Atlantic Ocean and the Pacific. Such histories have been written, and are being written by historians of Diné, Lakota, Mohawk, Tlingit, Muskogee, Anishinaabe, Lumbee, Inuit, Kiowa, Cherokee, Hopi, and other Indigenous communities and nations that have survived colonial genocide. This book attempts to tell the story of the United States as a colonialist settler-state, one that, like colonialist European states, crushed and subjugated the original civilizations in the territories it now rules. Indigenous peoples, now in a colonial relationship with the United States, inhabited and thrived for millennia before they were displaced to fragmented reservations and economically decimated.

This is a history of the United States.

ONE

FOLLOW THE CORN

Carrying their flints and torches, Native Americans
were living in balance with Nature—
but they had their thumbs on the scale.

—Charles C. Mann, *1491*

Humanoids existed on Earth for around four million years as hunters and gatherers living in small communal groups that through their movements found and populated every continent. Some two hundred thousand years ago, human societies, having originated in Sub-Saharan Africa, began migrating in all directions, and their descendants eventually populated the globe. Around twelve thousand years ago, some of these people began staying put and developed agriculture—mainly women who domesticated wild plants and began cultivating others.

As a birthplace of agriculture and the towns and cities that followed, America is ancient, not a "new world." Domestication of plants took place around the globe in seven locales during approximately the same period, around 8500 BC. Three of the seven were in the Americas, all based on corn: the Valley of Mexico and Central America (Mesoamerica); the South-Central Andes in South America; and eastern North America. The other early agricultural centers were the Tigris-Euphrates and Nile River systems, Sub-Saharan Africa, the Yellow River of northern China, and the Yangtze River of southern China. During this time, many of the same human societies began domesticating animals. Only in the American continents was the parallel domestication of animals eschewed in favor of game management, a kind of animal husbandry different from that developed in Africa and Asia. In these seven areas, agriculture-based "civilized" societies developed in symbiosis with hunting, fishing, and gathering peoples on their peripheries, gradually enveloping many of the latter into the realms of their civilizations, except for those in regions inhospitable to agriculture.

THE SACRED CORN FOOD

Indigenous American agriculture was based on corn. Traces of cultivated corn have been identified in central Mexico dating back ten thousand years. Twelve to fourteen centuries later, corn production had spread throughout the temperate and tropical Americas from the southern tip of South America to the subarctic of North America, and from the Pacific to the Atlantic Ocean on both continents. The wild grain from which corn was cultivated has never been identified with certainty, but the Indigenous peoples for whom corn was and is their sustenance believe it was a sacred gift from their gods. Since there is no evidence of corn on any other continent prior to its post-Columbus dispersal, its development is a unique invention of the original American agriculturalists. Unlike most grains, corn cannot grow wild and cannot exist without attentive human care.

Along with multiple varieties and colors of corn, Mesoamericans cultivated squash and beans, which were extended throughout the hemisphere, as were the many varieties and colors of potato cultivated by Andean farmers beginning more than seven thousand years ago. Corn, being a summer crop, can tolerate no more than twenty to thirty days without water and even less time in high temperatures. Many of the areas where corn was the staple were arid or semiarid, so its cultivation required the design and construction of complex irrigation systems—in place at least two thousand years before Europeans knew the Americas existed. The proliferation of agriculture and cultigens could not have occurred without centuries of cultural and commercial interchange among the peoples of North, Central, and South America, whose traders carried seeds as well as other goods and cultural practices.

The vast reach and capacity of Indigenous grain production impressed colonialist Europeans. A traveler in French-occupied North America related in 1669 that six square miles of cornfields surrounded each Iroquois village. The governor of New France, following a military raid in the 1680s, reported that he had destroyed more than a million bushels (forty-two thousand tons) of corn belonging to four Iroquois villages.[1] Thanks to the nutritious triad of corn, beans, and squash—which provide a complete protein—the Americas were densely populated when the European monarchies began sponsoring colonization projects there.

The total population of the hemisphere was about one hundred million at the end of the fifteenth century, with about two-fifths in North America, including Mexico. Central Mexico alone supported some thirty million people. At the same time, the population of Europe as far east as the Ural Mountains was around fifty million. Experts have observed that such population densities in precolonial America were supportable because the peoples had created a relatively disease-free paradise.[2] There certainly were diseases and health problems, but the practice of herbal medicine and even surgery and dentistry, and most importantly both hygienic and ritual bathing, kept diseases at bay. Settler observers in all parts of the Americas marveled at the frequent bathing even in winter in cold climates. One commented that the Native people "go to the river and plunge in and wash themselves before they dress daily." Another wrote: "Men, women, and children, from early infancy, are in the habit of bathing." Ritual sweat baths were common to all Native North Americans, having originated in Mexico.[3] Above all, the majority of the Indigenous peoples of the Americas had healthy, mostly vegetarian diets based on the staple of corn and supplemented by wild fish, fowl, and four-legged animals. People lived long and well with abundant ceremonial and recreational periods.

UP FROM MEXICO

As on the two other major continental landmasses—Eurasia and Africa—civilization in the Americas emerged from certain population centers, with periods of vigorous growth and integration interspersed with periods of decline and disintegration. At least a dozen such centers were functioning in the Americas when Europeans intervened. Although this is a history of the part of North America that is today the United States, it is important to follow the corn to its origins and briefly consider the peoples' history of the Valley of Mexico and Central America, often called Mesoamerica. Influences from the south powerfully shaped the Indigenous peoples to the north (in what is now the United States) and Mexicans continue to migrate as they have for millennia but now across the arbitrary border that was established in the US war against Mexico in 1846–48.

The first great cultivators of corn were the Mayans, initially centered in present-day northern Guatemala and the Mexican state of Tabasco. Extending to the Yucatán peninsula, the Mayans of the tenth century built city-states—Chichen-Itzá, Mayapán, Uxmal, and many others—as far south as Belize and Honduras. Mayan villages, farms, and cities extended from tropical forests to alpine areas to coastal and interior plains. During the five-century apex of Mayan civilization, a combined priesthood and nobility governed. There was also a distinct commercial class, and the cities were densely populated, not simply bureaucratic or religious centers. Ordinary Mayan villages in the far-flung region retained fundamental features of clan structures and communal social relations. They worked the nobles' fields, paid rent for use of land, and contributed labor and taxes to the building of roads, temples, nobles' houses, and other structures. It is not clear whether these relations were exploitative or cooperatively developed. However, the nobility drew servants from groups such as war prisoners, accused criminals, debtors, and even orphans. Although servile status was not hereditary, this was forced labor. Increasingly burdensome exploitation of labor and higher taxes and tribute produced dissension and uprisings, resulting in the collapse of the Mayan state, from which decentralized polities emerged.

Mayan culture astonishes all who study it, and it is often compared to Greek (Athenian) culture. At its core was the cultivation of corn; religion was constructed around this vital food. The Mayan people developed art, architecture, sculpture, and painting, employing a variety of materials, including gold and silver, which they mined and used for jewelry and sculpture, not for use as currency. Surrounded by rubber trees, they invented the rubber ball and court ball games similar to modern soccer. Their achievements in mathematics and astronomy are the most impressive. By 36 BC they had developed the concept of zero. They worked with numbers in the hundreds of millions and used extensive dating systems, making possible both their observations of the cosmos and their unique calendar that marked the passage of time into the future. Modern astronomers have marveled at the accuracy of Mayan charts of the movements of the moon and planets, which were used to predict eclipses and other events. Mayan culture and science, as well as governmental and economic practices, were influential throughout the region.

During the same period of Mayan development, the Olmec civilization reigned in the Valley of Mexico and built the grand metropolis of Teotihuacán. Beginning in AD 750, Toltec civilization dominated the region for four centuries, absorbing the Olmecs. Colossal buildings, sculptures, and markets made up the Toltec cities, which housed extensive libraries and universities. They created multiple cities, the largest being Tula. The Toltecs' written language was based on the Mayan form, as was the calendar they used in scientific research, particularly in astronomy and medicine. Another nation in the Valley of Mexico, the Culhua, built the city-state of Culhuacán on the southern shore of Lake Texcoco, as well as the city-state of Texcoco on the eastern shore of the lake. In the late fourteenth century, the Tepanec people rose in an expansionist drive and subjugated Culhuacán, Texcoco, and all their subject peoples in the Valley of Mexico. They proceeded to conquer Tenochtitlán, which was located on an island in the middle of the immense Lake Texcoco and had been built around 1325 by the Nahuatl-speaking Aztecs who had migrated from northern Mexico (today's Utah). The Aztecs had entered the valley in the twelfth century and been involved in toppling the Toltecs.[4]

In 1426, the Aztecs of Tenochtitlán formed an alliance with the Texcoco and Tlacopan peoples and overthrew Tepanec rule. The allies proceeded to wage war against neighboring peoples and eventually succeeded in gaining control over the Valley of Mexico. The

Aztecs emerged as dominant in the Triple Alliance and moved to bring all the peoples of Mexico under their tributary authority. These events paralleled ones in Europe and Asia during the same period, when Rome and other city-states were demolished and occupied by invading Germanic peoples, while the Mongols of the Eurasian steppe overran much of Russia and China. As in Europe and Asia, the invading peoples assimilated and reproduced civilization.

The economic basis for the powerful Aztec state was hydraulic agriculture, with corn as the central crop. Beans, pumpkins, tomatoes, cocoa, and many other food crops flourished and supported a dense population, much of it concentrated in large urban centers. The Aztecs also grew tobacco and cotton, the latter providing the fiber for all cloth and clothing. Weaving and metalwork flourished, providing useful commodities as well as works of art. Building techniques enabled construction of enormous stone dams and canals, as well as fortress-like castles made of brick or stone. There were elaborate markets in each city and a far-flung trade network that used routes established by the Toltecs.

Aztec merchants acquired turquoise from Pueblos who mined it in what is now the US Southwest to sell in central Mexico where it had become the most valued of all material possessions and was used as a means of exchange or a form of money.[5] Sixty-five thousand turquoise artifacts in Chaco Canyon, New Mexico, are evidence of the importance of turquoise as a major precolonial commodity. Other items were also valuable marketable commodities in the area, salt being close to turquoise in value. Ceramic trade goods involved interconnected markets from Mexico City to Mesa Verde, Colorado. Shells from the Gulf of California, tropical bird feathers from the Gulf Coast area of Mexico, obsidian from Durango, Mexico, and flint from Texas were all found in the ruins of Casa Grande (Arizona), the commercial center of the northern frontier. Turquoise functioning as money was traded to acquire macaw and parrot feathers from tropical areas for religious rituals, seashells from coastal peoples, and hides and meat from the northern plains. The stone has been found in precolonial sites in Texas, Kansas, and Nebraska, where the Wichitas served as intermediaries, carrying turquoise and other goods farther east and north. Crees in the Lake

Superior region and communities in what is today Ontario, Canada, and in today's Wisconsin acquired turquoise through trade.[6]

Traders from Mexico were also transmitters of culture and features such as the Sun Dance religion in the Great Plains, and the cultivation of corn by the Algonquin, Cherokee, and Muskogee (Creek) peoples of the eastern half of North America were transmitted from Central America. The oral and written histories of the Aztecs, Cherokees, and Choctaws record these relations. Cherokee oral history tells of their ancestors' migrations from the south and through Mexico, as does Muskogee history.[7]

Although Aztecs were apparently flourishing culturally and economically, as well as being militarily and politically strong, their dominance was declining on the eve of Spanish intrusion. Being pressed for tribute through violent attacks, peasants rebelled and there were uprisings all over Mexico. Montezuma II, who came to power in 1503, might have succeeded in his attempt to reform the regime, but the Spanish overthrew him before he had the opportunity. The Mexican state was crushed and its cities leveled in Cortés's three-year genocidal war. Cortés's recruitment of resistant communities all over Mexico as allies aided in toppling the central regime. Cortés and his two hundred European mercenaries could never have overthrown the Mexican state without the Indigenous insurgency he co-opted. The resistant peoples who allied with Cortés to overthrow the oppressive Aztec regime could not yet have known the goals of the gold-obsessed Spanish colonizers or the European institutions that backed them.

THE NORTH

What is now the US Southwest once formed, with today's Mexican states of Sonora, Sinaloa, and Chihuahua, the northern periphery of the Aztec regime in the Valley of Mexico. Mostly an alpine, arid, and semiarid region cut with rivers, it is a fragile land base with rainfall a scarce commodity and drought endemic. Yet, in the Sonora Desert of present-day southern Arizona, communities were practicing agriculture by 2100 BC and began digging irrigation canals as early as

1250 BC. The earliest evidence of corn in the area dates from 2000 BC, introduced by trade and migration between north and south. Farther north, people began cultivating corn, beans, squash, and cotton around 1500 BC. Their descendants, the Akimel O'odham people (Pimas), call their ancestors the Huhugam (meaning "those who have gone"), which English speakers have rendered as "Hohokam." The Hohokam people left behind ball courts similar to those of the Mayans, multistory buildings, and agricultural fields. Their most striking imprint on the land is one of the most extensive networks of irrigation canals in the world at that time. From AD 900 to 1450, the Hohokams built a canal system of more than eight hundred miles of trunk lines and hundreds more miles of branches serving local sites. The longest known canal extended twenty miles. The largest were seventy-five to eighty-five feet across and twenty feet deep, and many were leak-proof, lined with clay. One canal system carried enough water to irrigate an estimated ten thousand acres.[8] Hohokam farmers grew surplus crops for export and their community became a crossroads in a trade network reaching from Mexico to Utah and from the Pacific Coast to New Mexico and into the Great Plains. By the fourteenth century, Hohokams had dispersed, living in smaller communities.

The Ancestral Puebloans of Chaco Canyon on the Colorado Plateau—in the present-day Four Corners region of Arizona, New Mexico, Colorado, and Utah—thrived from AD 850 to 1250. Ancestors of the Pueblos of New Mexico, they constructed more than four hundred miles of roads radiating out from Chaco. Averaging thirty feet wide, these roads followed straight courses, even through difficult terrain such as hills and rock formations. The highways connected some seventy-five communities. Around the thirteenth century, the Ancient Puebloans abandoned the Chaco area and migrated, building nearly a hundred smaller agricultural city-states along the northern Rio Grande valley and its tributaries. Northernmost Taos Pueblo was an important trade center, handling buffalo products from the plains, tropical bird products, copper and shells from Mexico, and turquoise from New Mexican mines. Pueblo trade extended as far west as the Pacific Ocean, as far east as the Great Plains, and as far south as Central America.

Other major peoples in the region, the Navajos (Diné) and Apaches, are of Athabascan heritage, having migrated to the region from the subarctic several centuries before Columbus. The majority of the Diné people did not migrate and remain in the original homeland in Alaska and northwestern Canada. Originally a hunting and trading people, they interacted and intermarried with the Pueblos and became involved in conflicts between villages engendered by disputes over water usage, with Diné and Apache groups allied with one or another of the riverine city-states.[9]

The island peoples of the Gulf of Mexico and the Caribbean Basin were an integral part of the cultural, religious, and economic exchanges with the peoples from today's Guyana, Venezuela, Colombia, Panama, Costa Rica, Nicaragua, Honduras, Guatemala, Mexico, Texas, Louisiana, Mississippi, Alabama, and Florida. Water, far from presenting a barrier to trade and cultural relations, served as a means of connecting the region's peoples. Precolonial Caribbean cultures and cultural connections have been very little studied, since many of these peoples, the first victims of Columbus's colonizing missions, were annihilated, enslaved and deported, or later assimilated enslaved African populations with the advent of the Atlantic slave trade. The best known are the Caribs, Arawaks, Tainos, and the Chibchan-speaking peoples. Throughout the Caribbean islands and rim are also descendants of Maroons—mixed Indigenous and African communities—who successfully liberated themselves from slavery, such as the Garifuna people ("Black Caribs") along the coast of the western Caribbean.[10]

From the Atlantic Ocean to the Mississippi River and south to the Gulf of Mexico lay one of the most fertile agricultural belts in the world, crisscrossed with great rivers. Naturally watered, teeming with plant and animal life, temperate in climate, the region was home to multiple agricultural nations. In the twelfth century, the Mississippi Valley region was marked by one enormous city-state, Cahokia, and several large ones built of earthen, stepped pyramids, much like those in Mexico. Cahokia supported a population of tens of thousands, larger than that of London during the same period. Other architectural monuments were sculpted in the shape of gigantic birds, lizards, bears, alligators, and even a 1,330-foot-long serpent. These feats of monumental construction testify to the levels of civic and social organization. Called "mound builders" by European settlers, the people of this civilization had dispersed before the European invasion, but their influence had spread throughout the eastern half of the North American continent through cultural influence and trade.[11] What European colonizers found in the southeastern region of the continent were nations of villages with economies based on agriculture and corn the mainstay. This was the territory of the nations of the Cherokee, Chickasaw, and Choctaw and the Muskogee Creek and Seminole, along with the Natchez Nation in the western part, the Mississippi Valley region.

To the north, a remarkable federal state structure, the Haudenosaunee confederacy—often referred to as the Six Nations of the Iroquois Confederacy—was made up of the Seneca, Cayuga, Onondaga, Oneida, and Mohawk Nations and, from early in the nineteenth century, the Tuscaroras. This system incorporated six widely dispersed and unique nations of thousands of agricultural villages and hunting grounds from the Great Lakes and the St. Lawrence River to the Atlantic, and as far south as the Carolinas and inland to Pennsylvania. The Haudenosaunee peoples avoided centralized power by means of a clan-village system of democracy based on collective stewardship of the land. Corn, the staple crop, was stored in granaries and distributed equitably in this matrilineal society by the clan mothers, the oldest women from every extended family. Many other nations flourished in the Great Lakes region where now the US-Canada border cuts through their realms. Among them, the Anishinaabe Nation (called by others Ojibwe and Chippewa) was the largest.

The peoples of the prairies of central North America spanned an expanse of space from West Texas to the subarctic between the Mississippi River and the Rocky Mountains. Several centers of development in that vast region of farming and bison-dependent peoples may be identified: in the prairies of Canada, the Crees; in the Dakotas, the Lakota and Dakota Sioux; and to their west and south, the Cheyenne and Arapaho peoples. Farther south were the Ponca, Pawnee, Osage, Kiowa, and many other nations, with buffalo numbering sixty million. Territorial disputes inevitably occurred, and diplomatic skills as well as trade were highly developed for conflict resolution.

In the Pacific Northwest, from present-day Alaska to San Francisco, and along the vast inland waterways to the mountain barriers, great seafaring and fishing peoples flourished, linked by culture, common ceremonies, and extensive trade. These were wealthy peoples living in a comparative paradise of natural resources, including the sacred salmon. They invented the potlatch, the ceremonial distribution or destruction of accumulated goods, creating a culture of reciprocity. They crafted gigantic wooden totems, masks, and lodges carved from giant sequoias and redwoods. Among these communities speaking many languages were the Tlingit people in Alaska and the salmon-fishing Salish, Makah, Hoopa, Pomo, Karok, and Yurok people.

The territory between the Sierra Nevada and Rocky Mountains in the West, now called the Great Basin, was a harsh environment that supported small populations before European colonization, as it does today. Yet the Shoshone, Bannock, Paiute, and Ute peoples there managed the environment and built permanent villages.

GOVERNANCE

Each Indigenous nation or city-state or town comprised an independent, self-governing people that held supreme authority over internal affairs and dealt with other peoples on equal footing. Among the factors that integrated each nation, in addition to language, were shared belief systems and rituals and clans of extended families that spanned more than one town. The system of decision making was based on consensus, not majority rule. This form of decision making later baffled colonial agents who could not find Indigenous officials to bribe or manipulate. In terms of international diplomacy, each of the Indigenous peoples of western North America was a sovereign nation. First the Spanish, French, and British colonizers, and then the US colonizers, made treaties with these Indigenous governments.

Indigenous governance varied widely in form.[12] East of the Mississippi River, towns and federations of towns were governed by family lineages. The male elder of the most powerful clan was the executive. His accession to that position and all his decisions were subject to the approval of a council of elders of the clans that were represented in the town. In this manner, the town had sovereign authority over its internal affairs. In each sovereign town burned a sacred fire symbolizing its relationship with the spirit beings. A town could join other towns under the leadership of a single leader. English colonists termed such groupings of towns "confederacies" or "federations." The Haudenosaunee people today retain a fully functioning government of this type. It was the Haudenosaunee constitution, called the Great Law of Peace, that inspired essential elements of the US Constitution.[13] Oren Lyons, who holds the title of Faithkeeper of the Turtle Clan and is a member of the Onondaga Council of Chiefs, explains the essence of that constitution: "The first principle is peace. The second principle, equity, justice for the people. And third, the power of the good minds, of the collective powers to be of one mind: unity. And health. All of these were involved in the basic principles. And the process of discussion, putting aside warfare as a method of reaching decisions, and now using intellect."[14]

The Muskogees (Creeks), Seminoles, and other peoples in the Southeast had three branches of government: a civil administration, a military, and a branch that dealt with the sacred. The leaders of each branch were drawn from the elite, and other officials were drawn from prominent clans. Over the centuries preceding European colonialism, ancient traditions of diplomacy had developed among the Indigenous nations. Societies in the eastern part of the continent had an elaborate ceremonial structure for diplomatic meetings among representatives of disparate governments. In the federations of sovereign towns, the leading town's fire represented the entire group, and each member town sent a representative or two to the federation's council. Thus everyone in the federation was represented in the government's decision making. Agreements reached in such meetings were considered sacred pledges that the representatives made not only to one another but also to the powerful spirit looking on. The nations tended to hold firm to such treaties out of respect for the sacred power that was party to the agreements. Relations with the spirit world were thus a major factor in government.[15]

The roles of women varied among the societies of eastern North America. Among the Muskogees and other southern nations, women hardly participated in governmental affairs. Haudenosaunee and Cherokee women, on the other hand, held more political authority. Among the Mohawks, Oneidas, Onondagas, Cayugas, Senecas, and Tuscaroras, certain female lineages controlled the choice of male representatives for their clans in their governing councils. Men were the representatives, but the women who chose them had the right to speak in the council, and when the chosen representative was too young or inexperienced to be effective, one of the women might participate in council on his behalf. Haudenosaunee clan mothers held the power to recall unsatisfactory representatives. Charles C. Mann, author of *1491: New Revelations of the Americas before Columbus*, calls it "a feminist dream."[16]

According to the value system that drove consensus building and decision making in these societies, the community's interest overrode individual interests. After every member of a council had had his or her say, any member who still considered a decision incorrect might nevertheless agree to abide by it for the sake of the community's cohesion. In the rare cases in which consensus could not be reached, the segment of the community represented by dissenters might withdraw from the community and move away to found a new community. This was similar to the practice of the nearly one hundred autonomous towns of northern New Mexico.

STEWARDS OF THE LAND

By the time of European invasions, Indigenous peoples had occupied and shaped every part of the Americas, established extensive trade networks and roads, and were sustaining their populations by adapting to specific natural environments, but they also adapted nature to suit human ends. Mann relates how Indigenous peoples used fire to shape and tame the precolonial North American landscape. In the Northeast, Indigenous farmers always carried flints. One English observer in 1637 noted that they used the flints "to set fire of the country in all places where they come."[17] They also used torches for night hunting and rings of flame to encircle animals to kill. Rather than domesticating animals for hides and meat, Indigenous communities created havens to attract elk, deer, bear, and other game. They burned the undergrowth in forests so that the young grasses and other ground cover that sprouted the following spring would entice greater numbers of herbivores and the predators that fed on them, which would sustain the people who ate them both. Mann describes these forests in *1491*: "Rather than the thick, unbroken, monumental snarl of trees imagined by Thoreau, the great eastern forest was an ecological kaleidoscope of garden plots, blackberry rambles, pine barrens, and spacious groves of chestnut, hickory, and oak." Inland a few miles from the shore of present-day Rhode Island, an early European explorer marveled at the trees that were spaced so that the forest "could be penetrated even by a large army." English mercenary John Smith wrote that he had ridden a galloping horse through the Virginia forest. In Ohio, the first English squatters on Indigenous lands in the mid-eighteenth century encountered forested areas that resembled English parks, as they could drive carriages through the trees.

Bison herds roamed the East from New York to Georgia (it's no accident that a settler city in western New York was named Buffalo). The American bison was indigenous to the northern and southern plains of North America, not the East, yet Native peoples imported them east along a path of fire, as they transformed forest into fallows for the bison to survive upon far from their original habitat. Historian William Cronon has written that when the Haudenosaunee hunted buffalo, they were "harvesting a foodstuff which they had consciously been instrumental in creating." As for the "Great American Desert," as Anglo-Americans called the Great Plains, the occupants transformed that too into game farms. Using fire, they extended the giant grasslands and maintained them. When Lewis and Clark began their trek up the Missouri River in 1804, ethnologist Dale Lott has observed, they beheld "not a wilderness but a vast pasture managed by and for Native Americans." Native Americans created the world's largest gardens and grazing lands—and thrived.[18]

Native peoples left an indelible imprint on the land with systems of roads that tied nations and communities together across the entire landmass of the Americas. Scholar David Wade Chambers writes:

> The first thing to note about early Native American trails and roads is that they were not just paths in the woods following along animal tracks used mainly for hunting. Neither can they be characterized simply as the routes that nomadic peoples followed during seasonal migrations. Rather they constituted an extensive system of roadways that spanned the Americas, making possible short, medium and long distance travel. That is to say, the Pre-Columbian Americas were laced together with a complex system of roads and paths which became the roadways adopted by the early settlers and indeed were ultimately transformed into major highways.[19]

Roads were developed along rivers, and many Indigenous roads in North America tracked the Mississippi, Ohio, Missouri, Columbia, and Colorado Rivers, the Rio Grande, and other major streams. Roads also followed seacoasts. A major road ran along the Pacific coast from northern Alaska (where travelers could continue by boat to Siberia) south to an urban area in western Mexico. A branch of that road ran through the Sonora Desert and up onto the Colorado Plateau, serving ancient towns and later communities such as those of the Hopis and Pueblos on the northern Rio Grande.

From the Pueblo communities, roads eastward carried travelers onto the semiarid plains along tributaries of the Pecos River and up to the communities in what is now eastern New Mexico, the Texas Panhandle, and West Texas. There were also roads from the northern Rio Grande to the southern plains of western Oklahoma by way of the Canadian and Cimarron Rivers. The roads along those rivers and their tributaries led to a system of roads that followed rivers from the Southeast. They also connected with ones that turned southwestward toward the Valley of Mexico.

The eastern roads connected Muskogee (Creek) towns in present-day Georgia and Alabama. From the Muskogee towns, a major route led north through Cherokee lands, the Cumberland Gap, and the Shenandoah Valley region to the confluence of the Ohio and

Scioto Rivers. From that northeastern part of the continent, a traveler could reach the West Coast by following roads along the Ohio River to the Mississippi, up the Mississippi to the mouth of the Missouri, and along the Missouri westward to its headwaters. From there, a road crossed the Rocky Mountains through South Pass in present-day Wyoming and led to the Columbia River. The Columbia River road led to the large population center at the river's mouth on the Pacific Ocean and connected with the Pacific Coast road.

CORN

North America in 1492 was not a virgin wilderness but a network of Indigenous nations, peoples of the corn. The link between peoples of the North and the South can be seen in the diffusion of corn from Mesoamerica. Both Muskogees and Cherokees, whose original homelands in North America are located in the Southeast, trace their lineage to migration from or through Mexico. Cherokee historian Emmet Starr wrote:

> The Cherokees most probably preceded by several hundred years the Muskogees in their exodus from Mexico and swung in a wider circle, crossing the Mississippi River many miles north of the mouth of the Missouri River as indicated by the mounds. . . . The Muskogees were probably driven out of Mexico by the Aztecs, Toltecs or some other of the northwestern tribal invasions of the ninth or preceding centuries. This is evidenced by the customs and devices that were long retained by the Creeks.[20]

Another Cherokee writer, Robert Conley, tells about the oral tradition that claims Cherokee origins in South America and subsequent migration through Mexico. Later, with US military invasions and relocations of the Muskogee and Cherokee peoples, many groups split off and sought refuge in Mexico, as did others under pressure, such as the Kickapoos.[21]

Although practiced traditionally throughout the Indigenous agricultural areas of North America, the Green Corn Dance remains strongest among the Muskogee people. The elements of the ritual dance are similar to those of the Valley of Mexico. Although the dance takes various forms among different communities, the core of it is the same, a commemoration of the gift of corn by an ancestral corn woman. The peoples of the corn retain great affinities under the crust of colonialism.

This brief overview of precolonial North America suggests the magnitude of what was lost to all humanity and counteracts the settler-colonial myth of the wandering Neolithic hunter. These were civilizations based on advanced agriculture and featuring polities. It is essential to understand the migrations and Indigenous peoples' relationships prior to invasion, North and South, and how colonialism cut them off, but, as we will see, the relationships are being reestablished.

TWO

CULTURE OF CONQUEST

*The discovery of gold and silver in America, the extirpation,
enslavement and entombment in mines of the aboriginal
population, the beginning of the conquest and looting
of the East Indies, the turning of Africa into a warren
for the commercial hunting of black-skins, signaled the
rosy dawn of the era of capitalist production. These idyllic
proceedings are the chief moments of prior accumulation.*

—Karl Marx, from "Genesis of the Industrial Capitalist," *Capital*

HOW IT BEGAN

The late anthropologist Edward H. Spicer wrote that the initial Europeans who participated in colonization of the Americas were heirs to rich and ancient cultures, social relations, and customs in their lands of origin, whether Spain, France, Holland, or England. In the passage to the Americas and encountering the Indigenous inhabitants, they largely abandoned the webs of European social relations. What each actually participated in was a culture of conquest—violence, expropriation, destruction, and dehumanization.[1]

Spicer's observation is true, but the culture of conquest didn't start with Europeans crossing the Atlantic. European institutions and the worldview of conquest and colonialism had formed several centuries before that. From the eleventh through the thirteenth centuries, Europeans conducted the Crusades to conquer North Africa and the Middle East, leading to unprecedented wealth in the hands of a few. This profit-based religion was the deadly element that European merchants and settlers brought to the Americas. In addition to seeking personal wealth, colonizers expressed a Christian zeal that justified colonialism. Along with that came the militaristic tradition that had also developed in western Europe during the Crusades (literally, "carrying of the cross"). Although the popes, beginning with Urban II, called for most of the ventures, the crusading armies were mercenary outfits that promised the soldiers the right to sack and loot Muslim towns and cities, feats that would gain them wealth and prestige back home. Toward the end of the thirteenth century, the papacy began directing such mercenaries to crush domestic "enemies" in their midst, as well—pagans and commoners in general, especially women (as ostensible witches) and heretics. In this way, knights and noblemen could seize land and force the commoners living on it into servitude. Historian Peter Linebaugh notes that whereas the anti-Muslim Crusades were attempts to control the lucrative Muslim trade routes to the Far East, the domestic crusades against heretics and commoners were carried out to terrorize poor people and at the same time to enlist them in the lucrative and adventurous yet holy venture: "Crusading was thus a murderous device to resolve a contradiction by bringing baron and commoner together in the cauldron of religious war."[2]

The first population forcibly organized under the profit motive—whose labor was exploited well before overseas exploitation was possible—was the European peasantry. Once forced off their land, they had nothing to eat and nothing to sell but their labor. In addition, entire nations, such as Scotland, Wales, Ireland, Bohemia, the Basque Country, and Catalonia, were colonized and forced under the rule of various monarchies. The Moorish Nation and the Sephardic Jewish minority were conquered and physically deported by the Castilian/Aragon monarchy from the Iberian Peninsula—a long-term project culminating in group expulsions beginning in 1492, the year Columbus sailed to America.

The institutions of colonialism and methods for relocation, deportation, and expropriation of land had already been practiced, if not perfected, by the end of the fifteenth century.[3] The rise of the modern state in western Europe was based on the accumulation of wealth by means of exploiting human labor and displacing millions of subsistence producers from their lands. The armies that did this work benefited from technological innovations that allowed the development of more effective weapons of death and destruction. When these states expanded overseas to obtain even more resources, land, and labor, they were not starting anew. The peoples of West Africa, the Caribbean, Mesoamerica, and the Andes were the first overseas victims. South Africa, North America, and the rest of South America followed. Then came all of Africa, the Pacific, and Asia.

The sea voyages of European explorers and merchants in the late fifteenth and early sixteenth centuries were not the first of their kind. These voyagers borrowed the techniques for long-distance sea travel from the Arab world. Before the Arabs ventured into the Indian Ocean, Inuits (Eskimos) plied the Arctic Circle in their kayaks for centuries and made contacts with many peoples, as did Norse, South Asian, Chinese, Japanese, Peruvian, and Melanesian and Polynesian fishing peoples of the Pacific. Egyptian and Greek knowledge of the seas most likely extended beyond the Mediterranean, into the Atlantic and Indian Oceans. Western European seagoing merchants and the monarchies that backed them would differ only in that they had developed the bases for colonial domination and exploitation of labor in those colonies that led to the capture and enslavement of millions of Africans to transport to their American colonies.

LAND AS PRIVATE PROPERTY

Along with the cargo of European ships, especially of the later British colonizing ventures, came the emerging concept of land as private property. Esther Kingston-Mann, a specialist in Russian land tenure history, has reconstructed the elevation of land as private property to "sacred status" in sixteenth-century England.[4] The English used the term "enclosure" to denote the privatization of the commons. During this time, peasants, who constituted a large majority of the population, were evicted from their ancient common lands. For centuries the commons had been their pasture for milk cows and for running sheep and their source for water, wood for fuel and construction, and edible and medicinal wild plants. Without these resources they could not have survived as farmers, and they did not survive as farmers after they lost access to the commons. Not only were the commons privatized during the sixteenth and seventeenth centuries, they were also transformed into grazing lands for commercial sheep production, wool being the main domestic and export commodity, creating wealth for a few and impoverishment for the many. Denied access to the former commons, rural subsistence farmers and even their children had no choice but to work in the new woolen textile factories under miserable conditions—that is, when they could find such work for unemployment was high. Employed or not, this displaced population was available to serve as settlers in the North American British colonies, many of them as indentured servants, with the promise of land. After serving their terms of indenture, they were free to squat on Indigenous land and become farmers again. In this way, surplus labor created not only low labor costs and great profits for the woolens manufacturers but also a supply of settlers for the colonies, which was an "escape valve" in the home country, where impoverishment could lead to uprisings of the exploited. The sacred status of property in the forms of land taken from Indigenous farmers and of Africans as chattel was seeded into the drive for Anglo-American independence from Britain and the founding of the United States.

Privatization of land was accompanied by an ideological drive to paint the commoners who resisted as violent, stupid, and lazy. The English Parliament, under the guise of fighting backwardness, criminalized former rights to the commons. Accompanying and facilitating the privatization of the commons was the suppression of women, as feminist theorist Silvia Federici has argued, by conjuring witchcraft. Those accused of witchcraft were poor peasant women, often widows, while the accusers tended to be wealthier, either their landlords or employers, individuals who controlled local institutions or had ties to the national government. Neighbors were encouraged to accuse one another.[5] Witchcraft was considered mainly a female crime, especially at the peak of the witch hunts between 1550 and 1650, when more than 80 percent of those who were charged with witchcraft, tried, convicted, and executed were women. In England, those accused of witchcraft were mostly elderly women, often beggars, sometimes the wives of living laborers but usually widows.

Actions and local occurrences said to indicate witchcraft included nonpayment of rent, demand for public assistance, giving the "evil-eye," local die-offs of horses or other stock, and mysterious deaths of children. Also among the telltale actions were practices related to midwifery and any kind of contraception. The service that women provided among the poor as healers was one of a number of vestiges from pre-Christian, matrilineal institutions that once predominated in Europe. It is no surprise that those who had held on to and perpetuated these communal practices were those most resistant to the enclosure of the commons, the economic base of the peasantry, as well as women's autonomy.[6]

The traumatized souls thrown off the land, as well as their descendants, became the land-hungry settlers enticed to cross a vast ocean with the promise of land and attaining the status of gentry. English settlers brought witch hunting with them to Jamestown, Virginia, and to Salem, Massachusetts. In language reminiscent of that used to condemn witches, they quickly identified the Indigenous populations as inherently children of Satan and "servants of the devil" who deserved to be killed.[7] Later the Salem authorities would justify witch trials by claiming that the English settlers were inhabiting land controlled by the devil.

WHITE SUPREMACY AND CLASS

Also part of the Christian colonizers' outlook was a belief in white supremacy. As an 1878 US Protestant evangelical hymn suggests— "Are your garments spotless? / Are they white as snow? / Are they washed in the blood of the lamb?"—whiteness as an ideology involves much more than skin color, although skin color has been and continues to be a key component of racism in the United States. White supremacy can be traced to the colonizing ventures of the Christian Crusades in Muslim-controlled territories and to the Protestant colonization of Ireland. As dress rehearsals for the colonization of the Americas, these projects form the two strands that merge in the geopolitical and sociocultural makeup of US society.

The Crusades in the Iberian Peninsula (Spain and Portugal today) and expulsion of Jews and Muslims were part of a process that created the core ideology for modern colonialism—white supremacy—and its justification for genocide. The Crusades gave birth to the papal law of *limpieza de sangre*—cleanliness of blood—for which the Inquisition was established by the Church to investigate and determine. Before this time the concept of biological race based on "blood" is not known to have existed as law or taboo in Christian Europe or anywhere else in the world.[8] As scapegoating and suspicion of Conversos (Jews who had converted to Christianity) and Moriscos (Muslims who had converted to Christianity) intensified over several centuries in Christian-controlled Spain, the doctrine of *limpieza de sangre* was popularized. It had the effect of granting psychological and increasingly legal privileges to "Old Christians," both rich and poor, thus obscuring the class differences between the landed aristocracy and land-poor peasants and shepherds. Whatever their economic station, the "Old Christian" Spanish were enabled to identify with the nobility. As one Spanish historian puts it, "The common people looked upwards, wishing and hoping to climb, and let themselves be seduced by chivalric ideals: honour, dignity, glory, and the noble life."[9] Lope de Vega, a sixteenth-century contemporary of Cervantes, wrote: "Soy un hombre, / aunque de villana casta, / limpio de sangre y jamas / de hebrea o mora manchada" (I am a man, although of lowly status, yet clean of blood and with no mixture of Jewish or Moorish blood).

This cross-class mind-set can be found as well in the stance of descendants of the old settlers of British colonization in North America. This then is the first instance of class leveling based on imagined racial sameness—the origin of white supremacy, the essential ideology of colonial projects in America and Africa. As Elie Wiesel famously observed, the road to Auschwitz was paved in the earliest days of Christendom. Historian David Stannard, in *American Holocaust*, adds the caveat that the same road led straight through the heart of America.[10] The ideology of white supremacy was paramount in neutralizing the class antagonisms of the landless against the landed and distributing confiscated lands and properties of Moors and Jews in Iberia, of the Irish in Ulster, and of Native American and African peoples.

Great Britain, emerging as an overseas colonial power a century after Spain did, absorbed aspects of the Spanish racial caste system into its colonialist rationalizations, particularly regarding African slavery, but it did so within the context of Protestantism, which imagined a chosen people founding and raising a New Jerusalem. The English did not just adapt the habits and experiences of Spanish colonization; they had their own prior experience, which actually constituted overseas imperialism. During the early seventeenth century the English conquered Ireland and declared a half-million acres of land in the north open to settlement. The settlers who served early settler colonialism came mostly from western Scotland. England had previously conquered Wales and Scotland, but it had never before attempted to remove so large an Indigenous population and plant settlers in their place as in Ireland. The ancient Irish social system was systematically attacked, traditional songs and music forbidden, whole clans exterminated, and the remainder brutalized. A "wild Irish" reservation was even attempted. The "plantation" of Ulster was as much a culmination of, as it was a departure from, centuries of intermittent warfare in Ireland. In the sixteenth century, the official in charge of the Irish province of Munster, Sir Humphrey Gilbert, ordered that

> the heddes of all those (of what sort soever thei were) which were killed in the daie, should be cutte off from their bodies and brought to the place where he [Gilbert] incamped at night, and should there bee laied on the ground by eche side of the waie ledying into his owne tente so that none could come into his tente for any cause but commonly he muste passe through a lane of heddes which he used ad terrorem. . . . [It brought] greate terrour to the people when thei sawe the heddes of their dedde fathers, brothers, children, kindsfolke, and friends.[11]

The English government paid bounties for the Irish heads. Later only the scalp or ears were required. A century later in North America, Indian heads and scalps were brought in for bounty in the same manner. Although the Irish were as "white" as the English, transforming them into alien others to be exterminated previewed what came to be perceived as racialist when applied to Indigenous peoples of North America and to Africans.

At that conjuncture, both in the Christian Crusades against Muslims and England's invasion of Ireland, the transition from religious wars to the genocidal mode of colonialism is apparent. The Irish under British colonial rule, well into the twentieth century, continued to be regarded as biologically inferior. During the mid-nineteenth century, influenced by social Darwinism, some English scientists peddled the theory that the Irish (and all people of color) had descended from apes, while the English were descendants of "man," who had been created by God "in his own image." Thus the English were "angels" and the Irish (and other colonized peoples) were a lower species, which today US "Christian Identity" white supremacists call "mud people," inferior products of the process of evolution.[12] The same Sir Humphrey Gilbert who had been in charge of the colonization of Ulster planted the first English colonial settlement in North America in Newfoundland in the summer of 1583. In the lead-up to the formation of the United States, Protestantism uniquely refined white supremacy as part of a politico-religious ideology.

TERMINAL NARRATIVES

According to the current consensus among historians, the wholesale transfer of land from Indigenous to Euro-American hands that occurred in the Americas after 1492 is due less to European invasion, warfare, and material acquisitiveness than to the bacteria that the invaders unwittingly brought with them. Historian Colin Calloway is among the proponents of this theory, and he writes that "epidemic diseases would have caused massive depopulation in the Americas whether brought by European invaders or brought home by Native American traders."[13] Such an absolutist assertion renders any other fate for the Indigenous peoples improbable. Professor Calloway is a careful and widely respected historian of Indigenous North

America, but his conclusion articulates a default assumption. The thinking behind the assumption is both ahistorical and illogical in that Europe itself lost a third to one-half of its population to infectious disease during medieval pandemics. The principal reason the consensus view is wrong and ahistorical is that it erases the effects of settler colonialism with its antecedents in the Spanish "Reconquest" and the English conquest of Scotland, Ireland, and Wales. By the time Spain, Portugal, and Britain arrived to colonize the Americas, their methods of eradicating peoples or forcing them into dependency and servitude were ingrained, streamlined, and effective. If disease could have done the job, it is not clear why the European colonizers in America found it necessary to carry out unrelenting wars against Indigenous communities in order to gain every inch of land they took from them—nearly three hundred years of colonial warfare, followed by continued wars waged by the independent republics of the hemisphere.

Whatever disagreement may exist about the size of precolonial Indigenous populations, no one doubts that a rapid demographic decline occurred in the sixteenth and seventeenth centuries, its timing from region to region depending on when conquest and colonization began. Nearly all the population areas of the Americas were reduced by 90 percent following the onset of colonizing projects, decreasing the targeted Indigenous populations of the Americas from one hundred million to ten million. Commonly referred to as the most extreme demographic disaster—framed as natural—in human history, it was rarely called genocide until the rise of Indigenous movements in the mid-twentieth century forged questions.

US scholar Benjamin Keen acknowledges that historians "accept uncritically a fatalistic 'epidemic plus lack of acquired immunity' explanation for the shrinkage of Indian populations, without sufficient attention to the socioeconomic factors . . . which predisposed the natives to succumb to even slight infections."[14] Other scholars agree. Geographer William M. Denevan, while not ignoring the existence of widespread epidemic diseases, has emphasized the role of warfare, which reinforced the lethal impact of disease. There were military engagements directly between European and Indigenous nations, but many more saw European powers pitting one Indigenous nation against another or factions within nations, with European allies aiding one or both sides, as was the case in the colonization of the peoples of Ireland, Africa, and Asia. Other killers cited by Denevan are overwork in mines, frequent outright butchery, malnutrition and starvation resulting from the breakdown of Indigenous trade networks, subsistence food production and loss of land, loss of will to live or reproduce (and thus suicide, abortion, and infanticide), and deportation and enslavement.[15] Anthropologist Henry Dobyns has pointed to the interruption of Indigenous peoples' trade networks. When colonizing powers seized Indigenous trade routes, the ensuing acute shortages, including food products, weakened populations and forced them into dependency on the colonizers, with European manufactured goods replacing Indigenous ones. Dobyns has estimated that all Indigenous groups suffered serious food shortages one year in four. In these circumstances, the introduction and promotion of alcohol proved addictive and deadly, adding to the breakdown of social order and responsibility.[16] These realities render the myth of "lack of immunity," including to alcohol, pernicious.

Historian Woodrow Wilson Borah focused on the broader arena of European colonization, which also brought depopulation in the Pacific Islands, Australia, western Central America, and West Africa.[17] Sherburne Cook—associated with Borah in the revisionist Berkeley School, as it was called—studied the attempted destruction of the California Indians. Cook estimated 2,245 deaths among peoples in Northern California—the Wintu, Maidu, Miwak, Omo, Wappo, and Yokuts Nations—in late-eighteenth-century armed conflicts with the Spanish, while some 5,000 died from disease and another 4,000 were relocated to missions. Among the same people in the second half of the nineteenth century, US armed forces killed 4,000, and disease killed another 6,000. Between 1852 and 1867, US citizens kidnapped 4,000 Indian children from these groups in California. Disruption of Indigenous social structures under these conditions and dire economic necessity forced many of the women into prostitution in goldfield camps, further wrecking what vestiges of family life remained in these matriarchal societies.[18]

Proponents of the default position emphasize attrition by disease despite other causes equally deadly, if not more so. In doing so they refuse to accept that the colonization of America was genocidal by plan, not simply the tragic fate of populations lacking immunity to disease. In the case of the Jewish Holocaust, no one denies that more Jews died of starvation, overwork, and disease under Nazi incarceration than died in gas ovens, yet the acts of creating and maintaining the conditions that led to those deaths clearly constitute genocide.

Anthropologist Michael V. Wilcox asks, "What if archaeologists were asked to explain the continued presence of descendant communities five hundred years after Columbus instead of their disappearance or marginality?" Cox calls for the active dismantling of what he terms "terminal narratives"—"accounts of Indian histories which explain the absence, cultural death, or disappearance of Indigenous peoples."[19]

GOLD FEVER

Searching for gold, Columbus reached many of the islands of the Caribbean and mapped them. Soon, a dozen other soldier-merchants mapped the Atlantic coast from the northern Maritimes to the tip of South America. From the Iberian Peninsula came merchants, mercenaries, criminals, and peasants. They seized the land and property of Indigenous populations and declared the territories to be extensions of the Spanish and Portuguese states. These acts were confirmed by the monarchies and endorsed by the papal authority of the Roman Catholic Church. The Treaty of Tordesillas in 1494 divided the "New World" between Spain and Portugal with a line drawn from Greenland south through what is now Brazil. Called the Doctrine of Discovery, it claimed that possession of the entire world west of that line would be open to Spanish conquest and all east of it to Portuguese conquest.

The story is well known. In 1492, Columbus sailed with three ships on his first voyage at the behest of Ferdinand, King of Aragon, and Isabella, Queen of Castille. The marriage of Ferdinand and Isabella in 1469 had led to the merger of their kingdoms into what would become the core of the Spanish state. Columbus planted a colony of forty of his men on "Española" (now the Dominican Republic and Haiti) and returned to Spain with Indigenous slaves and gold. In 1493, Columbus returned to the Caribbean with seventeen ships, more than a thousand men, and supplies. He found that the men he had left on the first trip had subsequently been killed by the Indigenous inhabitants. After planting another settlement, Columbus returned to Spain with four hundred Arawak slaves. With seven ships, Columbus returned to the Caribbean in 1498, reaching what is now Venezuela, and he made a fourth and final voyage in 1502, this time touching the Caribbean coast of Central America. In 1513, Vasco Núñez de Balboa crossed the Isthmus of Panama and charted the Pacific coast of the Americas. Juan Ponce de León claimed the Florida peninsula for Spain in 1513. In 1521, following a three-year bloodbath and overthrow of the Aztec state, Hernando Cortés proclaimed Mexico as New Spain. Parallel with the crushing of Mexican resistance were Ferdinand Magellan's explorations and charting of the Atlantic coast of the South American continent, followed by Spanish wars against the Inca Nation of the Andes. In both Mexico and Peru, the conquistadors confiscated elaborate artwork and statuary made of gold and silver to be melted down for use as money. During the same period, the Portuguese laid waste to what is today Brazil and began a thriving slave trade that would funnel millions of enslaved Africans to South America, beginning the lucrative Atlantic slave trade.

The consequences of this amassing of fortunes were first felt in the catastrophe experienced by small farmers in Europe and England. The peasants became impoverished, dependent workers crowded into city slums. For the first time in human history, the majority of Europeans depended for their livelihood on a small wealthy minority, a phenomenon that capitalist-based colonialism would spread worldwide. The symbol of this new development, indeed its currency, was gold. Gold fever drove colonizing ventures, organized at first in pursuit of the metal in its raw form. Later the pursuit of gold became more sophisticated, with planters and merchants establishing whatever conditions were necessary to hoard as much gold as possible. Thus was born an ideology: the belief in the inherent value of gold despite its relative uselessness in reality. Investors, monarchies, and parliamentarians devised methods to control the processes of wealth accumulation and the power that came with it, but the ideology behind gold fever mobilized settlers to cross the Atlantic to an unknown fate. Subjugating entire societies and civilizations, enslaving whole countries, and slaughtering people village by village did not seem too high a price to pay, nor did it appear inhumane. The systems of colonization were modern and rational, but its ideological basis was madness.

THREE

CULT OF THE COVENANT

For all the land which thou seest,
to thee will I give it and to thy seed forever.

—Genesis 13:15

And I will establish my covenant between me and thee and
thy seed after thee in their generations for an everlasting
covenant, to be a God unto thee, and to thy seed after thee.

—Genesis 17:7

MYTH OF THE PRISTINE WILDERNESS

With the onset of colonialism in North America, control of the land was wrenched away from the Indigenous peoples, and the forests grew dense, so that later European settlers were unaware of the former cultivation and sculpting and manicuring of the landscape. Abandoned fields of corn turned to weeds and bushes. Settlers chopped down trees in New England until the landscape was nearly bare.[1] One geographer notes, "Paradoxical as it may seem, there was undoubtedly much more 'forest primeval' in 1850 than in 1650."[2] Anglo-Americans who did observe Native habitat management in action misunderstood what they saw. Captain John Palliser, traveling through the prairies in the 1850s, complained about the Indians' "disastrous habit of setting the prairie on fire for the most trivial and worse than useless reasons." In 1937, Harvard naturalist Hugh Raup claimed that the "open, park-like woods" written about in earlier times had been, "from time immemorial, characteristic of vast areas in North America" and could not have been the result of human management.[3]

In the founding myth of the United States, the colonists acquired a vast expanse of land from a scattering of benighted peoples who were hardly using it—an unforgivable offense to the Puritan work ethic. The historical record is clear, however, that European colonists shoved aside a large network of small and large nations whose governments, commerce, arts and sciences, agriculture, technologies, theologies, philosophies, and institutions were intricately developed, nations that maintained sophisticated relations with one another and with the environments that supported them. By the early seventeenth century, when British colonists from Europe began to settle in North America, a large Indigenous population had long before created "a humanized landscape almost everywhere," as William Denevan puts it.[4] Native peoples had created town sites, farms, monumental earthworks, and networks of roads, and they had devised a wide variety of governments, some as complex as any in the world. They had developed sophisticated philosophies of government, traditions of diplomacy, and policies of international relations. They conducted trade along roads that crisscrossed the landmasses and waterways of the American continents. Before the arrival of Europeans, North America was indeed a "continent of villages," but also a continent of nations and federations of nations.[5]

Many have noted that had North America been a wilderness, undeveloped, without roads, and uncultivated, it might still be so, for the European colonists could not have survived. They appropriated what had already been created by Indigenous civilizations. They stole already cultivated farmland and the corn, vegetables, tobacco, and other crops domesticated over centuries, took control of the deer parks that had been cleared and maintained by Indigenous communities, used existing roads and water routes in order to move armies to conquer, and relied on captured Indigenous people to identify the locations of water, oyster beds, and medicinal herbs. Historian Francis Jennings was emphatic in addressing what he called the myth that "America was virgin land, or wilderness, inhabited by nonpeople called savages":

European explorers and invaders discovered an inhabited land. Had it been pristine wilderness then, it would possibly be so still today, for neither the technology nor the social organization of Europe in the sixteenth and seventeenth centuries had the capacity to maintain, of its own resources, outpost colonies thousands of miles from home. Incapable of conquering true wilderness, the Europeans were highly competent in the skill of conquering other people, and that is what they did. They did not settle a virgin land. They invaded and displaced a resident population.

This is so simple a fact that it seems self-evident.[6]

THE CALVINIST ORIGIN STORY

All modern nation-states claim a kind of rationalized origin story upon which they fashion patriotism or loyalty to the state. When citizens of modern states and their anthropologists and historians look at what they consider "primitive" societies, they identify their "origin myths," quaint and endearing stories, but fantastic ones, not grounded in "reality." Yet many US scholars seem unable (or unwilling) to subject their own nation-state's founding story to the same objective examination. The United States is not unique among nations in forging an origin myth, but most of its citizens believe it to be exceptional among nation-states, and this exceptionalist ideology has been used to justify appropriation of the continent and then domination of the rest of the world. It is one of the few states founded on the covenant of the Hebrew Torah, or the Christian borrowing of it in the Old Testament of the Bible. Other covenant states are Israel and the now-defunct apartheid state of South Africa, both of which were founded in 1948.[7] Although the origin stories of these three covenant states were based on Judeo-Christian scripture, they were not founded as theocracies. According to the myths, the faithful citizens come together of their own free will and pledge to each other and to their god to form and support a godly society, and their god in turn vouchsafes them prosperity in a promised land.

The influence of the scriptures was pervasive among many of the Western social and political thinkers whose ideas the founders of the first British colonies in North America drew upon. Historian

Donald Harman Akenson points to the way that "certain societies, in certain eras of their development," have looked to the scriptures for guidance, and likens it to the way "the human genetic code operates physiologically. That is, this great code has, in some degree, directly determined what people would believe and when they would think and what they would do."[8] Dan Jacobson, a citizen of Boer-ruled South Africa, whose parents were immigrants, observes that,

> like the Israelites, and their fellow Calvinists in New England, [the Boers] believed that they had been called by their God to wander through the wilderness, to meet and defeat the heathen, and to occupy a promised land on his behalf. . . . A sense of their having been summoned by divine decree to perform an ineluctable historical duty has never left the Boers, and has contributed to both their strength and their weakness.[9]

Founders of the first North American colonies and later of the United States had a similar sense of a providential opportunity to make history. Indeed, as Akenson reminds us, "it is from [the] scriptures that western society learned how to think historically." The key moment in history according to covenant ideology "involves the winning of 'the Land' from alien, and indeed evil, forces."[10]

The principal conduit of the Hebrew scriptures and covenant ideology to European Christians was John Calvin, the French religious reformer whose teachings coincided with the advent of the European invasion and colonization of the Americas. The Puritans drew upon Calvinist ideology in founding the Massachusetts Bay Colony, as did the Dutch Calvinist settlers of the Cape of Good Hope in founding their South African colony during the same period. Calvinism was a Protestant Christian movement with a strong separatist political component. In accord with the doctrine of predestination, Calvin taught that human free will did not exist. Certain individuals are "called" by God and are among the "elect." Salvation therefore has nothing to do with one's actions; one is born as part of the elect or not, according to God's will. Although individuals could not know for certain if they were among the elect, outward good fortune, especially material wealth, was taken to be a manifestation of election; conversely, bad fortune and poverty, not to speak of dark skin, were taken as evidence of damnation. "The attractiveness of such a doctrine to a group of invading colonists . . . is obvious," Akenson observes, "for one could easily define the natives as immutably profane, and damned, and oneself as predestined to virtue."[11]

Since another sign of justification was a person's ability to abide by the laws of a well-ordered society, Calvin preached the obligation of citizens to obey lawful authority. In fact, they should do so even when that authority was lodged in poor leaders (one of the seeds for "my country right or wrong"). Calvin led his Huguenot followers across the border into Geneva, took political control of the city-state, and established it as a republic in 1541. The Calvinist state enacted detailed statutes governing every aspect of life and appointed functionaries to enforce them. The laws reflected Calvin's interpretation of the Old Testament; dissenters were forced to leave the republic, and some were even tortured and executed.

Although the US Constitution represents for many US citizens a covenant with God, the US origin story goes back to the Mayflower Compact, the first governing document of the Plymouth Colony, named for the ship that carried the hundred or so passengers to what is now Cape Cod, Massachusetts, in November 1620. Forty-one of the "Pilgrims," all men, wrote and signed the compact. Invoking God's name and declaring themselves loyal subjects of the king, the signatories announced that they had journeyed to northern "Virginia," as the eastern seaboard of North America was called by the English, "to plant the First Colony" and did therefore "Covenant and Combine ourselves together in a Civil Body Politic" to be governed by "just and equal Laws" enacted "for the general good of the Colony, unto which we promise all due submission and obedience." The original settlers of Massachusetts Bay Colony, founded in 1630, adopted an official seal designed in England before their journey. The central image depicts a near-naked native holding a harmless, flimsy-looking bow and arrow and inscribed with the plea, "Come over and help us."[12] Nearly three hundred years later, the official seal of the US military veterans of the "Spanish-American War" (the invasion and occupation of Puerto Rico, Cuba, and the Philippines) showed a naked woman kneeling before an armed US soldier and a sailor, with a US battleship in the background. One may trace this recurrent altruistic theme into the early twenty-first century, when the United States still invades countries under the guise of rescue.

In other modern constitutional states, constitutions come and go, and they are never considered sacred in the manner patriotic US citizens venerate theirs. Great Britain has no written constitution. The Magna Carta arguably comes close, but it does not reflect a covenant. US citizens did not inherit their cult-like adherence to their constitution from the English. From the Pilgrims to the founders of the United States and continuing to the present, the cultural persistence of the covenant idea, and thus the bedrock of US patriotism, represents a deviation from the main course in the development of national identities. Arguably, both the 1948 birth of the state of Israel and advent of Nationalist Party rule of South Africa were emulations of the US founding; certainly many US Americans closely identify with the state of Israel, as they did with Afrikaner-ruled South Africa. Patriotic US politicians and citizens take pride in "exceptionalism." Historians and legal theorists characterize US statecraft and empire as those of a "nation of laws," rather than one dominated by a particular class or group of interests, suggesting a kind of holiness.

The US Constitution, the Mayflower Compact, the Declaration of Independence, the writings of the "Founding Fathers," Lincoln's Gettysburg Address, the Pledge of Allegiance, and even Martin Luther King Jr.'s "I Have a Dream" speech are all bundled into the covenant as sacred documents that express the US state religion. An aspect of this most visible in the early twenty-first century is the burgeoning "gun lobby," based on the sanctity of the Second Amendment to the Constitution. In the forefront of these Second Amendment adherents are the descendants of the old settlers who say that they represent "the people" and have the right to bear arms in order to overthrow any government that does not in their view adhere to the God-given covenant.

Parallel to the idea of the US Constitution as covenant, politicians, journalists, teachers, and even professional historians chant like a mantra that the United States is a "nation of immigrants." From its beginning, the United States has welcomed—indeed, often solicited, even bribed—immigrants to repopulate conquered territories "cleansed" of their Indigenous inhabitants. From the mid-nineteenth century, immigrants were recruited to work mines, raze forests, construct canals and railroads, and labor in sweatshops, factories, and commercial farm fields. In the late twentieth century, technical and medical workers were recruited. The requirements for their formal citizenship were simple: adhere to the sacred covenant through taking the Citizenship Oath, pledging loyalty to the flag, and regarding those outside the covenant as enemies or potential enemies of the exceptional country that has adopted them, often after they escaped hunger, war, or repression, which in turn were often caused by US militarism or economic sanctions. Yet no matter how much immigrants might strive to prove themselves to be as hardworking and patriotic as descendants of the original settlers, and despite the rhetoric of *E pluribus unum*, they are suspect. The old stock against which they are judged inferior includes not only those who fought in the fifteen-year war for independence from Britain but also, and perhaps more important, those who fought and shed (Indian) blood, before and after independence, in order to acquire the land. These are the descendants of English Pilgrims, Scots, Scots-Irish, and Huguenot French—Calvinists all—who took the land bequeathed to them in the sacred covenant that predated the creation of the independent United States. These were the settlers who fought their way over the Appalachians into the fertile Ohio Valley region, and it is they who claimed blood sacrifice for their country. Immigrants, to be accepted, must prove their fidelity to the covenant and what it stands for.

SETTLER COLONIALISM AND THE ULSTER-SCOTS

The core group of frontier settlers were the Ulster-Scots—the Scots-Irish, or "Scotch-Irish," as they called themselves.[13] Usually the descendants of these Scots-Irish say their ancestors came to the British colonies from Ireland, but their journey was more circuitous than that. The Scots-Irish were Protestants from Scotland who were recruited by the British as settlers in the six counties of the province of Ulster in northern Ireland. The British had seized these half-million acres from Ireland in the early seventeenth century, driven the indigenous Irish farmers from it, and opened it to settlement under English protection. This coincided with the English plantation of two colonies on the Atlantic coast of North America and the beginning of settler colonialism there. These early settlers came mostly from the Scottish lowlands. Scotland itself, along with Wales, had preceded Ireland as colonial notches in the belt of English expansion. Britain's colonization of Indigenous lands in North America was foreshadowed by its colonization of northern Ireland. By 1630 the new settlers in Ulster—21,000 Britons, including some Welsh, and 150,000 Lowland Scots—were more numerous than British settlers in all of North America at the time. In 1641, the indigenous Irish rebelled and killed ten thousand of the settlers, yet Protestant Scots settlers continued to pour in. In some formerly Irish areas, they formed a majority of the population. They brought with them the covenant ideology of Calvinism that had been the work of the Scotsman John Knox. Later John Locke, also a Scot, would secularize the covenant idea into a "contract," the social contract, whereby individuals sacrifice their liberty only through consent. An insidiously effective example, the US economic system, was based on Locke's theories.[14]

So it was that the Ulster-Scots were already seasoned settler colonialists before they began to fill the ranks of settlers streaming toward the North American British colonies in the early eighteenth century, many of them as indentured servants. Before ever meeting Indigenous Americans, the Ulster settlers had perfected scalping for bounty, using the indigenous Irish as their victims. As this chapter and the following one show, the Scots-Irish were the foot soldiers of British empire building, and they and their descendants formed the shock troops of the "westward movement" in North America, the expansion of the US continental empire and the colonization of its inhabitants. As Calvinists (mostly Presbyterian), they added to and transformed the Calvinism of the earlier Puritan settlers into the unique ideology of the US settler class.[15]

In one of history's great migrations, nearly a quarter-million Scots-Irish left Ulster for British North America between 1717 and 1775. Although a number left for religious reasons, the majority were losers in the struggle over Britain's Irish policies, which brought economic ruin to Ireland's wool and linen industries. Hard times were magnified by prolonged drought, and so the settlers pulled up stakes and moved across the Atlantic. This is a story that would repeat itself time and time again in settler treks across North America, the majority of migrants ending up landless losers in the Monopoly game of European settler colonialism.

The majority of Ulster-Scot settlers were cash-poor and had to indenture themselves to pay for their passage to North America. Once settled, they came to predominate as soldier-settlers. Most initially landed in Pennsylvania, but large numbers soon migrated to the southern colonies and to the backcountry, the British colonies' western borders, where they squatted on unceded Indigenous lands. Among frontier settlers, Scots-Irish predominated among settlers of English and German descent. Although the majority remained landless and poor, some became merchants and owners of plantations worked by slaves, as well as politically powerful. Seventeen presidents of the United States have been of Ulster-Scots lineage, from Andrew Jackson, founder of the Democratic Party, to Ronald Reagan, the Bushes, Bill Clinton, and Barack Obama on his mother's side. Theodore Roosevelt characterized his Scots-Irish ancestors as "a stern, virile, bold and hardy people who formed the kernel of that American stock who were the pioneers of our people in the march westwards."[16] Perhaps as influential as their being presidents, educators, and businessmen, the Scots-Irish engendered a strong set of individualist values that included the sanctity of glory in warfare. They made up the officer corps and were soldiers of the regular army, as well as the frontier-ranging militias that cleared areas for settlement by exterminating Indigenous farmers and destroying their towns.

The Seven Years' War between the British and the French (1754–63) was fought both in Europe and in North America, where the British colonists called it the French and Indian War because it was mainly a British war against the Indigenous peoples, some of whom formed alliances with the French. The British colonial militias consisted largely of frontier Scots-Irish settlers who wanted access to Indigenous farmland in the Ohio Valley region. By the time of US independence, Ulster-Scots made up 15 percent of the population of the thirteen colonies, and most were clustered in majority numbers in the backcountry. During the war for settler independence from Britain, most settlers who had emigrated directly from Scotland remained loyal to the British Crown and fought on that side. In contrast, the Scots-Irish were in the forefront of the struggle for independence and formed the backbone of Washington's fighting forces. Most of the names of soldiers at Valley Forge were Scots-Irish. They saw themselves, and their descendants see themselves, as the true and authentic patriots, the ones who spilled rivers of blood to secure independence and to acquire Indigenous lands—gaining blood rights to the latter as they left bloody footprints across the continent.[17]

During the last two decades of the eighteenth century, first- and second-generation Scots-Irish continued to pour westward into the Ohio Valley region, West Virginia, Kentucky, and Tennessee. They were the largest ethnic group in the westward migration, and they maintained many of their Scots-Irish ways. They tended to move three or four times, acquiring and losing land before settling at least somewhat permanently. Scots-Irish settlers were overwhelmingly farmers rather than explorers or fur traders. They cleared forests, built log cabins, and killed Indians, forming a human wall of colonization for the new United States and, in wartime, employing their fighting skills effectively. Historian Carl Degler writes that "these hardy, God-fearing Calvinists made themselves into a veritable human shield of colonial civilization."[18] The next chapter explores the kind of counterinsurgent warfare they perfected, which formed the basis of US militarism into the twenty-first century.

The Calvinist religion of the Scots-Irish, Presbyterianism, was in numbers of faithful soon second only to those of New England's Congregationalist Church. But on the frontier, Scots-Irish devotion to the formal Presbyterian Church waned. New evangelical offshoots refashioned Calvinist doctrines to decentralize and do away with the Presbyterian hierarchy. Although they continued to regard themselves as chosen people of the covenant, commanded by God to go into the wilderness to build the new Israel, the Scots-Irish also saw themselves, as their descendants see themselves, as the true and authentic patriots, entitled to the land through their blood sacrifice.

SACRED LAND BECOMES REAL ESTATE

The land won through North American bloodshed was not necessarily conceived in terms of particular parcels for a farm that would be passed down through generations. Most of the settlers who fought for it kept moving on nearly every generation. In the South many lost their holdings to land companies that then sold it to planters seeking to increase the size of their slave-worked plantations. Without the unpaid forced labor of enslaved Africans, a farmer growing cash crops could not compete on the market. Once in the hands of settlers, the land itself was no longer sacred, as it had been for the Indigenous. Rather, it was private property, a commodity to be acquired and sold—every man a possible king, or at least wealthy. Later, when Anglo-Americans had occupied the continent and urbanized much of it, this quest for land and the sanctity of private property were reduced to a lot with a house on it, and "the land" came to mean the country, the flag, the military, as in "the land of the free" of the national anthem, or Woody Guthrie's "This Land Is Your Land." Those who died fighting in foreign wars were said to have sacrificed their lives to protect "this land" that the old settlers had spilled blood to acquire. The blood spilled was largely Indigenous.

These then were the settlers upon which the national myths are based, the ultimately dispensable cannon fodder for the taking of the land and the continent, the foot soldiers of empire, the "yeoman farmers" romanticized by Thomas Jefferson. They were not of the ruling class, although a few slipped through and later were drawn in by the ruling class as elected officials and military officers, thereby maintaining the facade of a classless society and a democratic empire. The founders were English patricians, slave owners, large land barons, or otherwise successful businessmen dependent on the slave trade and exports produced by enslaved Africans and on property sales. When descendants of the settler class, overwhelmingly Presbyterian or otherwise Calvinist Protestant, were accepted into the ruling class, they usually became Episcopalians, members of an elite church linked to the state Church of England. As we look at the bloody deeds of the settlers in acquiring and maintaining land, the social class context is an essential element.

FOUR

BLOODY FOOTPRINTS

For the first 200 years of our military heritage, then, Americans depended on arts of war that contemporary professional soldiers supposedly abhorred: razing and destroying enemy villages and fields; killing enemy women and children; raiding settlements for captives; intimidating and brutalizing enemy noncombatants; and assassinating enemy leaders. . . . In the frontier wars between 1607 and 1814, Americans forged two elements—unlimited war and irregular war—into their first way of war.

—John Grenier, *The First Way of War*

Within days of the assassination of Osama bin Laden, on May 2, 2011, it was revealed that the Navy SEAL team executing the mission had used the code name Geronimo for its target.[1] A May 4 report in the *New York Daily News* commented, "Along with the unseen pictures of Osama Bin Laden's corpse and questions about what Pakistan knew, intelligence officials' reasons for dubbing the Al Qaeda boss 'Geronimo' remain one of the biggest mysteries of the Black Ops mission." The choice of that code name was not a mystery to the military, which also uses the term "Indian Country" to designate enemy territory and identifies its killing machines and operations with such names as UH-1B/C Iroquois, OH-58D Kiowa, OV-1 Mohawk, OH-6 Cayuse, AH-64 Apache, S-58/H-34 Choctaw, UH-60 Black Hawk, Thunderbird, and Rolling Thunder. The last of these is the military name given to the relentless carpet-bombing of Vietnam peasants in the mid-1960s. There are many other current and recent examples of the persistence of the colonial-ist and imperialist sensibilities at the core of a military grounded in wars against the Indigenous nations and communities of North America.

On February 19, 1991, Brigadier General Richard Neal, briefing reporters in Riyadh, Saudi Arabia, stated that the US military wanted to be certain of speedy victory once it committed land forces to "Indian Country." The following day, in a little-publicized statement of protest, the National Congress of American Indians pointed out that fifteen thousand Native Americans were serving as combat troops in the Persian Gulf. Neither Neal nor any other military authority apologized for the statement. The term "Indian Country" in cases such as this is not merely an insensitive racial slur, tastelessly but offhandedly employed to refer to the enemy. It is, rather, a technical military term, like "collateral damage" or "ordnance," that appears in military training manuals and is regularly used to mean "behind enemy lines." It is often shortened to "In Country." This usage recalls the origins and development of the US military, as well as the nature of US political and social history as a colonialist project. Furthermore, "Indian Country" is a legal term that identifies Native jurisdiction under US colonial laws but is also an important tool for Native nations to use in maintaining and expanding their land bases in the process of decolonization. "Indian Country," the legal term, includes not only federally recognized reservation territories, but also informal reservations, dependent Native communities and allotments, and specially designated lands.[2]

ROOTS OF GENOCIDE

In *The First Way of War: American War Making on the Frontier, 1607–1814*, military historian John Grenier offers an indispensable analysis of the colonialist warfare against the Indigenous peoples of the North American territories claimed by Great Britain. The way of war largely devised and enacted by settlers formed the basis for the founding ideology and colonialist military strategy of the independent United States, and this approach to war is still in force in the twenty-first century.[3] Grenier writes that he began his study with the goal of tracing the historical roots of the use of unlimited war by the United States, war whose purpose is to destroy the will of the enemy people or their capacity to resist, employing any means necessary but mainly by attacking civilians and their support systems, such as food supply. Today called "special operations" or "low-intensity conflict," that kind of warfare was first used against Indigenous communities by colonial militias in Virginia and Massachusetts. These irregular forces, made up of settlers, sought to disrupt every aspect of resistance as well as to obtain intelligence through scouting and taking prisoners. They did so by destroying Indigenous villages and fields and intimidating and slaughtering enemy noncombatant populations.[4]

Grenier analyzes the development of the US way of war from 1607–1814, during which the US military was forged, leading to its reproduction and development into the present. US historian Bernard Bailyn calls the period "barbarous" and a "conflict of civilizations," but Bailyn represents the Indigenous civilization as "marauders" that the European settlers needed to get rid of.[5] From this formative period, Grenier argues, emerged problematic characteristics of the US way of war and thereby the characteristics of its civilization, which few historians have come to terms with.

In the beginning, Anglo settlers organized irregular units to brutally attack and destroy unarmed Indigenous women, children, and old people using unlimited violence in unrelenting attacks. During nearly two centuries of British colonization, generations of settlers, mostly farmers, gained experience as "Indian fighters" outside any organized military institution. Anglo-French conflict may appear to have been the dominant factor of European colonization in North America during the eighteenth century, but while large regular armies fought over geopolitical goals in Europe, Anglo settlers in North America waged deadly irregular warfare against the Indigenous communities. Much of the fighting during the fifteen-year settlers' war for independence, especially in the Ohio Valley region and western New York, was directed against Indigenous resisters who realized it was not in their interest to have a close enemy of settlers with an independent government, as opposed to a remote one in Great Britain. Nor did the fledgling US military in the 1790s carry out operations typical of the state-centered wars occurring in

Europe at the time. Even following the founding of the professional US Army in the 1810s, irregular warfare was the method of the US conquest of the Ohio Valley and Mississippi Valley regions. Since that time, Grenier notes, irregular methods have been used in tandem with operations of regular armed forces.

The chief characteristic of irregular warfare is that of the extreme violence against civilians, in this case the tendency to seek the utter annihilation of the Indigenous population. "In cases where a rough balance of power existed," Grenier observes, "and the Indians even appeared dominant—as was the situation in virtually every frontier war until the first decade of the 19th century—[settler] Americans were quick to turn to extravagant violence."[6]

Many historians who acknowledge the exceptional one-sided colonial violence attribute it to racism. Grenier argues that rather than racism leading to violence, the reverse occurred: the out-of-control momentum of extreme violence of unlimited warfare fueled race hatred. "Successive generations of Americans, both soldiers and civilians, made the killing of Indian men, women, and children a defining element of their first military tradition and thereby part of a shared American identity. Indeed, only after seventeenth- and early-eighteenth-century Americans made the first way of war a key to being a white American could later generations of 'Indian haters,' men like Andrew Jackson, turn the Indian wars into race wars." By then, the Indigenous peoples' villages, farmlands, towns, and entire nations formed the only barrier to the settlers' total freedom to acquire land and wealth. Settler colonialists again chose their own means of conquest. Such fighters are often viewed as courageous heroes, but killing the unarmed women, children, and old people and burning homes and fields involved neither courage nor sacrifice.

So it was from the planting of the first British colonies in North America. Among the initial leaders of those ventures were military men—mercenaries—who brought with them their previous war experiences in Britain's imperialist, anti-Muslim Crusades. Those who put together and led the first colonial armies, such as John Smith in Virginia, Myles Standish at Plymouth, John Mason in Connecticut, and John Underhill in Massachusetts, had fought in the bitter, brutal, and bloody religious wars ongoing in Europe at the time of the first settlements. They had long practiced burning towns and fields and killing the unarmed and vulnerable. "Tragically for the Indian peoples of the Eastern Seaboard," Grenier observes, "the mercenaries unleashed a similar way of war in early Virginia and New England."[7]

SETTLER-PARASITES CREATE THE VIRGINIA COLONY

The first Jamestown settlers lacked a supply line and proved unable or unwilling to grow crops or hunt for their own sustenance. They decided that they would force the farmers of the Powhatan Confederacy—some thirty polities—to provide them with food. Jamestown military leader John Smith threatened to kill all the women and children if the Powhatan leaders would not feed and clothe the settlers as well as provide them with land and labor. The leader of the confederacy, Wahunsonacock, entreated the invaders:

> Why should you take by force that from us which you can have by love? Why should you destroy us, who have provided you with food? What can you get by war? . . . What is the cause of your jealousy? You see us unarmed, and willing to supply your wants, if you will come in a friendly manner, and not with swords and guns, as to invade an enemy.[8]

Smith's threat was carried out: war against the Powhatans started in August 1609 and the destruction of the Powhatans became the order of the day. The war dragged on for a year until the English governor, Thomas Gage, ordered forces mobilized by George Percy, a mercenary who had fought in the Netherlands, "to take revenge" and destroy the Indigenous population. In his report following the assault, Percy gloated over the gruesome details of killing all the children. Despite the terrorizing tactics of the settlers, the Powhatans were able to protect their grain storage buildings and force the Jamestown settlers to shelter within their colonial fortress.[9] Meanwhile the Powhatans organized a stronger confederacy. In 1622, they attacked all the English settlements along the James River, killing 350—a third of the settler population. Unable to eliminate the Indigenous population by force of arms, the colonists resorted to a "feedfight," as Grenier identifies it—systematic destruction of all the Indigenous agricultural resources.[10] A dozen years later an even greater conflict broke out, the Tidewater War (1644–46). Hardly a war, it consisted rather of settlers continuously raiding Indigenous villages and fields with the goal of starving the people out of the area. There followed three decades of peace, from which the settlers inferred that total war and expulsion of the Indigenous people worked. The few Indigenous families that remained in eastern Virginia were under the absolute dominance of the English. It was clear, Grenier points out, that "the English would tolerate Indians within and near their settlements provided they essentially neither saw nor heard them."[11] In the absence of Indigenous sources of food and labor, the colonists brought in enslaved Africans and indentured European servants to do the work.

By 1676, the settler population of Virginia had mushroomed and English tobacco farmers were encroaching on the lands of the Susquehannock people. When the Susquehannocks resisted, a war broke out that went badly for the English. In 1676, the Virginia House of Burgesses formed a mounted force of 125 men to range through a particular cluster of Indigenous villages and thereby overcome Susquehannock resistance.[12] This was the immediate background of Bacon's Rebellion, so beloved by populist US historians and those who search for the onset of racialized servitude in the British colonies. The rebellion occurred when Anglo settler-farmers along with landless indentured servants—both Anglo and African—took into their own hands the slaughter of Indigenous farmers with the aim of taking their land. The plantation owners who ruled the colony were troubled, to be sure, by the interracial aspect of the uprising. Soon after, Virginia law made greater distinction between indentured servants and slaves and codified the permanent status of slavery for Africans.[13] The point is an important one, but there is a larger issue. Bacon's Rebellion affected the development of genocidal policies aimed at the Indigenous peoples—namely, the creation of wealth in the colonies based on landholding and the use of landless or land-poor settler-farmers as foot soldiers for moving the settlement frontier deeper into Indigenous territories.[14] That the rebellion's leader, Nathaniel Bacon, was a wealthy planter reveals the relationship between the wealthy landed settlers and the poorer, often landless, settlers. Historian Eric Foner rightly concludes that the rebellion was a power play by Bacon against the Virginia governor William Berkeley and his planter allies, as Bacon's financial backers included other wealthy planters opposed to Berkeley.[15]

IN THE NAME OF GOD

What transpired up the coast in the founding and growth of the New England colony was different, at least at first. Just before the 1620 landing of the *Mayflower*, smallpox had spread from English trading ships off the coast to the Pequot fishing and farming communities on land, greatly reducing the population of the area the Plymouth Colony would occupy. King James attributed the epidemic to God's "great goodness and bounty toward us."[16] Consequently, those who survived in the Indigenous communities had little means to immediately resist the settlers' expropriation of their lands and resources. Sixteen years later, however, the Indigenous villages had recovered and were considered a barrier to the settlers moving into Pequot territory in Connecticut. A single violent incident triggered a devastating Puritan war against the Pequots in what the colony's annals and subsequent history texts call the Pequot War.

The Puritan settlers, as if by instinct, jumped immediately into a hideous war of annihilation, entering Indigenous villages and killing women and children or taking them hostage. The Pequots responded by attacking English settlements, including Fort Saybrook in Connecticut. Connecticut authorities commissioned mercenary John Mason to lead a force of soldiers from that colony and Massachusetts to one of the two Pequot strongholds on the Mystic River. Pequot fighters occupied one of the forts, while the other one contained only women, children, and old men. The latter was the one John Mason targeted. Slaughter ensued. After killing most of the Pequot defenders, the soldiers set fire to the structures and burned the remaining inhabitants alive.[17]

This kind of war was alien to the Indigenous peoples.[18] According to their ways of war, when relations between groups broke down
and conflict came, warfare was highly ritualized, with quests for
individual glory, resulting in few deaths. Colonial wars inevitably
drew other Indigenous communities in on one side or the other. During the Pequot War, neighboring Narragansett villages allied with
the Puritans in hopes of reaping a large harvest of captives, booty,
and glory. But after the carnage was done, the Narragansetts left the
Puritan side in disgust, saying that the English were "too furious"
and "slay[ed] too many men." After having made the Pequots the enemy, the settlers set out to complete the destruction. Fewer than two
hundred half-starved Pequots remained of the two thousand at the
beginning of the war. Although they had ceased fighting and were
without any means of defense, the settlers started a new attack on
the Pequots. The colony commissioned the mercenary Mason and
his murderous crew of forty men to burn the few remaining homes
and fields.[19] Puritan William Bradford wrote at the time in his *History of Plymouth Plantation*:

> Those that scaped the fire were slaine with the sword; some
> hewed to peeces, others rune throw with their rapiers, so as
> they were quickly dispatchte, and very few escaped. It was
> conceived they thus destroyed about 400 at this time. It was a
> fearful sight to see them thus frying in the fyer, and the streams
> of blood quenching the same, and horrible was the stincke and
> sente there of, but the victory seemed a sweete sacrifice, and
> they gave the prayers thereof to God, who had wrought so
> wonderfully for them, thus to inclose their enemise in their
> hands, and give them so speedy a victory over so proud and
> insulting an enimie.[20]

The other Indigenous nations of the region assessed what was in
store for them and accepted tributary status under the colonial authority.

During the late seventeenth century, Anglo settlers in New England began the routine practice of scalp hunting and what Grenier identifies as "ranging"—the use of settler-ranger forces. By

that time, the non-Indigenous population of the English colony in North America had increased sixfold, to more than 150,000, which meant that settlers were intruding on more of the Indigenous homelands. Indigenous resistance followed in what the settlers called King Philip's War.[21] Wampanoag people and their Indigenous allies attacked the settlers' isolated farms, using a method of guerrilla warfare that relied on speed and caution in striking and retreating. The settlers scorned this kind of resistance as "skulking," and responded by destroying Indigenous villages—again extirpation. But Indigenous guerrilla attacks continued, and so the commander of the Plymouth militia, Benjamin Church, studied Indigenous tactics in order to develop a more effective kind of preemption. He petitioned the colony's governor for permission to choose sixty to seventy settlers to serve as scouts, as he called them, for what he termed "wilderness warfare." In July 1676, the first settler-organized ranger force was the result. The rangers—60 settlers and 140 colonized Indigenous men—were to "discover, pursue, fight, surprise, destroy, or subdue" the enemy, in Church's words. The inclusion of Indigenous fighters on the colonists' side has marked settler colonialism and foreign occupations ever since.[22] The settler-rangers could learn from their Native aides, then discard them. In the following two decades, Church perfected his evolving method of annihilation.

"REDSKINS"

Indigenous people continued to resist by burning settlements and killing and capturing settlers. As an incentive to recruit fighters, colonial authorities introduced a program of scalp hunting that became a permanent and long-lasting element of settler warfare against Indigenous nations.[23] During the Pequot War, Connecticut and Massachusetts colonial officials had offered bounties initially for the heads of murdered Indigenous people and later for only their scalps, which were more portable in large numbers. But scalp hunting became routine only in the mid-1670s, following an incident on the northern frontier of the Massachusetts colony. The practice began in earnest in 1697 when settler Hannah Dustin, having murdered ten of her Abenaki captors in a nighttime escape, presented their ten scalps to the Massachusetts General Assembly and was rewarded with bounties for two men, two women, and six children.[24]

Dustin soon became a folk hero among New England settlers. Scalp hunting became a lucrative commercial practice. The settler authorities had hit upon a way to encourage settlers to take off on their own or with a few others to gather scalps, at random, for the reward money. "In the process," John Grenier points out, "they established the large-scale privatization of war within American frontier communities."[25] Although the colonial government in time raised the bounty for adult male scalps, lowered that for adult females, and eliminated that for Indigenous children under ten, the age and gender of victims were not easily distinguished by their scalps nor checked carefully. What is more, the scalp hunter could take the children captive and sell them into slavery. These practices erased any remaining distinction between Indigenous combatants and noncombatants and introduced a market for Indigenous slaves. Bounties for Indigenous scalps were honored even in absence of war. Scalps and Indigenous children became means of exchange, currency, and this development may even have created a black market. Scalp hunting was not only a profitable privatized enterprise but also a means to eradicate or subjugate the Indigenous population of the Anglo-American Atlantic seaboard.[26] The settlers gave a name to the mutilated and bloody corpses they left in the wake of scalp-hunts: redskins.

This way of war, forged in the first century of colonization—destroying Indigenous villages and fields, killing civilians, ranging, and scalp hunting—became the basis for the wars against the Indigenous across the continent into the late nineteenth century.[27]

COLONIAL EXPANSION

Having cleared the Indigenous populations from much of the coastal region from New England to the Carolinas, another wave of settlers employed the same kind of warfare in establishing the colony of Georgia beginning in 1732. Technically, it was the part of Spanish-occupied Florida called Guale. From the time the first settlers squatted on Indigenous land in Georgia, rangers were in the forefront of ethnic cleansing, clearing the region for British settlement. Brigadier General James Oglethorpe, commander in chief of the Georgia colony, tried but failed to turn his own small regular army into rangers, so he commissioned Hugh Mackay Jr. to organize the regulars into a Highland ranger force. A settler agent for the Georgia colony, Mackay was a former British army officer and a Scots Highlander. The Highlanders were reputed to be tough, fearless fighters—in other words, brutal killers. It was unusual at the time to put a local militia officer in command of army regulars.[28]

The Indigenous population of Georgia consisted primarily of the Cherokee Nation. The colonizers realized it would be impossible to persuade the Cherokees to accept or defend Georgia settlers if war broke out between Britain and Spain over British encroachment into Spanish Guale. Traders from Carolina had already brought smallpox and rum to the Cherokees, which had killed many in their villages and made them suspicious of all English people. Oglethorpe himself visited Cherokee towns but was rebuffed. Meanwhile Spanish agents were also trying to win over the Cherokees to fight on their side against the British. In the fall of 1739, on the verge of war, Oglethorpe won commitment from some Cherokee villages in exchange for corn, but he was aware that, like other Indigenous nations, the Cherokees would likely play one colonial power against the other for their own interests and could change sides at any moment. In December, English invasion farther into Spanish territory began. Anglo and Scots rangers and their Indigenous allies destroyed Spanish plantations and intimidated the Maroon communities in northern Florida composed of local Indigenous families and escaped African slaves from the British colonies. The rangers sacked and looted, burned and pillaged, while hunting scalps of Spanish-allied Indigenous people and runaway slaves. Lasting nearly a month, the operations ravaged Florida, in part because the Spanish put up little fight. During the 1740s, the British War Office and Parliament commissioned two companies of colonial rangers and authorized more than a hundred men for full-time duty in the Highland Rangers in Georgia.[29] Ranging, looting, and scalp hunting continued.

WAR THAT TURNS THE TIDE

The decade leading up to the outbreak of the French and Indian War (1754–63), known in Europe as the Seven Years' War, saw conflict on the British-French frontiers in New England, New York, and Nova Scotia, all of which were well populated with Indigenous villages of various nations as well as French settlers called Acadians.[30] A clash of interests among British settlers, Indigenous communities, and Acadians in the region of the present-day Canadian Maritime Provinces led to a four-year conflict that the British called King George's War. Although Britain had gained nominal possession of Nova Scotia, it could not control the population of Acadians and the mixed communities of intermarried Acadians and Mi'kmaq and Malisset people. The Acadian-Indigenous villages insisted on neutrality in the British and French disputes, and the powerful Haudenosaunee confederacy supported them in that stance. But British imperialists wanted the land, and they permitted Anglo-American settlers to play a prominent role in the fighting, which included ranging and scalp hunting. By the end of the war, settler-rangers dominated the British military presence in Nova Scotia, setting off sustained Acadian-Indigenous resistance against British rule.[31]

At the outbreak of the French and Indian War, while the British regular army and navy focused on French imperial positions in the Maritimes, the settler militia forces continued ranging against the Acadian-Indigenous villages, which led to an expulsion of the Acadians, sometimes known today as the Great Upheaval. In a period of weeks, British army forces and colonial militias forced four thousand noncombatants out of Nova Scotia, and at least half that number died in the Acadian diaspora. Some eight thousand escaped deportation by fleeing into the woods. The Acadians thus became the largest population of European settlers in North American history to be forcibly dispersed. This feat was accomplished with slaughter, intimidation, and plunder. By this time, there was no hesitation on the part of Anglo settlers to consider unarmed civilians of all ages as appropriate targets of violence.

Major General Jeffery Amherst—after whom Amherst, Massachusetts is named—commanded the British army in the North American theater of the Seven Years' War. In 1759, Amherst appointed Major Robert Rogers, the seasoned leader of New England's Rogers's Rangers and perhaps the most famous and admired ranger in frontier lore, to lead a force of settler-rangers, British volunteers, and allied Stockbridge Indigenous scouts—all to be handpicked by Rogers. Amherst ordered them to attack a resistant Abenaki village in the St. Lawrence River Valley. Although Amherst ordered Rogers not to allow torture or killing of women or children, the commander would have known about these rangers' reputation of sparing no one in their blood-drenched raids on Indigenous villages. In commissioning Rogers, Amherst effectively sanctioned settler-ranger counterinsurgent warfare. In general, the British military not only tolerated but made use of the settlers' dirty war, in the Cherokee war, the subsequent French and Indian War, and in the effort to crush Pontiac's Rebellion of 1763, in which Amherst is best known for his support of using germ warfare against Indigenous people.[32] "Could it not be contrived," Amherst wrote to a subordinate officer, "to Send the Small Pox among those Disaffected Tribes of Indians? We must, on this occasion, Use Every Stratagem in our power to Reduce them." The colonel promised to do his best.[33] Amherst then gave orders "to bring them [Pontiac's forces and allies] to a proper Subjection" until "there was not an Indian Settlement within a thousand Miles of our Country."[34]

In the southern part of the French and Indian War, the British in 1760 found their war-making capacity overwhelmed by the Cherokee Nation. So here too they turned to rangers. In the spring, when the Cherokee Nation challenged British authority, Amherst rushed regular regiments to Charleston under the command of Colonel Archibald Montgomery with orders to punish the Cherokees as quickly as possible so the soldiers could return north and join in the imminent attack on Montreal. In previous wars against Indigenous nations, British commanders had assigned ranger groups specific missions, but in the Cherokee war, the British military forces, including regulars, would target noncombatants. A few months earlier, the North Carolina governor had conjured the strategy that would be used:

In Case a War must be proclaimed, the three Southern Provinces of Virginia and the Carolinas should exert their whole
force, enter into and destroy all the [Cherokee] Towns of those
at War with us, and make as many of them as we should take
their Wives and Children Slaves, by sending them to the Islands
[West Indies] if above 10 years old . . . and to allow 10 lbs sterling for every prisoner taken and delivered in each Province.[35]

This was the plan adopted. Commander Montgomery was well
aware that even with irregular warfare the military could not defeat
the Cherokees in their own country and that he would need settlers and Indigenous allies serving as scouts and guides. He added to
his troop strength three hundred settler-rangers, forty local militia
members, and fifty Catawba allies. The Cherokee Nation had not
succeeded in forming a confederation with the Muskogees or Chickasaws, so their villages were vulnerable. The first target was the autonomous Cherokee town of Estatoe, comprising some two hundred
homes and two thousand people. Montgomery's forces set all the
homes and buildings afire, picking off individuals who tried to flee,
while others who hid inside were burned alive. One after another,
towns were set ablaze until the Cherokees organized a resistance
strong enough to drive out the attackers. The British claimed to have
crushed Cherokee resistance, but they had not, and the Cherokees
laid siege to British forts. A year later, British forces struck again, this
time even harder, and overwhelmed the Cherokees in their capital of
Etchoe and destroyed it. The British then moved on to the other Cherokee towns, burning them too. During the month-long, one-sided
battle of annihilation, the British razed fifteen towns and burned
fourteen hundred acres of corn. Five thousand Cherokees were made
homeless refugees, and the number of deaths remained uncounted.[36]

Another weapon of war was alcohol, accelerating in the eighteenth century. In 1754, a Catawba leader known as King Hagler by
English colonists petitioned the North Carolina authorities:

Brothers, here is one thing you yourselves are to blame very
much in; that is you rot your grain in tubs, out of which you
take and make strong spirits.

You sell it to our young men and give it [to] them, many times; they get very drunk with it [and] this is the very cause that they oftentimes commit those crimes that is offensive to you and us and all through the effect of that drink. It is also very bad for our people, for it rots their guts and causes our men to get very sick and many of our people has lately died by the effects of that strong drink, and I heartily wish you would do something to prevent your people from daring to sell or give them any of that strong drink, upon any consideration whatever, for that will be a great means of our being free from being accused of those crimes that is committed by our young men and will prevent many of the abuses that is done by them through the effect of that strong drink.[37]

King Hagler continued to petition for years for an embargo on liquor without succeeding.

Britain's victory at the end of the French and Indian War in 1763 led to English domination of world trade, sea power, and colonial holdings for a century and a half.[38] In the Treaty of Paris (1763) France ceded Canada and all claims east of the Mississippi to Britain. In the course of the war, Anglo settlers had gained strength in numbers and security in relation to Indigenous peoples just outside the British-occupied colonies. Even there, significant numbers of settlers had squatted on Indigenous lands beyond the colonies' putative boundaries, reaching into the Ohio Valley region. To the settlers' dismay, soon after the Treaty of Paris was signed, King George III issued a proclamation that prohibited British settlement west of the Allegheny-Appalachian mountain barrier, ordering those who had settled there to relinquish their claims and move back east of the line. However, British authorities did not commit enough troops to the frontier to enforce the edict effectively. As a result, thousands more settlers poured over the mountains and squatted on Indigenous lands.

By the early 1770s, terror against Indigenous people on the part of Anglo settlers increased in all the colonies, and speculation in western lands was rampant. In the southern colonies especially, farmers who had lost their land in competition with larger, more efficient, slave-worked plantations rushed for western land. These settler-farmers thus set, as Grenier writes, "a prefigurative pattern of U.S. annexation and colonization of Indigenous nations across the continent for the following century: a vanguard of farmer-settlers led by seasoned 'Indian fighters,' calling on authorities/militias of the British colonies, first, and the U.S. government/army later, to defend their settlements, forming the core dynamic of U.S. 'democracy.'"[39]

The French and Indian War would later be seen as the trigger for independence of the settler population, in which the distinctly "American" nation was born. This mythology was expressed in the 1826 novel *The Last of the Mohicans: A Narrative of 1757*, in which the author—land speculator James Fenimore Cooper—created a us-able settler-colonial history. Blockbuster Hollywood adaptations of the book in 1932 and 1992 reinforced the mythology. But the 1940 film, based on the best-selling novel *Northwest Passage*, which is considered a classic and remains popular due to repeated television showings, goes even further in portraying the bloodthirsty merce-naries, Rogers's Rangers, as heroes for their annihilation of a village of Abenakis.[40]

THE OHIO COUNTRY

The settlers' war for independence from Britain paralleled a decade of "Indian wars" (1774–83), all with settler-rangers using extreme violence against Indigenous noncombatants with the goals of total subjugation or expulsion. The British governor of Virginia, John Murray, the Fourth Earl of Dunmore, sided with British settlers who wanted land in the Ohio Country (in part because he was himself a land speculator). In his view, no royal policy could prevent settlers' seizure of Indigenous land. In early 1774, the Shawnee Nation in the Ohio Valley region responded to settler encroachment on its farm-lands and hunting grounds by raiding illicit settlements and chasing out land surveyors. The settlers seem to have been waiting for just such an excuse to retaliate viciously. Dunmore commissioned 150 Virginia settler-rangers to destroy Shawnee towns, and he mobilized the Virginia militia to invade the Ohio Valley and to "proceed directly to their Towns, and if possible destroy their Towns and magazines and distress them in every other way that is possible."[41]

During "Lord Dunmore's War," Shawnees and other Indigenous peoples in what the Anglo separatists would soon call the Northwest Territory realized that they were in a life-or-death struggle with these murdering bands of settlers who were led by a wealthy land speculator, intent on destroying their nation and wiping them from the face of the earth. This realization led to another recurrent factor in the onslaught of European colonial ventures: the appearance of an accommodationist faction within the Shawnee Nation that accepted a humiliating peace agreement. Dunmore demanded all the Shawnee hunting grounds in what would later become, following US independence, the state of Kentucky.[42] Although Virginia did not get all the land Dunmore demanded, Dunmore's War was only the beginning of a three-decade war against the Shawnee Nation and its allies. That alliance was led militarily in its resistance by the great Tecumseh, born in 1768, who had grown up in the midst of unrelenting warfare against his people, along with his brother, Tenskwatawa, also known as the Prophet and the movement's spiritual leader.[43]

Dunmore's War pushed the Shawnees into an alliance with the British against the separatists in 1777. Indigenous warriors struck scattered squatter settlements throughout the Upper Ohio Valley region, driving hundreds of settlers from Shawnee territory. But the tide of war between the British and the separatists turned, allowing the Continental Congress to focus on the Ohio Country and organize an offensive to annihilate the Shawnee Nation. Five hundred separatist fighters, composed of both militiamen and regulars, waged a genocidal war. Rampaging against combatants and noncombatants alike, the ranger force fell on the staunchly neutral towns of the Delaware Nation, torturing and killing women and children. In one particularly twisted incident, the settler troops slaughtered a Delaware boy who had been bird hunting alone. A near-riot ensued among the troops over who had the right to claim the "honor" of the kill. The Continental Congress sent a thousand more fighters with orders to "proceed, without delay, to destroy such towns of hostile tribes of Indians as he [Brigadier General Lachlan

McIntosh] in his discretion shall think will most effectually chastise and terrify the savages, and check their ravages on the frontiers." The Shawnees moved out of the way of the raiders to avoid the attacks, but the killing went on unabated.[44]

The settlers' escalation of extreme violence in the Ohio Country led to perhaps the most outrageous war crime, which showed that Indigenous conversion to Christianity and pacifism was no protection from genocide. Moravian missionizing among the ravaged Delaware communities in Pennsylvania had produced three Moravian Indian villages in the decades before the war for independence had begun. Residents of one of the settlements, named Gnadenhütten, in eastern Ohio, were displaced by British troops during fighting in the area, but were able to return to harvest their corn. Soon afterward, in March 1782, a settler militia from Pennsylvania under the command of David Williamson appeared and rounded up the Delawares, telling them they had to evacuate for their own safety. There were forty-two men, twenty women, and thirty-four children in the group of Delawares. The militiamen searched their belongings to confiscate anything that could be used as a weapon, then announced that they were all to be killed, accusing them of having given refuge to Delawares who had killed white people. They were also accused of stealing the household items and tools they possessed, because such items should only belong to white people. Condemned to death, the Delawares spent the night praying and singing hymns. In the morning, Williamson's men marched over ninety people in pairs into two houses and methodically slaughtered them. One killer bragged that he personally had bludgeoned fourteen victims with a cooper's mallet, which he had then handed to an accomplice. "My arm fails me," he was said to have announced. "Go on with the work."[45] This action set a new bar for violence, and atrocities that followed routinely surpassed even that atrocity.[46]

A year earlier, the Delaware leader Buckongeahelas had addressed a group of Christianized Delawares, saying that he had known some good white men, but that the good ones were a small number:

> They do what they please. They enslave those who are not of their color, although created by the same Great Spirit who

created us. They would make slaves of us if they could, but as they cannot do it, they kill us. There is no faith to be placed in their words. They are not like the Indians, who are only enemies while at war, and are friends in peace. They will say to an Indian: "My friend, my brother." They will take him by the hand, and at the same moment destroy him. And so you will also be treated by them before long. Remember that this day I have warned you to beware of such friends as these. I know the long knives; they are not to be trusted.[47]

HOW THE SETTLERS WON INDEPENDENCE

Both the British and their settler separatist opponents realized that the key to victory on the southern frontier of the thirteen colonies was an alliance with the Cherokee Nation. Despite constant attacks on its villages and crops, and with refugees and disease, the enormous Cherokee Nation remained intact with a well-functioning government. To win the Cherokees to their side, British authorities provided weaponry and money to Cherokee towns while separatist representatives tried to persuade the towns to remain neutral by threatening their complete destruction. Neutrality was the most the settlers could hope for. The settlers' viciousness toward Indigenous people caused them to be despised and spurred some Cherokees to take sides against them. A few Cherokee towns that had been hit hardest by settler-rangers responded by attacking squatter settlements, destroying several in the Carolinas in 1776. Following such attacks, separatists quickly announced their determination to destroy the Cherokee Nation. The North Carolina delegation to the Continental Congress declared, "The gross infernal breach of faith which they [the Cherokees] have been guilty of shuts them out from every pretension to mercy, and it is surely the policy of the Southern Colonies to carry fire and Sword into the very bowels of their country and sink them so low that they may never be able again to rise and disturb the peace of their Neighbors."[48]

In the summer and fall of 1776, more than five thousand settler-rangers from Virginia, Georgia, and North and South Carolina stormed through Cherokee territory.[49] William Henry Drayton, a leader of the Anglo separatists from Charleston, had met with the Cherokees in 1775. After the Cherokee attack that prompted the separatists' 1776 scorched-earth campaign, he recommended that "the nation be extirpated, and the lands become the property of the public. For my part, I shall never give my voice for a peace with the Cherokee Nation upon any other terms than their removal beyond the mountains."[50] As Cherokees fled, abandoning their towns and fields, the soldiers seized, killed, and scalped women and children, taking no prisoners.[51]

In mid-1780, eighty Virginia separatist settler-rangers attacked the Shawnees in southern Ohio and spent a month destroying and looting their towns and fields. At the same time, the Cherokee Nation regained momentum in its resistance, raiding squatters' settlements within its territory. In retaliation, North Carolina sent five hundred mounted rangers to burn Cherokee towns, with orders to "chastise that nation and reduce them to obedience." During the winter of 1780–81, the separatist seven-hundred-man Virginia militia wreaked destruction again in the Cherokee Nation. On Christmas Day, the militia commander wrote to Thomas Jefferson, then a Virginia delegate to the Continental Congress, that a detachment had "surprised a party of Indians, [and taken] one scalp, and Seventeen Horses loaded with clothing and skins and House furnishings"—a clear sign that these were noncombatant refugees trying to flee. The commander also reported that his forces had thus far destroyed the principal Cherokee towns of Chote, Scittigo, Chilhowee Togue, Micliqua, Kai-a-tee, Sattoogo, Telico, Hiwassee, and Chistowee, along with several smaller villages.

All told, more than a thousand homes had been laid waste, and some fifty thousand bushels of corn and other provisions either burned or looted.[52] At this point, the Virginia and North Carolina separatist authorities pooled their manpower and matériel and organized a force that effected a broad sweep of annihilation through the Cherokee towns, driving residents out into present-day middle Tennessee and northern Alabama, where they exterminated Indigenous families and burned down the towns in that area too.

Throughout the war between separatist settlers and the forces of the monarchy, armed settlers waged total war against Indigenous people, largely realizing their objectives. The Cherokees were forced to accept tributary status, yet the attacks continued. It would take nearly a half century after US independence was won to forcibly remove the Cherokee Nation from the South, but the effort was un-relenting. For the settlers squatting on Indigenous lands across the 1763 Proclamation Line of King George III, the wars waged by set-tlers during the war of independence were a continuation of those their ancestors and other predecessors had waged since the early seventeenth century. Some historians portray the British as the or-ganizers of Indigenous resistance during this period. The separatist colonial oligarchy that drew up the Declaration of Independence in 1776 certainly took that view. Yet, as Grenier points out, the Indigenous people were well aware that negotiating with a faraway empire would yield much better outcomes than would dealing with the government of extermination-minded settlers.[53]

THE HAUDENOSAUNEE

On the western edge of the colony of New York, as in the southern colonies, settlers were invading and squatting on the territory of the Haudenosaunee (Six Nations Iroquois) by the mid-1770s. As with the Cherokee Nation, the British and the separatists knew that the Haudenosaunee would be an important factor in their war, and, as with the Cherokee Nation, both parties sent representatives to the Haudenosaunee councils to appeal for their support. Each member nation of the confederacy had its own specific interests because each had had different experiences in the previous century and a half of British and French intrusion. Much of the French and Indian War had been fought in their territories, with Indigenous people doing most of the actual fighting on both sides. In 1775, the Mohawk Na-tion allied with the British against the separatist settlers. The Sen-eca Nation had early on considered the British to be an intractable enemy but with the separatist war looming was more afraid of the settlers, and so the Senecas followed the Mohawks' lead into a Brit-ish alliance. The Cayuga, Tuscarora, and Onondaga Nations did not choose sides. Only the Christianized Oneidas conceded support for the separatist settlers.

In response to the decisions by five of the Iroquois Nations, General George Washington wrote instructions to Major General John Sullivan to take peremptory action against the Haudenosaunee, "to lay waste all the settlements around . . . that the country may not be merely *overrun* but *destroyed*. . . . [Y]ou will not by any means, listen to any overture of peace before the total ruin of their settlements is effected. . . . Our future security will be in their inability to injure us . . . and in the terror with which the severity of the chastisement they receive will inspire them." Sullivan replied, "The Indians shall see that there is malice enough in our hearts to destroy everything that contributes to their support."[54]

By 1779, the Continental Congress had decided to start with the Senecas. Three armies were mustered to scorch the earth across New York and converge at Tioga, the principal Seneca town, in what is now northern Pennsylvania. Their orders were to wipe out the Senecas and any other Indigenous nation that opposed their separatist project, burning and looting all the villages, destroying the food supply, and turning the inhabitants into homeless refugees. The separatist governments of the New York and Pennsylvania colonies offered rangers for the project, and, as an incentive for enlistment, the Pennsylvania assembly authorized a bounty on Seneca scalps, without regard to sex or age. This combination of Continental Army regulars, settler-rangers, and commercial scalp hunters ravaged most of Seneca territory.

With the Iroquois Confederacy disunited regarding the war, the Continental Army forces were practically unimpeded in their triumphal and deadly march. In another scenario typically resulting from European and Anglo-American colonialism and neocolonialism, civil war erupted within the Iroquois Confederacy itself, with Mohawks destroying Oneida villages. The Oneidas could no longer give their separatist allies intelligence. "By 1781," Grenier observes, "after three seasons of the Indian war, New York's frontier had become a no-man's-land."[55]

FIVE

THE BIRTH OF A NATION

*Our nation was born in genocide. . . . We are perhaps
the only nation which tried as a matter of national
policy to wipe out its indigenous population. Moreover,
we elevated that tragic experience into a noble crusade.
Indeed, even today we have not permitted ourselves
to reject or feel remorse for this shameful episode.*

—Martin Luther King Jr.

The British withdrew from the fight to maintain their thirteen colonies in 1783, in order to redirect their resources to the conquest of South Asia. The British East India Company had been operating in the subcontinent since 1600 in a project parallel to Britain's colonization of the North American Atlantic Coast. Britain's transfer to the United States of its claim to the Ohio Country spelled a nightmarish disaster for all Indigenous peoples east of the Mississippi. Britain's withdrawal in 1783 did not end military actions against Indigenous peoples but rather was a prelude to unrestrained violent colonization of the continent. In negotiations to end the war, Britain did not insist on consideration for the Indigenous nations that resisted the settlers' war of secession. In the resulting 1783 Treaty of Paris, the Crown transferred to the United States ownership of all its territory south of the Great Lakes, from the Mississippi to the Atlantic, and north of Spanish-occupied Florida. Muskogee Creek leader Alexander McGillivray expressed the general Indigenous view: "To find ourselves and country betrayed to our enemies and divided between the Spaniards and Americans is cruel and ungenerous."[1]

THE NEW ORDER

Wars continued for another century, unrelentingly and without pause, and the march across the continent used the same strategy and tactics of scorched earth and annihilation with increasingly deadly firepower. Somehow, even "genocide" seems an inadequate description for what happened, yet rather than viewing it with horror, most Americans have conceived of it as their country's manifest destiny.

With the consolidation of the new state, the United States of America, by 1790, the opportunity for Indigenous nations to negotiate alliances with competing European empires against the despised settlers who intended to destroy them was greatly narrowed. Nevertheless, Indigenous nations had defied the founding of the independent United States in a manner that allowed for their survival and created a legacy—a culture of resistance—that has persisted. By the time of the birth of the US republic, Indigenous peoples in what is now the continental United States had been resisting European colonization for two centuries. They had no choice given the aspirations of the colonizers: total elimination of Native nations or survival. Precolonial Indigenous societies were dynamic social systems with adaptation built into them. Fighting for survival did not require cultural abandonment. On the contrary, the cultures used already existing strengths, such as diplomacy and mobility, to develop new mechanisms required to live in nearly constant crisis. There is always a hard core of resistance in that process, but the culture of resistance also includes accommodations to the colonizing social order, including absorbing Christianity into already existing religious practices, using the colonizer's language, and intermarrying with settlers and, more importantly, with other oppressed groups, such as escaped African slaves. Without the culture of resistance, surviving Indigenous peoples under US colonization would have been eliminated through individual assimilation.

A new element was added in the independent Anglo-American legal regime: treaty making. The US Constitution specifically refers to Indigenous nations only once, but significantly, in Article 1, Section

8: "[Congress shall have Power] to regulate Commerce with foreign Nations and among the several States, and with the Indian Tribes." In the federal system in which all powers not specifically reserved for the federal government go to the states, relations with Indigenous nations are unequivocally a federal matter.

Although not mentioned as such, Native peoples are implied in the Second Amendment. Male settlers had been required in the colonies to serve in militias during their lifetimes for the purpose of raiding and razing Indigenous communities, the southern colonies included, and later states' militias were used as "slave patrols." The Second Amendment, ratified in 1791, enshrined these irregular forces into law: "A well regulated Militia, being necessary to the security of a free State, the right of the people to keep and bear Arms, shall not be infringed." The continuing significance of that "freedom" specified in the Bill of Rights reveals the settler-colonialist cultural roots of the United States that appear even in the present as a sacred right.[2]

US genocidal wars against Indigenous nations continued unabated in the 1790s and were woven into the very fabric of the new nation-state. The fears, aspirations, and greed of Anglo-American settlers on the borders of Indigenous territories perpetuated this warfare and influenced the formation of the US Army, much as the demands and actions of backcountry settlers had shaped the colonial militias in North America. Owners of large, slave-worked plantations sought to expand their landholdings while small farm owners who were unable to compete with the planters and were pushed off their land now desperately sought cheap land to support their families. The interests of both settler groups were in tension with those of state and military authorities who sought to build a new professional military based on Washington's army. Just as the US government and its army were taking form, a number of settlements on the peripheries of Indigenous nations threatened to secede, prompting the army to make rapid expansion into Indigenous territories a top priority. Brutal counterinsurgency warfare would be the key to the army's destruction of the Indigenous peoples' civilization in the Ohio Country and the rest of what was then called the Northwest over the first quarter-century of US independence.[3]

TOTAL WAR IN OHIO SETS THE STAGE

The first Washington administration was consumed by the crisis engendered by its inability to quickly conquer and colonize the Ohio Country over which it claimed sovereignty.[4] During the Confederation period, before the US Constitution was written and ratified, the Indigenous nations in that region had access to a constant supply of British arms and had formed effective political and military alliances, the first of them forged by Mohawk leader Joseph Brant during the 1780s. Washington's administration determined that only war, not diplomacy, would break up the Indigenous alliances. Secretary of War Henry Knox told the army commander of Fort Washington (where Cincinnati is today) that "to extend a defensive and efficient protection to so extensive a frontier, against solitary, or small parties of enterprising savages, seems altogether impossible. No other remedy remains, but to extirpate, utterly, if possible, the said Banditti."[5] These orders could not be implemented with a conventional army engaged in regular warfare. Although federal officers commanded the army, the fighters were nearly all drawn from militias made up primarily of squatter settlers from Kentucky. They were unaccustomed to army discipline but fearless and willing to kill to get a piece of land to grab or some scalps for bounty.

The army found the Miami villages they planned to attack already deserted, so they set up a base in one of the villages and waited for a Miami assault. But the assault was not forthcoming. When the commander sent out small units to find the Miamis, these search-and-destroy missions were ambushed and sent fleeing by allied Miamis and Shawnees under the leadership of Little Turtle (Meshekinnoqquah) and Blue Jacket (Weyapiersenwah). The deserted towns had been bait to lure the invaders into ambushes. The commander reported to the War Department that his forces had burned three hundred buildings and destroyed twenty thousand bushels of corn. Those were likely facts, but his claim to have broken up the Indigenous political and military organization was not accurate. Knox apparently knew that more than food and property destruction would be needed to quell resistance. He ordered the commanders to recruit five hundred weathered Kentucky mounted rangers to burn and loot Miami towns and fields along the Wabash River. They were to capture women and children as hostages to use as terms of surrender.

In carrying out these orders, the marauding rangers demonstrated what they could accomplish with unmitigated violence and a total lack of scruples and respect for noncombatants. They destroyed the Miamis' two largest towns and took forty-one women and children captive, then sent warnings to the other towns that the same would be their lot unless they surrendered unconditionally: "Your warriors will be slaughtered, your towns and villages ransacked and destroyed, your wives and children carried into captivity, and you may be assured that those who escape the fury of our mighty chiefs shall find no resting place on this side of the great lakes." Yet the Indians of the Ohio Country continued to fight, well aware of the likely consequences. The Seneca leader Cornplanter called the colonizers the "town destroyers." He described how, during the destruction and suffering that troops wreaked on the western Iroquois, Seneca "women look behind them and turn pale, and our children cling close to the necks of their mothers."[6]

Despite the primary use of settler militias, President Washington insisted that the new government had to develop a professional army that would enhance US prestige in the eyes of European countries. He also thought that the cost of using mercenaries, at four times that of regular troops, was too high. But whenever regular troops were sent into the Ohio Country, the Indigenous resisters drove them out. Reluctantly, Washington resigned himself to the necessity of using what were essentially vicious killers to terrorize the region, thereby annexing land that could be sold to settlers. The sale of confiscated land was the primary revenue source for the new government.

In late 1791, the War Department notified Ohio squatters to call out their rangers for an offensive. Major General "Mad" Anthony Wayne was charged with restructuring the units of the army under his command to function as irregular forces. Washington and other officials were aware that Wayne was unreliable and an alcoholic, but it appeared that such characteristics might be useful for the dirty war ahead. Between 1792 and 1794, Wayne put together a combined force of regulars with a large contingent of experienced rangers. He enthusiastically embraced such counterinsurgent tactics as destroying food supplies and murdering civilians.

Among the fifteen hundred mounted rangers in the first mission was the talented William Wells with his group of rangers. When he was thirteen, Wells had been captured by the Miamis and then had lived with them for nine years, marrying Little Turtle's daughter. Under his father-in-law's command, Wells had fought the invading settlers and the US Army. In 1792, Wells was chosen to represent the Miami Nation in a negotiation with the United States, but on arrival for talks he encountered a brother from the family he had been separated from for a decade. He was persuaded to return to Kentucky and served as a ranger for the US Army.[7]

Wayne's troops and rangers managed to enter the Ohio Country and establish a base they called Fort Defiance (in northwestern Ohio), in what had been the heart of the Indigenous alliance led by Little Turtle.[8] Wayne then made an ultimatum to the Shawnees: "In pity to your innocent women and children, come and prevent the further effusion of your blood." The Shawnee leader Blue Jacket refused submission, and the US forces began destroying Shawnee villages and fields and murdering women, children, and old men. On August 20, 1794, at Fallen Timbers, the main Shawnee fighting force was overpowered. Even after this US victory, the rangers continued for three days laying waste to Shawnee houses and cornfields. After creating a fifty-mile swath of devastation, the invading forces returned to Fort Defiance. The defeat at Fallen Timbers was a severe blow to the Indigenous nations of the Ohio Country, but they would reorganize their resistance during the following decade.

The US conquest of southern Ohio was formalized in the 1795 Treaty of Greenville, a victory based on vicious irregular warfare. The nations of the region no longer had the British and the French and the settlers to play against one another, but rather were now faced with the determined imperialist thrust of an independent republic that had to coddle settlers if they were to recruit any into their service.[9]

TECUMSEH

Over the following decade, more settlers poured over the Appalachians, squatting on Indigenous lands, and even building towns, anticipating that the US military, land speculators, and civilian institutions would follow.

In the Ohio Country, the Shawnee brothers Tecumseh and Tenskwatawa began building a concerted Indigenous resistance in the early nineteenth century. From their organizing center, Prophet's Town, founded in 1807, Tenskwatawa and his fellow organizers traveled throughout Shawnee towns calling for a return to their cultural roots, which had been eroded by the assimilation of Anglo-American practices and trade goods, especially alcohol.[10] Abuse of alcohol (and drugs) is epidemic like diseases in communities subjected to colonization or other forms of domination, particularly in crowded and miserable refugee situations. This is the case in all parts of the world, not only among Native peoples of North America. Alcohol was an item in the tool kit of colonialists who made it readily and cheaply available. Christian missionaries often took advantage of these dysfunctional conditions to convert, offering not only food and housing but also discipline to avoid alcohol. But this was itself a form of colonial submission.

Significantly, Tecumseh did not limit his vision to the Ohio Country but also envisaged organizing all the peoples west to the Mississippi, north into the Great Lakes region, and south to the Gulf of Mexico. He visited other Indigenous nations, calling for unity in defiance of the squatters' presence on their lands. He presented a program that would end all sales of Indigenous land to settlers. Only then would settlers' migrations in search of cheap land cease and the establishment of the United States in the West be prevented. An alliance of all Indigenous nations could then manage Indigenous lands as a federation. His program, strategy, and philosophy mark the beginning of pan-Indigenous movements in Anglo-colonized North America that established a model for future resistance. Joseph Brant and Pontiac had originated the strategy in the 1780s, but Tecumseh and Tenskwatawa forged a pan-Indigenous framework made all the more potent by combining Indigenous spirituality and politics while respecting the particular religions and languages of each nation.[11]

The evolving Indigenous alliance posed a serious barrier to continued Anglo-American squatting and land speculation and acquisitions in the trans-Appalachian region. With previous Indigenous resistance movements, such as those led by Little Turtle and Blue Jacket, during peace negotiations in the wake of ruinous US wars of annihilation, leaders of factions had become "agency chiefs" who agreed to land sales without the consent of those they purported to represent. The colonized communities had fallen into economic dependency on trade goods and federal annuities, incurring debts that led to the forfeiture of what land remained in their hands. The emerging younger generation was contemptuous of such chiefs, whom they perceived as selling out their people. Anglo-American settlers and speculators exerted increased pressure and issued new threats of annihilation, provoking anger and calls for retaliation but also a renewed spirit of resistance.

By 1810, new Indigenous alliances challenged squatter settlers in the Indiana and Illinois Territories at a time when war between the United States and Great Britain was looming. Fearing that the British would unite with the Indigenous alliances to prevent the US imperialist goal to dominate the continent, these settlers drafted a petition to President James Madison, demanding that the government act preemptively: "The safety of the persons and property of this frontier can never be effectually secured, but by the breaking up of the combination formed by the Shawnee Prophet on the Wabash."[12]

In 1809, Indiana's territorial governor, William Henry Harrison, badgered and bribed a few destitute Delaware, Miami, and Potawatomi individuals to sign the Treaty of Fort Wayne, according to which these nations would hand over their land in what is now southern Indiana for an annual annuity. Tecumseh promptly condemned the treaty and those who signed it without the approval of the peoples they represented. Harrison met with Tecumseh at Vincennes in 1810, along with other delegates of the allied Shawnee, Kickapoo, Wyandot, Peoria, Ojibwe, Potawatomi, and Winnebago

Nations. The Shawnee leader informed Harrison that he was leaving for the South to bring the Muskogees, Choctaws, and Chickasaws into the alliance.

Harrison, now convinced that Tecumseh's brother Tenskwatawa, the Prophet, was the source of the renewed Indigenous militancy, reasoned that destroying Prophet's Town would crush the resistance. It would present a clear choice to the many Indigenous people who supported the militant leaders: cede more land to the United States and take the money and trade goods, or suffer further annihilation. He decided to strike in Tecumseh's absence. Having served as General Wayne's aide-de-camp in the Fallen Timbers attacks, Harrison knew how to keep his regular army forces from being ambushed. He assembled Indiana and Kentucky rangers—seasoned Indian killers —and some US Army regulars. At the site of what is today Terre Haute, Indiana, the soldiers constructed Fort Harrison on Shawnee land—a symbol of their intention to remain permanently. The people in Prophet's Town were aware of the military advance, but Tecumseh had warned them not to be drawn into a fight, because the alliance was not yet ready for war. Tenskwatawa sent scouts to observe the enemy's movements. The US forces arrived on the edge of Prophet's Town at dawn on November 6, 1811. Seeing no alternative to overriding his brother's instructions, Tenskwatawa led an assault before dawn the following morning. Only after some two hundred of the Indigenous residents had fallen did the troops overpower them, burning the town, destroying the granary, and looting, even digging up graves and mutilating the corpses. This was the famous "battle" of Tippecanoe that made Harrison a frontier hero to the settlers and later helped elect him president.[13]

The US Army's destruction of the capital of the alliance outraged Indigenous peoples all over the Old Northwest, prompting fighters of the Kickapoos, Winnebagos, Potawatamis, and even Creeks from the South to converge on a British garrison at Fort Malden in Canada to obtain supplies with which to fight. Contrary to the false US assumption that Tecumseh was a mere tool of the British, he had been unwilling to enter into a British alliance because Europeans had proved so unreliable in the past. But now he spoke for unified and coordinated Indigenous-led war on the United States that the

British could support if they wished but not control. President Madison, speaking to Congress in seeking a declaration of war against Great Britain, argued: "In reviewing the conduct of Great Britain toward the United States our attention is necessarily drawn to the warfare just renewed by the savages on one of our extensive frontiers—a warfare which is known to spare neither age nor sex and to be distinguished by features peculiarly shocking to humanity."[14]

During the summer of 1812, the Indigenous alliance struck US installations and squatter settlements with little help from the British. The US forts at present-day Detroit and Dearborn fell. Among the inhabitants of Fort Dearborn, Kentucky ranger William Wells was killed and his body mutilated as that of a despised turncoat. In the fall, Indigenous forces attacked Anglo-American squatter settlements all over Illinois and Indiana Territories. The US rangers attempting to track and kill the Indigenous fighters found destroyed and abandoned Anglo-American settlements, with thousands of settlers driven from their homes. In response, Harrison turned the militias loose on Indigenous fields and villages with no restrictions on their behavior. The head of the Kentucky militia mustered two thousand armed and mounted volunteers to destroy Indigenous towns near today's Peoria, Illinois, but without success. A reversal came in the fall of 1813, when Tecumseh was killed in the Battle of the Thames and the Indigenous army was destroyed. Throughout the eighteen-month war, militias and rangers attacked Indigenous civilians and agricultural resources, leaving behind starving refugees.[15]

ASSAULT ON THE CHEROKEE NATION

In the unconquered Indigenous region of the Old Southwest, parallel resistance took place during the two decades following US independence, with similar tragic results, thanks to extirpative settler warfare. Tennessee (formerly claimed, but not settled, by the British colony of North Carolina) was carved out of the larger Cherokee Nation and became a state in 1796. Its eastern part, particularly the area around today's Knoxville, was a war zone. The mostly Scots-Irish squatters, attempting to secure and expand their settlements, were at war with the resistant Cherokees called "Chickamaugas." The settlers hated both the Indigenous people whom they were attempting to displace as well as the newly formed federal government. In 1784, a group of North Carolina settlers, led by settler-ranger John Sevier, had seceded from western Carolina and established the independent country of Franklin with Sevier as president. Neither North Carolina nor the federal government had exerted any control over the settlements in the eastern Tennessee Valley region. In the summer of 1788, Sevier ordered an unprovoked, preemptive attack on the Chickamauga towns, killing thirty villagers and forcing the survivors to flee south. Sevier's actions formed a template for settler-federal relations, with the settlers implementing the federal government's final solution, while the federal government feigned an appearance of limiting settler invasions of Indigenous lands.[16]

Facing the fierce resistance of Indigenous nations in the Ohio Country and the fighting between the Muskogee Nation and the state of Georgia, Washington's administration sought to contain Indigenous resistance in the South. Yet now the settlers were provoking the Cherokees in what would soon be the state of Tennessee. Secretary of War Knox claimed to believe that the thickness of settlers' development, converting Indigenous hunting grounds into farms, would slowly overwhelm the Indigenous nations and drive them out. He advised the squatters' leaders to continue building, which would attract more illegal settlers. This disingenuous view ignored the fact that the Indigenous farmers were well aware of the intentions of the settlers to destroy them and seize their territories.

In the 1785 Treaty of Hopewell between the federal government and the Cherokee Nation, the United States had agreed to restrict settlement to the east of the Blue Ridge Mountains. The several thousand squatter families who claimed nearly a million acres of land in precisely that zone were not about to abide by the treaty. Knox saw the situation as a showdown with the settlers and a test of federal authority west of the mountain chains, from Canada to Spanish Florida. The settlers did not believe that the federal government meant to protect their interests, which encouraged them to go it alone. In the face of constant attacks, the Cherokees were desperate to halt the destruction of their towns and fields. Many were starving, more without shelter, on the move as refugees, with only the Chickamauga fighters as a protective force fighting off the seasoned ranger-settler Indian killers. In July 1791, the Cherokees reluctantly signed the Treaty of Holston, agreeing to abandon any claims to land on which the Franklin settlements sat in return for an annual annuity of $100,000 from the federal government.[17]

The United States did nothing to halt the flow of squatters into Cherokee territory as the boundary was drawn in the treaty. A year after the treaty was signed, war broke out, and the Chickamaugas, under the leadership of Dragging Canoe, attacked squatters, even laying siege to Nashville.[18] The war continued for two years, with five hundred Chickamauga fighters joined by Muskogees and a contingent of Shawnees from Ohio, led by Cheeseekau, one of Tecumseh's brothers, who was later killed in the fighting. The settlers organized an offensive against the Chickamaugas. The federal Indian agent attempted to persuade the Chickamaugas to stop fighting, warning that the frontier settlers were "always dreadful, not only to the warriors, but to the innocent and helpless women and children, and old men." The agent also warned the settlers against attacking Indigenous towns, but he had to order the militia to disperse a mob of three hundred settlers, who, as he wrote, out of "a mistaken zeal to serve their country" had gathered to destroy "as many as they could of the Cherokee towns."[19] Sevier and his rangers invaded the Chickamaugas' towns in September 1793, with a stated mission of total destruction. Although forbidden by the federal agent to attack the villages, Sevier gave orders for a scorched-earth offensive.

By choosing to attack at harvesttime, Sevier intended to starve out the residents. The strategy worked. Soon after, the federal agent reported to the secretary of war that the region was pacified, with no Indigenous actions since "the visit General Sevier paid the [Cherokee] nation." A year later, Sevier demanded absolute submission from the Chickamauga villages lest they be wiped out completely. Receiving no response, a month later 1,750 Franklin rangers attacked two villages, burning all the buildings and fields—again near the harvest—and shooting those who tried to flee. Sevier then repeated his demand for submission, requiring the Chickamaugas to abandon their towns for the woods, taking only what they could transport. He wrote: "War will cost the United States much money, and some lives, but it will destroy the existence of your people, as a nation, forever." The remaining Chickamauga villages agreed to allow the settlers to remain in Cherokee country.

In squatter settlements, ruthless leaders like Sevier were not the exception but the rule. Once they had full control and got what they wanted, they made their peace with the federal government, which in turn depended on their actions to expand the republic's territory. Sevier went on to serve as a US representative from North Carolina and as governor of Tennessee. To this day, such men are idolized as great heroes, embodying the essence of the "American spirit." A bronze statue of John Sevier in his ranger uniform stands today in the National Statuary Hall of the US Capitol.[20]

MUSKOGEE RESISTANCE

The Muskogee Nation officially had remained neutral in the war between the Anglo-American settlers and the British monarchy. Nonetheless, many individual Muskogees had taken the opportunity to raid and harass squatters within their national territories in Georgia, Tennessee, and South Carolina. When the United States was formed, the Muskogee Nation turned to Spanish Florida for an alliance in trying to stop the flow of squatters into their territory. Spain had an interest in the alliance as a buffer to its holdings, which at the time included the lower Mississippi and the city of New Orleans. The squatters believed that the Muskogees and the Spanish officials, as well as the British, were in cahoots to keep them out of western Georgia and present-day Alabama and considered the Muskogee Nation to be the main barrier to their permanent settlement in the region, particularly Georgia. The Muskogees called the squatters *ecunnaunuxulgee* —"people greedily grasping after the lands of the red people."

The federal government negotiated with the Muskogee Nation for a new boundary and for more settlements and trade, in exchange for $60,000 a year in goods. The squatters did everything they could to provoke the Muskogees to war, while ignoring the treaty's provisions. They slaughtered hundreds of deer in the Muskogee deer parks, with the intention of wiping out the livelihood of Muskogee hunters, who also made up the resistance forces. But the War Department was complicit, using money due to the Muskogees under the treaty to divide them by bribing leaders (*miccos*) and thus isolating the insurgents from their communities. Eighty Muskogee fighters joined the Chickamaugas when they were still fighting, and together they attacked the Cumberland district of Tennessee in early 1792, while others struck Georgia squatters in Muskogee territory. It was then that Shawnee delegates, sent by Tecumseh, visited from the Ohio Country to encourage the Muskogees to drive the squatters from their lands, as the Shawnees had done successfully up to that time. Secretary of War Knox wrote to the federal agent in Georgia that he knew the Muskogee militants were "a Banditti, and do not implicate the whole nor any considerable part of that Nation. The hostilities of the Individuals arise from their own disposition, and are not probably dictated, either by the Chiefs, or by any Towns or other respectable classes of the Indians."[21]

By this time, in the process of the preceding British colonization and continuing with US colonization of the Muskogee Nation and other southeastern Indigenous nations, an Indigenous client class—called "compradors" by Africans, "caciques" in Spanish-colonized America—essential to colonialist projects, was firmly in place. This privileged class was dependent on their colonial masters for their personal wealth. This class division wracked the traditional relatively egalitarian and democratic Indigenous societies internally. This small elite in the Southeast embraced the enslavement of Africans, and a few even became affluent planters in the style of southern planters, mainly through intermarriage with Anglos. The trading posts established by US merchants further divided Muskogee society, pulling many deeply into the US economy through dependency and debt, and away from the Spanish and British trading firms, which had previously left their lands undisturbed. This method of colonization by co-optation and debt proved effective wherever employed by colonial powers in the world, but only when it was accompanied by extreme violence at any sign of indigenous insurgency. The United States moved across North America in this manner. While most Muskogees continued to follow their traditional democratic ways in their villages, the elite Muskogees were making decisions and compromises on their behalf that would bear tragic consequences for them all.

Federal authorities in 1793 identified five hundred Muskogee towns where they believed the majority of insurgents resided. Secretary of War Knox called on the Georgia militia for federal service. The federal Indian agent notified the War Department that the settlers were set on assaulting the Muskogees and asked that a thousand federal troops be deployed to occupy the insurgent Muskogee towns. Although the War Department rejected that idea and war was postponed, the restless Georgian militiamen deserted after having rushed to the Muskogee territory to loot, burn, and kill, only to be forced to wait. Persistent squatter attacks on Muskogee farmers, traders, and towns continued.

During the winter of 1793–94, Georgia border squatters formed an armed group of landless settlers. The leader, Elijah Clarke, was a veteran Indian killer and had been a major general in the Georgia militia during the war of independence, in which he commanded rangers to destroy Indigenous towns and fields. As a US patriot hero, Clarke was certain that his former troops would never take up arms against him. Clarke and his rangers declared the independence of their own republic, but Georgia state authorities captured him and destroyed the rebel stronghold. Still, Clarke's action sent a strong message to state and federal authorities that landless squatters were determined to take Indigenous lands. They would get the leader they needed for that purpose a decade later. Meanwhile, the elite of the Muskogee towns were successful in marginalizing the insurgents, while the federal government increased grants, and the wealthy class of Muskogees established trading posts, making whiskey cheaply available to impoverished Muskogees.[22]

THE DIE IS CAST

The successful settler intrusion into western Georgia made Alabama and Mississippi the next objectives for the rapidly expanding slave-worked plantation economy, which, along with land sales of occupied Indigenous lands by private speculators, was essential to the US economy as a whole. The plantation economy required vast swaths of land for cash crops, even before cotton was king, leaving in its wake destroyed Indigenous national territories and Anglo settlers who would fight and die driving out the Indigenous communities yet remain landless themselves, moving on to the next frontier to try again. US colonization produced the subsequent hideous slavery-based rule of the Old Southwest, which would flourish for seven more decades. Unlike in the Ohio Country, the Washington administration avoided force and in doing so alienated settlers in the region. By preventing them from wiping out the Muskogees, the federal government was seen as the enemy, just as the British authority had been for an earlier generation of determined settlers. But that would soon change with the Muskogee War of 1813–14, narrated in the following chapter, in which, as Robert V. Remini puts it in *Andrew Jackson and His Indian Wars*, "Tennessee frontiersman Andrew Jackson, commanding both regular Army troops and frontiersmen, personally guaranteed that the Creeks would feel the full brunt of total war."[23]

During 1810–15, then, two parallel wars were ongoing, one in the Ohio Country—the Old Northwest—which ended with the defeat of the Tecumseh-led alliance, and the other the war against the Muskogee Nation in 1813–14. Unlike the 1812–15 war between Britain and the United States, with which these wars overlapped, the situation did not return to things being as they had been before, but rather culminated in the elimination of Indigenous power east of the Mississippi. US conquest was not determined by the defeat of the British in battle in 1815, but rather by genocidal war and forced removal.[24]

US leaders brought counterinsurgency out of the pre-independence period into the new republic, imprinting on the fledgling federal army a way of war with formidable consequences for the continent and the world. Counterinsurgent warfare and ethnic cleansing targeting Indigenous civilians continued to define US war making throughout the nineteenth century, with markers such as the three US counterinsurgent wars against the Seminoles through the Sand Creek Massacre of 1864 to Wounded Knee in 1890. Early on, regular armies had incorporated these strategies and tactics as a way of war to which it often turned, although frequently the regular army simply stood by while local militias and settlers acting on their own used terror against Indigenous noncombatants.

Irregular warfare would be waged west of the Mississippi as it had been earlier against the Abenakis, Cherokees, Shawnees, Muskogees, and even Christian Indians. In the Civil War, these methods played a prominent role on both sides. Confederate regular forces, Confederate guerrillas such as William Quantrill, and General Sherman for the Union all engaged in waging total war against civilians. The pattern would continue in US military interventions overseas, from the Philippines and Cuba to Central America, Korea, Vietnam, Iraq, and Afghanistan. The cumulative effect goes beyond simply the habitual use of military means and becomes the very basis for US American identity. The Indian-fighting frontiersmen and the "valiant" settlers in their circled covered wagons are the iconic images of that identity. The continued popularity of, and respect for, the genocidal sociopath Andrew Jackson is another indicator. Actual men such as Robert Rogers, Daniel Boone, John Sevier, and David Crockett, as well as fictitious ones created by James Fenimore Cooper and other best-selling writers, call to mind D. H. Lawrence's "myth of the essential white American"—that the "essential American soul" is a killer.[25]

SIX

THE LAST OF THE MOHICANS AND ANDREW JACKSON'S WHITE REPUBLIC

The settler's work is to make even dreams of liberty impossible for the native. The native's work is to imagine all possible methods for destroying the settler.

—Frantz Fanon, *The Wretched of the Earth*

In 1803, the Jefferson administration, without consulting any affected Indigenous nation, purchased the Louisiana Territory from Napoleon Bonaparte. Louisiana comprised 828,000 square miles, and its addition doubled the size of the United States. The territory encompassed all or part of multiple Indigenous nations, including the Sioux, Cheyenne, Arapaho, Crow, Pawnee, Osage, and Comanche, among other peoples of the bison. It also included the area that would soon be designated Indian Territory (Oklahoma), the site of relocation of Indigenous peoples from west of the Mississippi. Fifteen future states would emerge from the taking: all of present-day Arkansas, Missouri, Iowa, Oklahoma, Kansas, and Nebraska; Minnesota west of the Mississippi; most of North and South Dakota; northeastern New Mexico and North Texas; the portions of Montana, Wyoming, and Colorado east of the Continental Divide; and Louisiana west of the Mississippi River, including the city of New Orleans. The territory pressed against lands occupied by Spain, including Texas and all the territory west of the Continental Divide to the Pacific Ocean. These would soon be next on the US annexation list.[1]

At the time, many US Americans saw the purchase as a strategic means of averting war with France while securing commerce on the Mississippi. But it was not long before some began eyeing it for settlement and others proposing an "exchange" of Indigenous lands in the Old Northwest and Old Southwest for lands west of the Mississippi.[2] Before turning to conquest and colonization west of the Mississippi, the slavery-based rule of the Southeast would be ethnically cleansed of Indigenous peoples. The man for the job was Andrew Jackson.

CAREER BUILDING THROUGH GENOCIDE

Neither superior technology nor an overwhelming number of settlers made up the mainspring of the birth of the United States or the spread of its power over the entire world. Rather, the chief cause was the colonialist settler-state's willingness to eliminate whole civilizations of people in order to possess their land. This trend of extermination became common in the twentieth century as the United States seized military and economic control of the world, capping five hundred years of European colonialism and imperialism.[3] The canny Prussian Otto von Bismarck, founder and first chancellor (1871–90) of the German empire, was prescient in observing, "The colonization of North America has been the decisive fact of the modern world."[4] Jefferson was its architect. Andrew Jackson was the implementer of the final solution for the Indigenous peoples east of the Mississippi.

Andrew Jackson was an influential Tennessee land speculator, politician, and wealthy owner of a slave-worked plantation, the Hermitage. He was also a veteran Indian killer. Jackson's family personified the Protestant Scots-Irish migration to the borderlands of empires. Jackson's Scots-Irish parents and two older brothers arrived in Pennsylvania from County Antrim in Northern Ireland in 1765. The Jacksons soon moved to a Scots-Irish community on the North Carolina border with South Carolina. Jackson's father died after a logging accident a few weeks before Andrew's birth in 1767. Life was hard for a single mother and three children on the frontier. At age thirteen, with little education, Jackson became a courier for the local regiment of the frontier secessionists in their war of independence from Britain. Jackson's mother and his brothers died during the war, leaving him an orphan. He worked at various jobs, then studied law and was admitted to the bar in the Western District of North Carolina, which would later become the state of Tennessee. Through his legal work, most of which related to disputed land claims, he acquired a plantation near Nashville worked by 150 slaves. He helped usher in Tennessee as a state in 1796, then was elected as its US senator, an office he quit after a year to become a judge in the Tennessee Supreme Court for six years.

As the most notorious land speculator in western Tennessee, Jackson enriched himself by acquiring a portion of the Chickasaw Nation's land. It was in 1801 that Jackson first took command of the Tennessee militia as a colonel and began his Indian-killing military career. After his brutal war of annihilation against the Muskogee Nation, Jackson continued building his national military and political career by tackling the resistant Seminoles in what are known as the Seminole Wars. In 1836, during the second of these wars, US Army general Thomas S. Jesup captured the popular Anglo attitude toward the Seminoles: "The country can be rid of them only by exterminating them." By then Jackson was finishing his second term as the most popular president in US history to that date, and the policy of genocide was embedded in the highest office of the US government.[5]

In the Southeast, the Choctaws and Chickasaws turned exclusively to US traders once the new US republic effectively cut off access to the Spanish in Florida. Soon they were trapped in the US trading world, in which they would run up debts and then have no way to pay other than by ceding land to creditors who were often acting as agents of the federal government. This was no accidental outcome but was foreseen and encouraged by Jefferson. In 1805, the Choctaws ceded most of their lands to the United States for $50,000, and the Chickasaws relinquished all their lands north of the Tennessee River for $20,000. Many Choctaws and Chickasaws thus became landless participants in the expanding plantation economy, burdened by debts and poverty.[6]

The division of the Muskogee (Creek) Nation and the rise of Andrew Jackson as a result led to his eventual elevation to the presidency and carrying out of the final solution—elimination of all the Indigenous communities east of the Mississippi through forced removal. After the Choctaws and Chickasaws lost most of their territories, only the Muskogees continued to resist the United States.

The Muskogee Nation was a federation of autonomous towns located in the valleys of the many rivers that crisscross what are now the states of Alabama, Tennessee, and parts of Georgia and Florida. The Lower Creeks inhabited and farmed in the eastern part of this region watered by the Chattahoochee, Flint, and Apalachicola Rivers, while the Upper Creeks lived west of them, in the valleys of the Coosa, Tallapoosa and Alabama Rivers. Following US independence, the Muskogees were divided by settler colonialism. Lower Creek villages became economically dependent on settlers and emulated settlers' values, including ownership of African slaves. This was largely due to two decades of diligent work on the part of US Indian agent Benjamin Hawkins. He was in charge of the US government's "civilization" project, lending the settler moniker "Five Civilized Tribes" to describe the great agricultural nations of the Southeast. Hawkins's mission was to instill Euro-American values and practices in Indigenous peoples—including the profit motive, privatization of property, debt, accumulation of wealth by a few, and slavery—allowing settlers to gain the land and assimilate the Muskogees. At the time of independence, hundreds of settlers were squatting illegally on lands of Muskogees of the Lower Creek towns, and that is where Hawkins concentrated, leaving the Muskogees upriver alone. However, traditionalists among the Upper Creeks, who had allied with Tecumseh and the Shawnee confederation, understood that they would be next, as they saw the twenty-year Hawkins project transforming some citizens of the Lower Creek towns into wealthy plantation and slave owners, while the majority became landless and poor.

Traditionalist fighters, called Red Sticks due to the color of their wooden spears, began an offensive against collaborating Upper Creeks and settlers that ended in civil war during 1813. The Red Sticks created chaos that affected Hawkins's scheme, as they attacked anyone associated with his program. Their effectiveness, however, provoked a genocidal counteroffensive not officially authorized by the federal government, led by Andrew Jackson who was then head of the Tennessee militias. Jackson threatened to form his own mercenary army to drive the Muskogees "into the ocean" if the government failed to eradicate the insurgents.[7] Although Jackson and his fellow Tennesseans made it clear that their goal was extermination of the Muskogee Nation, their rhetoric claimed self-defense. In a series of search-and-destroy missions over three months prior to the final assault on the Red Sticks, Jackson's mercenaries killed hundreds of Muskogee civilians, pursuing without mercy even homeless and starved refugees seeking shelter and safety. By this point, the Red Sticks had killed most of the Muskogee Nation livestock both to deprive US soldiers of food and to rid Muskogee culture of the colonizers' influence.[8]

Both Shawnee fighters and Africans who had freed themselves from slavery allied with the Red Sticks. With all their families they set up a fortified encampment at Tohopeka at the Horseshoe Bend on the Tallapoosa River in present-day Alabama. Jackson proceeded to mobilize Lower Creek fighters and some Cherokee allies against the Red Sticks. In March 1814, with seven hundred mounted militiamen and six hundred Cherokee and Lower Creek fighters, Jackson's armies attacked the Red Stick stronghold. The mercenaries captured three hundred Red Stick wives and children and held them as hostages to induce Muskogee surrender. Of a thousand Red Stick and allied insurgents, eight hundred were killed. Jackson lost forty-nine men.

In the aftermath of "the Battle of Horseshoe Bend," as it is known in US military annals, Jackson's troops fashioned reins for their horses' bridles from skin stripped from the Muskogee bodies, and they saw to it that souvenirs from the corpses were given "to the ladies of Tennessee."[9] Following the slaughter, Jackson justified his troops' actions: "The fiends of the Tallapoosa will no longer murder our women and children, or disturb the quiet of our borders. . . . They have disappeared from the face of the Earth. . . . How lamentable it is that the path to peace should lead through blood, and over the carcasses of the slain! But it is in the dispensation of that providence, which inflicts partial evil to produce general good."[10]

Horseshoe Bend marked the end of the Muskogees' resistance in their original homeland. As historian Alan Brinkley has observed, Jackson's political fortunes depended on the fate of the Indians—that is, their eradication.[11]

The surrender document the Muskogee Nation was forced to sign in 1814, the Treaty of Fort Jackson, asserted that they had lost under "principles of national justice and honorable war." Andrew Jackson, the only US negotiator of the treaty, insisted on nothing less than the total destruction of the Muskogee Nation, which the Muskogees had no power to refuse or negotiate. These terms of total surrender shocked the small group of Muskogee plantation and slave owners, who thought that they had been thoroughly accepted by the US Americans. They had fought alongside the Anglo militias against the majority Red Sticks in the war just concluded, yet all Muskogees were now to be punished equally. To no avail did the "friendlies" prostrate themselves before Jackson at the treaty meeting, begging that they and their holdings be spared. Jackson told them that the extreme punishment exacted upon them should teach all those who would try to oppose US domination. "We bleed our enemies in such cases," he explained, "to give them their senses."[12] Military historian Grenier observes that "Jackson's 'bleeding' of the Muskogees marks a culminating point in American military history as the end of the Transappalachian East's Indian wars. . . . The conquest of the West was not guaranteed by defeating the British Army in battle in 1815, but by defeating and driving the Indians from their homelands."[13]

The treaty obliged surviving Muskogees to move onto western remnants of their homelands, and Jackson, far from being reprimanded for his genocidal methods, won a commission from President James Madison as major general in the US Army. The territory that would become Alabama and Mississippi now lay open to Anglo-American settlement, an ominous green light to the expansion of plantation slavery. The Muskogee War thus inscribed a US policy of ethnic cleansing onto an entire Indigenous population. The policy originated by Andrew Jackson in that war would be reconfirmed politically when he became president in 1828.[14]

The Upper Creek Muskogees who remained in Alabama surren-

dered to Jackson and ceded twenty-three million acres of their ancestral lands to the United States in the Treaty of Fort Jackson. The Red
Sticks, however, joined the resistant Seminole Nation in the Florida
Everglades and three more decades of Muskogee resistance ensued.
During this period, Anglo-American slave owners, and Andrew
Jackson in particular, were determined to destroy the safe havens
that Seminole towns offered to Africans who escaped from slavery.[15] The Seminole Nation had not existed under that name prior
to European colonization. The ancestral towns of the Indigenous
people who became known as Seminoles were located along rivers
in a large area of what is today Alabama, Georgia, South Carolina,
and the Florida Panhandle. In the mid-eighteenth century, Waka-
puchasee (Cowkeeper) and his people separated from the Coweta
Muskogees and moved south into what was then Spanish-occupied
Florida. As Spain, Britain, and later the United States decimated
Indigenous towns throughout the Southeast, survivors, including
self-emancipated Africans, established a refuge in Seminole territory
in Spanish Florida in the Everglades. European incursions came in
the form of military attacks, disease, and disruption of trade routes,
causing collapse and realignments within and between the towns.[16]

The Seminole Nation was born of resistance and included the
vestiges of dozens of Indigenous communities as well as escaped
Africans, as the Seminole towns served as refuge. In the Caribbean
and Brazil, people in such escapee communities were called Maroons, but in the United States the liberated Africans were absorbed
into Seminole Nation culture. Then, as now, Seminoles spoke the
Muskogee language, and much later (in 1957) the US government
designated them an "Indian tribe." The Seminoles were one of the
"Five Civilized Tribes" ordered from their national homelands in
the 1830s to Indian Territory (later made part of the state of Oklahoma).

The United States waged three wars against the Seminole Nation between 1817 and 1858. The prolonged and fierce Second
Seminole War (1835–42) was the longest foreign war waged by the
United States up to the Vietnam War. The US military further developed its army, naval, and marine capabilities in again adopting a

counterinsurgency strategy, in this case against the Seminole towns in the Everglades. Once again US forces targeted civilians, destroyed food supplies, and sought to destroy every last insurgent. What US military annals call the First Seminole War (1817–19) began when US authorities entered Spanish Florida illegally in an attempt to re-cover US plantation owners' "property": former African slaves. The Seminoles repelled the invasion. In 1818, President James Monroe ordered Andrew Jackson, then a major general in the US Army, to lead three thousand soldiers into Florida to crush the Seminoles and retrieve the Africans among them. The expedition destroyed a num-ber of Seminole settlements and then captured the Spanish fort at Pensacola, bringing down the Spanish government, but it failed in destroying Seminole guerrilla resistance and the Seminoles did not agree to hand over any former slaves. "Armed occupation was the true way of settling a conquered country," Senator Thomas Hart Benton of Missouri said at the time, reflecting a popular blend of militarism and white-supremacist Christian identity. "The children of Israel entered the promised land, with implements of husbandry in one hand, and the weapons of war in the other."[17] The United States annexed Florida as a territory in 1819, opening it to Anglo-American settlement. In 1821 Jackson was appointed military com-mander of Florida Territory. The Seminoles never sued for peace, were never conquered, and never signed a treaty with the United States, and although some were rounded up and sent in 1832 to Oklahoma, where they were given a land base, the Seminole Nation has never ceased to exist in the Everglades.

THE MYTHICAL FOUNDATION OF SETTLER PATRIOTISM

Between 1814 and 1824, three-fourths of present-day Alabama and Florida, a third of Tennessee, a fifth of Georgia and Mississippi, and parts of Kentucky and North Carolina became the private property of white settlers—all of the land seized from Indigenous farmers. In 1824, the first permanent US colonial institution was established. First named the Office of Indian Affairs and placed tellingly within the Department of War, the agency was transferred to the Department of Interior twenty-five years later following the annexation of half of Mexico. In making this transfer, the federal government showed overconfidence in assuming that armed Indigenous resistance to US aggression and colonization had ended. Such resistance would continue for another half century.

Whereas white supremacy had been the working rationalization for British theft of Indigenous lands and for European enslavement of Africans, the bid for independence by what became the United States of America was more problematic. Democracy, equality, and equal rights do not fit well with dominance of one race by another, much less with genocide, settler colonialism, and empire. It was during the 1820s—the beginning of the era of Jacksonian settler democracy—that the unique US origin myth evolved reconciling rhetoric with reality. Novelist James Fenimore Cooper was among its initial scribes.

Cooper's reinvention of the birth of the United States in his novel *The Last of the Mohicans* has become the official US origin story. Herman Melville called Cooper "our national novelist."[18] Cooper was the wealthy son of a US congressman, a land speculator who built Cooperstown, named after himself, in upstate New York where he grew up. His hometown was christened all-American with the establishment of the National Baseball Hall of Fame there in 1936, during the Depression. Expelled from Yale, Cooper joined the navy, then married and began writing. In 1823, he published *The Pioneers*, the first book in his Leatherstocking Tales series, the other four being *The Last of the Mohicans*, *The Prairie*, *The Pathfinder*, and *The Deerslayer* (the last published in 1841). Each featured the character Natty Bumppo, also called variously, depending on his age, Leatherstocking, Pathfinder, or Deerslayer. Bumppo is a British settler on land appropriated from the Delaware Nation and is buddies with its fictional Delaware leader Chingachgook (the "last Mohican" in the myth). Together the Leatherstocking Tales narrate the mythical forging of the new country from the 1754–63 French and Indian War in *The Last of the Mohicans* to the settlement of the plains by migrants traveling by wagon train from Tennessee. At the end of the saga Bumppo dies a very old man on the edge of the Rocky Mountains, as he gazes east.[19]

The Last of the Mohicans, published in 1826, was a best seller throughout the nineteenth century and has been in print continuously since, with two Hollywood movies based on the story, the most recent made in 1992, the Columbus Quincentennial.[20] Cooper devised a fictional counterpoint of celebration to the dark underbelly of the new American nation—the birth of something new and wondrous, literally, the US American race, a new people born of the merger of the best of both worlds, the Native and the European, not biological merger but something more ephemeral, involving the dissolving of the Indian. In the novel, Cooper has the last of the "noble" and "pure" Natives die off as nature would have it, with the "last Mohican" handing the continent over to Hawkeye, the nativized settler, his adopted son. This convenient fantasy could be seen as quaint at best if it were not for its deadly staying power. Cooper had much to do with creating the US origin myth to which generations of historians have dedicated themselves, fortifying what historian Francis Jennings has described as "exclusion from the process of formation of American society and culture":

> In the first place they [US historians] exclude Amerindians (as also Afro-Americans) from participation, except as foils for Europeans, and thus assume that American civilization was formed by Europeans in a struggle against the savagery or barbarism of the nonwhite races. This first conception implies the second—that the civilization so formed is unique. In the second conception uniqueness is thought to have been created through the forms and processes of civilization's struggle on a specifically American frontier. Alternatively, civilization was able to triumph because the people who bore it were unique from the beginning—a Chosen People or a super race. Either way American culture is seen as not only unique but better than all other cultures, precisely because of its differences from them.[21]

US exceptionalism weaves through much of the literature produced in the United States, not only the writing of historians. Although

Wallace Stegner decried the devastation wrought by imperialism on Indigenous peoples and the land, he reinforced the idea of US uniqueness by reducing colonization to a twist of fate that produced some charming characteristics:

> Ever since Daniel Boone took his first excursion over Cumberland Gap, Americans have been wanderers. . . . With a continent to take over and Manifest Destiny to goad us, we could not have avoided being footloose. The initial act of emigration from Europe, an act of extreme, deliberate disaffiliation, was the beginning of a national habit.
>
> It should not be denied, either, that being footloose has always exhilarated us. It is associated in our minds with escape from history and oppression and law and irksome obligations, with absolute freedom, and the road has always led west. Our folk heroes and our archetypal literary figures accurately reflect that side of us. Leatherstocking, Huckleberry Finn, the narrator of Moby Dick, all are orphans and wanderers; any of them could say, "Call me Ishmael." The Lone Ranger has no dwelling place except the saddle.[22]

The British novelist and critic D. H. Lawrence, who lived in northern New Mexico for two years, conceptualized the US origin myth, invoking Cooper's frontiersman character Deerslayer: "You have there the myth of the essential white America. All the other stuff, the love, the democracy, the floundering into lust, is a sort of by-play. The essential American soul is hard, isolate, stoic, and a killer. It has never yet melted."[23]

Historian Wai-chee Dimock points out that nonfiction sources of the time reflected the same view:

> The *United States Magazine* and *Democratic Review* summed it up by arguing that whereas European powers "conquer only to enslave," America, being "a free nation," "conquers only to bestow freedom." . . . Far from being antagonistic, "empire" and "liberty" are instrumentally conjoined. If the former stands to safeguard the latter, the latter, in turn, serves to justify the former. Indeed, the conjunction of the two,

of freedom and dominion, gives America its sovereign place in history—its Manifest Destiny, as its advocates so aptly called it.[24]

Reconciling empire and liberty—based on the violent taking of Indigenous lands—into a usable myth allowed for the emergence of an enduring populist imperialism. Wars of conquest and ethnic cleansing could be sold to "the people"—indeed could be fought for by the young men of those very people—by promising to expand economic opportunity, democracy, and freedom for all.

The publication arc of the Leatherstocking Tales parallels the Jackson presidency. For those who consumed the books in that period and throughout the nineteenth century—generations of young white men—the novels became perceived fact, not fiction, and the basis for the coalescence of US American nationalism. Behind the legend was a looming real-life figure, the archetype that inspired the stories, namely, Daniel Boone, an icon of US settler colonialism. Boone's life spanned from 1734 to 1820, precisely the period covered in the Leatherstocking series. Boone was born in Berks County, Pennsylvania, on the edge of British settlement. He is an avatar of the moving colonial–Indigenous frontier. To the west lay "Indian Country," claimed through the Doctrine of Discovery by both Britain and France but free of European settlers save for a few traders, trappers, and soldiers manning colonial outposts.

Daniel Boone died in 1820 in Missouri, a part of the vast territory acquired in the 1803 Louisiana Purchase. When Missouri opened for settlement, the Boone family led the initial settlers there. His body was taken for burial in Frankfort, Kentucky, the covenant heart of the Ohio Country, Indian Country, for which the revolution had been fought and in which he had been the trekker superhero, almost a deity. Daniel Boone became a celebrity at age fifty in 1784, a year after the end of the war of independence. Real estate entrepreneur John Filson, seeking settlers to buy property in the Ohio Country, wrote and self-published *The Discovery, Settlement and Present State of Kentucke,* along with a map to guide illegal squatters. The book contained an appendix about Daniel Boone, purportedly written by Boone himself. That part of the book on Boone's "adventures" subsequently was published as "The Adventures of Col. Daniel Boone" in the *American Magazine* in 1787, then as a book. Thereby a superstar was born—the mythical hero, the hunter, the "Man Who Knows Indians," as Richard Slotkin has described this US American archetype:

> The myth of the hunter that had grown up about the figure of Filson's Daniel Boone provided a framework within which Americans attempted to define their cultural identity, social and political values, historical experience, and literary aspirations. . . . Daniel Boone, Washington, Franklin, and Jefferson were heroes to the whole nation because their experiences had reference to many or all of these common experiences. "The Hunters of Kentucky," a popular song that swept the nation in 1822–28, helped elect Andrew Jackson as President by associating him with Boone, the hero of the West.[25]

Yet the Leatherstocking's positive twist on genocidal colonialism was based on the reality of invasion, squatting, attacking, and colonizing of the Indigenous nations. Neither Filson nor Cooper created that reality. Rather, they created the narratives that captured the experience and imagination of the Anglo-American settler, stories that were surely instrumental in nullifying guilt related to genocide and set the pattern of narrative for future US writers, poets, and historians.

COMMANDER AND CHIEF

Andrew Jackson is enshrined in most US history texts in a chapter titled "The Age of Jackson," "The Age of Democracy," "The Birth of Democracy," or some variation thereon.[26] The Democratic Party claims Jackson and Jefferson as its founders. Every year, state and national Democratic organizations hold fund-raising events they call Jefferson-Jackson Dinners. They understand that Thomas Jefferson was the thinker and Jackson the doer in forging populist democracy for full participation in the fruits of colonialism based on the opportunity available to Anglo settlers.

Jackson carried out the original plan envisioned by the founders—particularly Jefferson—initially as a Georgia militia leader, then as an army general who led four wars of aggression against the Muskogees in Georgia and Florida, and finally as a president who engineered the expulsion of all Native peoples east of the Mississippi to the designated "Indian Territory." As the late Cherokee principal chief Wilma Mankiller wrote in her autobiography:

> The fledgling United States government's method of dealing with native people—a process which then included systematic genocide, property theft, and total subjugation—reached its nadir in 1830 under the federal policy of President Andrew Jackson. More than any other president, he used forcible removal to expel the eastern tribes from their land. From the very birth of the nation, the United States government truly had carried out a vigorous operation of extermination and removal. Decades before Jackson took office, during the administration of Thomas Jefferson, it was already cruelly apparent to many Native American leaders that any hope for tribal autonomy was cursed. So were any thoughts of peaceful coexistence with white citizens.[27]

It's not that Jackson had a "dark side," as his apologists rationalize and which all human beings have, but rather that Jackson *was* the Dark Knight in the formation of the United States as a colonialist, imperialist democracy, a dynamic formation that continues to constitute the core of US patriotism. The most revered presidents—Jefferson, Jackson, Lincoln, Wilson, both Roosevelts, Truman, Kennedy, Reagan, Clinton, Obama—have each advanced populist imperialism while gradually increasing inclusion of other groups beyond the core of descendants of old settlers into the ruling mythology. All the presidents after Jackson march in his footsteps. Consciously or not, they refer back to him on what is acceptable, how to reconcile democracy and genocide and characterize it as freedom for the people.

Jackson was a national military hero, but he was rooted in the Scots-Irish frontier communities, most of whose people, unlike him, remained impoverished. Their small farms were hard-pressed to compete with large plantations with thousands of acres of cotton planted and each tended by hundreds of enslaved Africans. Land-poor white rural people saw Jackson as the man who would save them, making land available to them by ridding it of Indians, thereby setting the pattern of the dance between poor and rich US Americans ever since under the guise of equality of opportunity. When Jackson was inaugurated in 1829, he opened the White House to the public, the majority in attendance being humble poor whites. Jackson was easily reelected in 1832, although landless settlers had acquired very little land, and what little they seized was soon lost to speculators, transformed into ever larger plantations worked by slave labor.

The late Jackson biographer Michael Paul Rogin observed:

> Indian removal was Andrew Jackson's major policy aim in the quarter-century before he became President. His Indian wars and treaties were principally responsible for dispossessing the southern Indians during those years. His presidential Indian removal finished the job. . . . During the years of Jacksonian Democracy, 1824–52, five of the ten major candidates for President had either won reputations as generals in Indian wars or served as Secretary of War, whose major responsibility in this period was relations with the Indians. Historians, however, have failed to place Indians at the center of Jackson's life. They have interpreted the Age of Jackson from every perspective but Indian destruction, the one from which it actually developed historically.[28]

Once elected president, Jackson lost no time in initiating the removal of all the Indigenous farmers and the destruction of all their towns in the South. In his first annual message to Congress, he wrote: "The emigration should be voluntary, for it would be as cruel as unjust to compel the aborigines to abandon the graves of their fathers and seek a home in a distant land. But they should be distinctly informed that if they remain within the limits of the States they must be subject to their laws. In return for their obedience as individuals they will without doubt be protected in the enjoyment of those possessions which they have improved by their industry."[29] This political code language barely veils the intention to forcibly remove the Cherokee, Chickasaw, Choctaw, Muskogee, and Seminole Nations, followed by all other Indigenous communities from east of the Mississippi River, except for the many who could not be rounded up and remained, without land, without acknowledgment, until the successful struggles of some of them for recognition in the late twentieth century.

The state of Georgia saw Jackson's election as a green light and claimed most of the Cherokee Nation's territory as public land. The Georgia legislature resolved that the Cherokee constitution and laws were null and void and that Cherokees were subject to Georgia law. The Cherokee Nation took a case against Georgia to the US Supreme Court. With Chief Justice John Marshall writing for the majority, the Court ruled in favor of the Cherokees. Jackson ignored the Supreme Court, however, in effect saying that John Marshall had made his decision and Marshall would have to enforce it if he could, although he, Jackson, had an army while Marshall did not.

While the case was working its way through the courts, gold was discovered in Georgia in 1829, which quickly brought some forty thousand eager gold seekers to run roughshod over Cherokee lands, squatting, looting, killing, and destroying fields and game parks. Under authority granted by the Indian Removal Act, passed by Congress in 1830, the United States drew up a treaty that would cede all Cherokee lands to the government in exchange for land in "Indian Territory." The US government held Cherokee leaders in jail and closed their printing press during negotiations with a few handpicked Cherokees, who provided the bogus signatures Jackson needed as a cover for forced removal.[30]

TRAILS OF TEARS

Not only the great southern nations were driven into exile, but also nearly all the Native nations east of the Mississippi were forced off their lands and relocated to Indian Territory, seventy thousand people in all. During the Jacksonian period, the United States made eighty-six treaties with twenty-six Indigenous nations between New York and the Mississippi, all of them forcing land sessions, including removals. Some communities fled to Canada and Mexico rather than going to Indian Territory.[31] When Sauk leader Black Hawk led his people back from a winter stay in Iowa to their homeland in Illinois in 1832 to plant corn, the squatter settlers there claimed they were being invaded, bringing in both Illinois militia and federal troops. The "Black Hawk War" that is narrated in history texts was no more than a slaughter of Sauk farmers. The Sauks tried to defend themselves but were starving when Black Hawk surrendered under a white flag. Still the soldiers fired, resulting in a bloodbath. In his surrender speech, Black Hawk spoke bitterly of the enemy:

> You know the cause of our making war. It is known to all white men. They ought to be ashamed of it. Indians are not deceitful. The white men speak bad of the Indian and look at him spitefully. But the Indian does not tell lies. Indians do not steal. An Indian who is as bad as the white men could not live in our nation; he would be put to death and eaten up by the wolves. . . . We told them to leave us alone, and keep away from us; they followed on, and beset our paths, and they coiled themselves among us, like the snake. They poisoned us by their touch. We were not safe. We lived in danger.[32]

The Sauks were rounded up and driven onto a reservation called Sac and Fox.

Most Cherokees had held out in remaining in their homeland despite pressure from federal administrations from Jefferson on to migrate voluntarily to the Arkansas-Oklahoma-Missouri area of the Louisiana Purchase territory. The Cherokee Nation addressed removal:

> We are aware that some persons suppose it will be for our advantage to remove beyond the Mississippi. We think otherwise. Our people universally think otherwise. . . . We wish to remain on the land of our fathers. We have a perfect and original right to remain without interruption or molestation. The

treaties with us, and laws of the United States made in pursu-
ance of treaties, guarantee our residence and our privileges,
and secure us against intruders. Our only request is, that these
treaties may be fulfilled, and these laws executed.[33]

A few contingents of Cherokees settled in Arkansas and what
became Indian Territory as early as 1817. There was a larger migration in 1832, which came after the Indian Removal Act. The 1838
forced march of the Cherokee Nation, now known as the Trail of
Tears, was an arduous journey from remaining Cherokee homelands
in Georgia and Alabama to what would later become northeastern Oklahoma. After the Civil War, journalist James Mooney interviewed people who had been involved in the forced removal. Based
on these firsthand accounts, he described the scene in 1838, when
the US Army removed the last of the Cherokees by force:

Under [General Winfield] Scott's orders the troops were dis-
posed at various points throughout the Cherokee country,
where stockade forts were erected for gathering in and holding the Indians preparatory to removal. From these, squads
of troops were sent to search out with rifle and bayonet every
small cabin hidden away in the coves or by sides of mountain
streams, to seize and bring in as prisoners all the occupants,
however or wherever they might be found. Families at dinner
were startled by the sudden gleam of bayonets in the doorway
and rose up to be driven with blows and oaths along the weary
miles of trail that led to the stockade. Men were seized in their
fields or going along the road, women were taken from their
wheels and children from their play. In many cases, on turning for one last look as they crossed the ridge, they saw their
homes in flames, fired by the lawless rabble that followed on
the heels of the soldiers to loot and pillage. So keen were these
outlaws on the scene that in some instances they were driving off the cattle and other stock of the Indians almost before
the soldiers had fairly started their owners in the other direction. Systematic hunts were made by the same men for Indian
graves, to rob them of the silver pendants and other valuables

deposited with the dead. A Georgia volunteer, afterward a colonel in the Confederate service, said: "I fought through the civil war and have seen men shot to pieces and slaughtered by thousands, but the Cherokee removal was the cruelest work I ever knew."[34]

Half of the sixteen thousand Cherokee men, women, and children who were rounded up and force-marched in the dead of winter out of their country perished on the journey.

The Muskogees and Seminoles suffered similar death rates in their forced transfer, while the Chickasaws and Choctaws lost around 15 percent of their people en route. An eyewitness account by Alexis de Tocqueville, the French observer of the day, captures one of thousands of similar scenes in the forced deportation of the Indigenous peoples from the Southeast:

> I saw with my own eyes several of the cases of misery which I have been describing; and I was the witness of sufferings which I have not the power to portray.
>
> At the end of the year 1831, whilst I was on the left bank of the Mississippi at a place named by Europeans Memphis, there arrived a numerous band of Choctaws (or Chactas, as they are called by the French in Louisiana). These savages had left their country, and were endeavoring to gain the right bank of the Mississippi, where they hoped to find an asylum which had been promised them by the American government. It was then the middle of winter, and the cold was unusually severe; the snow had frozen hard upon the ground, and the river was drifting huge masses of ice. The Indians had their families with them; and they brought in their train the wounded and sick, with children newly born, and old men upon the verge of death. They possessed neither tents nor wagons, but only their arms and some provisions. I saw them embark to pass the mighty river, and never will that solemn spectacle fade from my remembrance. No cry, no sob was heard amongst the assembled crowd; all were silent. Their calamities were of ancient date, and they knew them to be irremediable. The

Indians had all stepped into the bark which was to carry them across, but their dogs remained upon the bank. As soon as these animals perceived that their masters were finally leaving the shore, they set up a dismal howl, and, plunging all together into the icy waters of the Mississippi, they swam after the boat.[35]

In his biography of Jackson, Rogin points out that this was no endgame: "The dispossession of the Indians . . . did not happen once and for all in the beginning. America was continually beginning again on the frontier, and as it expanded across the continent, it killed, removed, and drove into extinction one tribe after another."[36]

Against all odds, some Indigenous peoples refused to be removed and stayed in their traditional homelands east of the Mississippi. In the South, the communities that did not leave lost their traditional land titles and status as Indians in the eyes of the government, but many survived as peoples, some fighting successfully in the late twentieth century for federal acknowledgment and official Indigenous status. In the north, especially in New England, some states had illegally taken land and created guardian systems and small reservations, such as those of the Penobscots and Passamaquoddies in Maine, both of which won lawsuits against the states and attained federal acknowledgment during the militant movements of the 1970s. Many other Native nations have been able to increase their land bases.

THE PERSISTENCE OF DENIAL

Andrew Jackson was born to squatters under British rule on Indigenous land. His life followed the trajectory of continental imperialism as he made his career of taking Indigenous land, from the time of Jefferson's presidency to the elimination of Indigenous nations east of the Mississippi. This process was the central fact of US politics and the basis for the US economy. Two-thirds of the US population of nearly four million at the time of independence lived within fifty miles of the Atlantic Ocean. During the following half century, more than four million settlers crossed the Appalachians, one of the largest and most rapid migrations in world history. Jackson was an actor who made possible the implementation of the imperialist project of the independent United States, but he was also an exponent of the Euro-American popular will that favored imperialism and the virtually free land it provided them.

During the period of Jackson's military and executive power, a mythology emerged that defined the contours and substance of the US origin narrative, which has weathered nearly two centuries and remains intact in the early twenty-first century as patriotic cant, a civic religion invoked in Barack Obama's presidential inaugural address in January 2009:

> In reaffirming the greatness of our nation, we understand that greatness is never a given. It must be earned. Our journey has never been one of shortcuts or settling for less.
>
> It has not been the path for the faint-hearted, for those who prefer leisure over work, or seek only the pleasures of riches and fame.
>
> Rather, it has been the risk-takers, the doers, the makers of things—some celebrated, but more often men and women obscure in their labor—who have carried us up the long, rugged path towards prosperity and freedom.
>
> For us, they packed up their few worldly possessions and traveled across oceans in search of a new life. For us, they toiled in sweatshops and settled the West, endured the lash of the whip and plowed the hard earth.
>
> For us, they fought and died in places like Concord and Gettysburg; Normandy and Khe Sanh.
>
> Time and again these men and women struggled and sacrificed and worked till their hands were raw so that we might live a better life. They saw America as bigger than the sum of our individual ambitions; greater than all the differences of birth or wealth or faction.
>
> This is the journey we continue today.[37]

Spoken like a true descendant of old settlers. President Obama raised another key element of the national myth in an interview a few days later with Al Arabiya television in Dubai. Affirming that the United States could be an honest broker in the Israeli-Palestinian conflict, he said: "We sometimes make mistakes. We have not been perfect. But if you look at the track record, as you say, America was not born as a colonial power."

The affirmation of democracy requires the denial of colonialism, but denying it does not make it go away.

SEVEN

SEA TO SHINING SEA

*These Spaniards [Mexicans] are the meanest looking
race of people I ever saw, don't appear more civilized
than our Indians generally. Dirty, filthy looking creatures.*

—Captain Lemuel Ford, 1835

*That the Indian race of Mexico must recede before us, is quite as
certain as that that is the destiny of our own Indians.*

—Waddy Thompson Jr., 1836

Captain Lemuel Ford of the First Dragoons, United States Army, made the above observation in his diary, referring to Comancheros, Mexican traders in northern Mexico who traded and intermarried primarily with Comanches on the plains. Waddy Thompson Jr. served as a US diplomat to Mexico from 1842 to 1844.[1] Army officers like Ford and diplomats like Thompson were not exceptional in their racist views. Indian hating and white supremacy were part and parcel of "democracy" and "freedom."

The populist poet of Jacksonian democracy, Walt Whitman, sang the song of manhood and the Anglo-American super race that had been steeled through empire. As an enthusiastic supporter of the US war against Mexico in 1846, Whitman proposed the stationing of sixty thousand US troops in Mexico in order to establish a regime change there "whose efficiency and permanency shall be guaranteed by the United States. This will bring out enterprise, open the way for manufacturers and commerce, into which the immense dead capital of the country [Mexico] will find its way."[2] Whitman explicitly grounded this prescription in racism: "The nigger, like the Injun, will be eliminated; it is the law of the races, history. . . . A superior grade of rats come and then all the minor rats are cleared out." The whole world would benefit from US expansion: "We pant to see our country and its rule far-reaching. What has miserable, inefficient Mexico . . . to do with the great mission of peopling the New World with a noble race?"[3] In September 1846, when General Zachary Taylor's troops captured Monterrey, Whitman hailed it as "another clinching proof of the indomitable energy of the Anglo-Saxon character."[4] Whitman's sentiments reflected the established US origin myth that had the frontier settlers replacing the Native peoples as historical destiny, adding his own theoretical twist of what would later be called social Darwinism.

US OVERSEAS IMPERIALISM

Traversing the continent "from sea to shining sea" was hardly a natural westward procession of covered wagons as portrayed in Western movies. The US invasion of Mexico was carried out by US marines, by sea, through Veracruz, and the early colonization of California initially progressed from the Pacific coast, reached from the Atlantic coast by way of Tierra del Fuego. Between the Mississippi River and the Rockies lay a vast region controlled by Indigenous nations that were neither conquered nor colonized by any European power, and although the United States managed to annex northern Mexico, large numbers of settlers could not reach the Northern California goldfields or the fertile Willamette Valley region of the Pacific Northwest without army regiments accompanying them. Why then does the popular US historical narrative of a "natural" westward movement persist? The answer is that those who still hold to the narrative remain captives of the ideology of "manifest destiny," according to which the United States expanded across the continent to assume its preordained size and shape. This ideology normalizes the successive invasions and occupations of Indigenous nations and Mexico as not being colonialist or imperialist, rather simply ordained progress. In this view, Mexico was just another Indian nation to be crushed.

The US invasion of Mexico has also been characterized as the first US "foreign" war, but it was not. By 1846, the United States had invaded, occupied, and ethnically cleansed dozens of foreign nations east of the Mississippi. Then there were the Barbary Wars. The opening lyric of the official hymn of the US Marine Corps, composed and adopted soon after the invasion of Mexico, "From the Halls of Montezuma to the shores of Tripoli," refers in part to 1801–5, when the marines were dispatched by President Thomas Jefferson to invade the Berber Nation of North Africa. This was the "First Barbary War," the ostensible goal of which was to persuade Tripoli to release US sailors it held hostage and to end "pirate" attacks on US merchant ships.[5] The "Second Barbary War," in 1815–16, ended when pasha Yusuf Karamanli, ruler of Tripoli, agreed not to exact fees from US ships entering their territorial waters.

By this time, throughout Spain's American colonies, wars of independence flamed, the leaders of these revolutions inspired by the French Revolution and the Haitian Revolution. A successful independence movement arose in France's Caribbean plantation slave colony of Haiti in 1801, when the majority enslaved African population overthrew the French planters and declared an independent nation-state. This was the first permanently successful national liberation movement against European colonialism in the world. The prevailing myth claims that the colonized peoples fighting for independence from Spain were inspired by successful US secession from Britain but this is a dubious claim.

Simon Bolívar was a major leader of the independence movements in South America. He visited liberated Haiti in 1815, a trip that sharpened his hatred for slavery and led to its abolishment in the independent nations that formed in South America. Bolívar and liberator José de San Martín were founders of the unitary republic they named Gran Colombia, which survived from 1819 to 1830 with Bolívar as president. Subsequently, Gran Colombia splintered into the nation-states of Venezuela, Colombia (which then included Panama), Ecuador, Peru, and Bolivia. A similar unitary nation formed in Central America called the United Provinces of Central America, with its capital in Guatemala City, which existed from 1821 to 1841, thereafter splitting into the present separate small states. In both cases the larger and stronger unitary federations were subject to economic intervention and domination by the British and US empires.

Father Miguel Hidalgo, a priest who was instrumental in the Mexican independence movement, was deeply assimilated into Indigenous society in Mexico, and the majority of the movement's insurgent fighters were drawn from Indigenous nations. Most of the actual fighters in the independence movements led by San Martín and Bolívar in South America were also Indigenous, representing their communities and nations, fighting for their own liberation as peoples. In striking contrast, the US war of independence targeted the Indigenous nations as enemies. The Indigenous communities in the new South American republics were soon dominated economically and politically by national landed elites that consolidated their power following the wars of independence. However, Indigenous peoples whose ancestors fought for liberation from Spanish colonialism have never forgotten their important role in those revolutionary movements and realize that the liberation process continues. The Indigenous peoples of Latin America feel they own those revolutions, whereas the US secession from Great Britain was the intentional founding of a white republic that planned elimination of the Indigenous peoples as territorial-based, collective societies.

The period of US intervention to annex and dominate former Spanish territories in the Americas began not in 1898 with the Spanish-American War, as most history texts claim, but rather nearly a century before, during Jefferson's presidency, with the Zebulon M. Pike expedition of 1806–7. Those historians who track "continental expansion" separately from clear actions of US imperialism rarely note the juxtaposition in time and presidential administration of the interventions in North Africa and Mexico on the eve of its liberation from Spain. Like the Lewis and Clark expedition, completed the same year that Pike set off, the Pike expedition was a military project ordered by President Jefferson. Lewis and Clark had headed into the far reaches of the newly acquired Louisiana Territory to gather intelligence on the Mandan, Hidatsa, Paiute, Shoshone, Ute, and many other nations in the huge swath of territory between the Rockies and the Pacific, bordered by Spanish-occupied territory on the west and south and British Canada on the north.[6] Pike and his small force of soldiers and Osage hostages had orders to illegally enter Spanish territory to gather information that would later be used for military invasion. Under the guise of having gone astray, Pike and his contingent found themselves inside Spanish-occupied northern New Mexico (today's southern Colorado), where they "discovered" Pikes Peak and built a fort. Ultimately, as they had undoubtedly planned, they were taken into custody by Spanish authorities who transported them to Chihuahua, Mexico, allowing Pike and his men to observe and make notes about northern Mexico on the way. More important, they collected information on Spanish military resources and behavior and the location of and relations among civilian populations. Pike was released, and in 1810 published his findings. Later titled *The Expeditions of Zebulon Montgomery Pike,* the book was a best seller.[7]

US COLONIZATION OF NORTHERN MEXICO

The instability of the impoverished new republic of Mexico, as it emerged in 1821 from more than three centuries of Spanish colonialism and an exhausting war of national liberation, put it in a weak position to defend its territory against US aggression. With Spain out of the way, the United States could pursue its own policy of imperialism without risking a difficult war with European imperialist powers—what George Washington had referred to in his farewell address when he warned against "foreign entanglements." Once Mexico was independent, its newly formed government immediately opened its borders to trade, something Spanish authorities had never allowed. US trader William Becknell arrived at Taos in the Mexican province of Nuevo México from St. Louis in 1821, and a US trading party led by Sylvester Pattie arrived in 1824.[8] Traders based in St. Louis, at the time the effective western frontier outpost of the United States, began extending their business to New Mexico. Until the publication of Pike's book in 1810, US merchants had shown little interest in trading in Mexico. Pike's account of the potential profits to be made inspired them to set out to capture that trade.[9]

US traders would help pave the way to US political control of northern Mexico through what came to be known as the "American party of Taos." Christopher Houston "Kit" Carson would play a major role in the success of the US invasion of northern Mexico as he continued work as a colonial mercenary. Born in 1809 in Kentucky, Carson was a fur trapper and entrepreneur, as well as a noted Indian hater and killer, who had left his family's homestead in Missouri for New Mexico at age sixteen. Most of the US citizens who made up the American party, including Carson, married into wealthy Spanish-identified families in New Mexico who had not favored independence from Spain, creating a strong Anglo affinity within the local ruling class. The goal of this clique was to attract, and thus monopolize, the trade in furs with Indigenous and other trappers, with the ultimate goal of US annexation. As a magnet, the traders would offer low-priced manufactured goods, from clothing to kitchenware, tools, and furniture. St. Louis was connected to transatlantic trading houses in cities on the East Coast, so it had the advantage of better variety and quality of goods than those of Chihuahua traders, who relied on the declining port of Veracruz. Bent's Fort (near present-day La Junta, Colorado) became the economic center for the fur trade in northern New Mexico, rivaling only John Jacob Astor's American Fur Company in North America. Missouri merchants circumvented the Mexican prohibition against exports of silver and gold (lifted briefly for silver between 1828 and 1835) through smuggling and bribery.[10]

St. Louis soon replaced Chihuahua as the entrepôt for the northern Mexico trade, and the elite of Mexico's northern provinces became parties to the US objective of incorporating the territory into the United States. As early as 1824, Missouri senator Thomas Hart Benton introduced a bill in the US Senate on behalf of citizens of Missouri for a US government survey of the Santa Fe Trail to the Mexican border. In 1832, President Andrew Jackson began using US troops to protect caravans of merchandise on the Santa Fe Trail going to northern Mexico from possible interference by Indigenous peoples whose territories they crossed without permission.

In addition to New Mexico, US citizen residents laid groundwork for the annexation of Mexico in Texas and California as well. The Spanish Cortes (parliament) had enacted a law in 1813 that authorized provincial authorities to make private property land grants, and this practice of granting land to individuals, including foreigners, was continued under the independent Mexican government until 1828. In 1823, Mexico's despotic ruler Agustín de Iturbide enacted a colonization law authorizing the national government to enter into a contract granting land to an *empresario*, or promoter, who was required to recruit a minimum of two hundred families to settle the grant. Only applied in the province of Texas, many such grants were sought by and granted to slave-owning Anglo-American entrepreneurs, despite slavery being illegal in Mexico, making possible their dominance in the province and leading to Mexico's loss of Texas in 1836.[11]

Senator Benton, his son-in-law Captain John C. Frémont, and Kit Carson also helped pave the way for the invasion of Northern California. In the early 1840s, Benton and his daughter, Jessie—Frémont's wife—built a booster press to entice settlers to the Oregon Territory as well as to settle in the Mexican province of California. At the same time, Frémont and his guide Carson mounted five expeditions to gather information, laying the groundwork for military conquest. The third expedition illegally entered the Sacramento Valley region from the north in early 1846, just before the United States declared war against Mexico. Frémont encouraged Anglo settlers in the Central Valley to side with the United States, promising military protection if war broke out. Once a US warship was positioned for war, Frémont was appointed lieutenant colonel of the California Battalion, as if it had all been planned in advance.[12]

Exploration and intelligence gathered by Pike, followed by infiltration and settlement of northern Mexican provinces preceded by US entrepreneurs, finally culminated in military invasion and war. US forces fought their way from Mexico's main commercial port of Veracruz on the Gulf of Mexico to the capital, Mexico City, nearly three hundred miles away. The US Army occupied the capital until the Mexican government agreed to cede its northern territories, codified in the 1848 Treaty of Guadalupe Hidalgo. Texas had become a

US state at the end of 1845. California quickly acquired statehood in 1850, followed by Nevada in 1864, Colorado in 1876, Wyoming in 1890, Utah in 1896, but the more densely populated Arizona and New Mexico not until 1912.

The Land Ordinance of 1785 had established a national system for surveying and distributing land, and as one historian has noted, "Under the May 1785 ordinance, Indian land would be auctioned off to the highest bidder."[13] The Northwest Ordinance of 1787, albeit guaranteeing Indigenous occupancy and title, set forth an evolutionary colonization procedure for annexation via military occupation, territorial status, and finally statehood. Conditions for statehood would be achieved when the settlers outnumbered the Indigenous population, which in the cases of both the Mexican cession area and the Louisiana Purchase territory required decimation or forced removal of Indigenous populations. In this US system, unique among colonial powers, land became the most important exchange commodity for the accumulation of capital and building of the national treasury. To understand the genocidal policy of the US government, the centrality of land sales in building the economic base of the US wealth and power must be seen. Apologists for US expansionism see the 1787 ordinance not as a reflection of colonialism, but rather as a means of "reconciling the problem of liberty with the problem of empire," in historian Howard Lamar's words.[14]

Following the Mexican War, the United States faced problems more pressing than that of reconciling conflicting ideologies. For one thing, the vast majority in the annexed territory were Indigenous peoples or Mexican farmers and ranchers, landed communities. As for the Navajos, Apaches, and Utes who had resisted for centuries all colonization efforts by the Spanish and then the Mexican authorities, they continued to resist the new colonial regime. To understand how the peoples of these regions responded to the US invasion and conquest, and to understand their particular relationship with the United States today, it is essential to understand their history under Spanish colonization.

INDIGENOUS PEOPLES OF
OCCUPIED NORTHERN MEXICO

Although the Spanish Crown had dispatched explorers such as Coronado, Cabeza de Baca, and others, and had established trading and military posts and towns along the North American Atlantic Coast and in Florida and along the Gulf Coast as far as the Mississippi, Spanish settler-colonialist rule did not begin north of the Rio Grande until 1598. The soldier-settler colonizing mission launched a brutal military assault on the Pueblo towns in New Mexico and imposed state and church institutions. The colonizers found a thriving irrigation-based agriculture supporting a population living in ninety-eight interrelated city-states (*pueblos*, the Spanish called them), and within two decades they reduced the towns to twenty-one.[15] Perhaps most provocative, given the Pueblos' extensive rituals and numerous religious feast days, the Franciscan missionaries forbade Pueblo religious practices and forced Christianity upon them. As Spanish repression and labor exploitation intensified, the Pueblos organized a revolution that also was supported by the unconquered Navajos, Apaches, and Utes, and the Hopi towns to the west in what is now Arizona. They were joined by the servant and laboring class of captive Indigenous and Mestizos in the Spanish capital at Santa Fe. In 1680, they drove the Spanish out of New Mexico, leaving the Pueblos free for twelve years before a new and permanent colonizing mission arrived.[16] During another 130 years of Spanish rule before Mexico's independence, the Pueblos were strictly controlled and forced to provide foot soldiers for Spanish forays against the Navajos, Apaches, and Utes who were never colonized by the Spanish. Mexico ousted the Franciscans and left the Pueblos to their own lives, although much of their territory had been lost to permanent settlers.

The two largest Mexican provinces annexed by the United States, Coahuila y Tejas (Texas) and California, were more sparsely populated and not as tightly centralized and organized as New Mexico. After 1692, as the Spanish Crown sent an army to invade and reoccupy the Rio Grande Pueblos, it also sought effective control and settlement of California and Texas, in part to create a large buffer with competing French, British, and Russian imperialism. After two centuries of dominance in the Americas, the Spanish state was crumbling politically and economically. Having experienced a depression in silver production in their American colonies and growing competition from other European powers, the Spanish settled on maintaining and expanding its northern holdings to hold back French and British encroachment into the mining areas of the interior of New Spain (Mexico).

In what is now the state of Texas, Spain built forts and expropriated land from the local Indigenous people, granting it to Spanish settlers to farm and ranch. The first Spanish town in Texas, San Antonio, was established in 1718, and Franciscan missionaries founded the Mission San Antonio de Valero (the Alamo). Spanish forts, missions, and settlements dotted the territory, especially along the Rio Grande from Matamoras to Laredo. The Indigenous peoples of Texas included the Lupin Apaches, Jumanos, Coahuiltecans, Tonkawas, Karankawas, and Caddos, all of whom were more vulnerable to colonization than the more mobile Comanches and Wichitas in West Texas. By the time of Mexican independence, the Indigenous population of the province was around fifty thousand, while Spanish settlers numbered around thirty thousand.

During the first decade of Mexican independence, some ten thousand Cherokees, Seminoles, Shawnees, and many other Indigenous communities east of the Mississippi avoided forced removal to Indian Territory and escaped the iron heel of the United States, taking refuge in Mexico. One such community was the people of the Coahuila Kikapú (Kickapoo) Nation, forced out of its homeland when Wisconsin was opened for settlement. The Tohono O'odam Nation did not move anywhere, but the redrawn 1848 border split their homeland. The independent Republic of Mexico provided land grants for their various communities. With Texas's independence from Mexico, then US annexation, many moved south of the imposed new border.[17]

The Republic of Mexico opened a door to US domination by granting land to Anglo immigrants. During the first decade of Mexican independence, some thirty thousand Anglo-American farmers and plantation owners, along with their slaves, poured into Texas, receiving development land grants. By the time Texas became a US state in 1845, Anglo settlers numbered 160,000.[18] Mexico abolished slavery in 1829, which affected the Anglo-American settlers' quest for wealth in building plantations worked by enslaved Africans. They lobbied the Mexican government for a reversal of the ban and gained only a one-year extension to settle their affairs and free their bonded workers—the government refused to legalize slavery. The settlers decided to secede from Mexico, initiating the famous and mythologized 1836 Battle of the Alamo, where the mercenaries James Bowie and Davy Crockett and slave owner William Travis were killed. Although technically an Anglo-American loss, the siege of the Alamo served to stir Anglo patriotic passions, and within a month at the decisive Battle of San Jacinto, Mexico handed over the province. This was a great victory for the Andrew Jackson administration, for the many Southern slave owners who became Texan planters, and especially for the alcoholic settler-warrior hero Sam Houston. The former governor of Tennessee, Houston was made commander in chief of the Texas army and president of the new "Texas republic," which he helped guide to US statehood in 1845. One of the first acts of the pro-slavery independent government was to establish a counterinsurgency force that—as its name, the Texas Rangers, suggests—followed the "American way of war" in destroying Indigenous towns, eliminating Native nations in Texas, pursuing ethnic cleansing, and suppressing protest from Tejanos, former Mexican citizens.[19]

Mission San Francisco de Asis, also called Mission Dolores, was a Spanish Franciscan mission established on the Pacific Coast at the same time as the Presidio (military base) at San Francisco—1776, the year that Anglo-Americans declared independence from Britain. The purpose of the garrison was twofold: to protect the mission from Indigenous inhabitants whose territory the Spanish were usurping and to round up those same people and force them to live and work for the Franciscan friars at the mission. Mission Dolores was the sixth of the twenty-one Franciscan missions established between 1769 and 1823, when Mexico disbanded the missions. The establishment of the missions and presidios from San Diego and Los Angeles and Santa Barbara to Carmel, San Francisco, and Sonoma, traces the colonization of California's Indigenous nations. The five-hundred-mile road that connected the missions was called El Camino Real, the Royal Highway.

The Spanish military in California was divided into four districts, each with Franciscan missions and strategically located presidios. The 1769 establishment of the first presidio in San Diego coincided with establishment of the first Franciscan mission in California. The second presidio was based in Monterey in 1770, to defend the six missions in the area as well as the mercury mines in the Santa Cruz Mountains. Monterey became the capital and the only port of entry for shipments to and from Spanish California, and it remained so until 1846, when the United States seized California.

These California Franciscan missions and their founder, Junípero Serra, are extravagantly romanticized by modern California residents and remain popular tourist sites. Very few visitors notice, however, that in the middle of the plaza of each mission is a whipping post. The history symbolized by that artifact is not dead and buried with the generations of Indigenous bodies buried under the California crust. The scars and trauma have been passed on from generation to generation. Putting salt in the wound, as it were, Pope John Paul II in 1988 beatified Junípero Serra, the first step toward sainthood. California Indigenous peoples were insulted by this act and organized to prevent the sanctification of a person they consider to have been an exponent of rape, torture, death, starvation, and humiliation of their ancestors and the attempted destruction of their cultures. Serra would take soldiers with him, randomly kidnapping Indigenous individuals and families, recording these captures in his diaries, as in this instance: "[When] one fled from between their [the soldiers'] hands, they caught the other. They tied him, and it was all necessary, for, even bound, he defended himself that they should not bring him, and flung himself on the ground with such violence that he scraped and bruised his thighs and knees. But at last they brought him. . . . He was most frightened and very disturbed."[20] In 1878, a old Kamia man named Janitin told an interviewer of his experience as a child: "When we arrived at the mission, they locked me in a room for a week. . . . Every day they lashed me unjustly because I did not finish what I did not know how to do, and thus I existed for many days until I found a way to escape; but I was tracked and they caught me like a fox." He was fastened to the stage and beaten to unconsciousness.

California Indigenous peoples resisted this totalitarian order. These insurgent actions are also recorded in official records and diaries, but they seem to have interested few historians until the civil rights era of the 1950s and 1960s, when California Indigenous peoples began to do their own research. They found that no mission escaped uprising from within or attacks from outside by communities of the imprisoned along with escapees. Guerrilla forces of up to two thousand formed. Without this resistance, there would be no descendants of the California Native peoples of the area colonized by the Spanish.[21]

Under the protection of the US Army, beginning in 1848, gold seekers from all over the world brought death, torture, rape, starvation, and disease to the Indigenous peoples whose ancestral territories included the sought-after goldfields north and east of San Francisco. As Alejandro Murguía describes it, unlike the Native peoples for whom gold was irrelevant, the forty-niners "hungered for gold with a sickness":

> They would do anything for it. They left families, homes, everything behind; they sailed for eight months aboard leaky, smelly ships to reach California; others, captains and sailors, jumped ship at San Francisco, leaving a fleet of abandoned brigs, barks, and schooners to rot by the piers. They slaughtered all the game they could find and so muddied the rivers and creeks with silt that the once plentiful salmon couldn't survive. The herds of elk and deer, the food source for Native Americans, were practically wiped out in one summer. The miners cheated and killed each other in the goldfields.[22]

In a true reign of terror, US occupation and settlement exterminated more than one hundred thousand California Native people in twenty-five years, reducing the population to thirty thousand by 1870—quite possibly the most extreme demographic disaster of all time.[23] Here too, against impossible odds, the Indigenous resisted and survived to tell the story. Had they not done so, there would be no Indigenous peoples remaining in Northern California, because the objective was to eradicate them. From the onset of the California gold rush, crazed "gold bugs" invaded Indigenous territories, terrorizing and brutally killing those who were in their path. These settlers seemed to require no military assistance in running roughshod over unarmed Indigenous residents of fishing communities in a bountiful paradise of woods, rivers, and mountains. The role left for the US Army was to round up the starving Indigenous refugees to transport them to established reservations in Oregon and Oklahoma.

THE WHITE MAN'S BURDEN

The two-year invasion and occupation of Mexico was a joyful experience for most US citizens, as evidenced by Walt Whitman's populist poetry. Its popularity was possible because of buoyant nationalism, and the war itself accelerated the spirit of nationalism and confirmed the manifest destiny of the United States. Besides new weapons of war and productive capacity brought about by the emerging industrial revolution, there was also an advance in printing and publishing techniques, which increased the book publishing market from $2.5 million in 1830 to $12.5 million in 1850. Most of the books published during the five-year period leading up to, during, and after the invasion were war-mongering tracts. Euro-American settlers were nearly all literate, and this was the period of the foundational "American literature," with writers James Fenimore Cooper, Walt Whitman, Edgar Allan Poe, John Greenleaf Whittier, Henry Wadsworth Longfellow, James Russell Lowell, Ralph Waldo Emerson, Henry David Thoreau, Nathaniel Hawthorne, and Herman Melville all active—each of whom remains read, revered, and studied in the twenty-first century, as national and nationalist writers, not as colonialists.

Although some of the writers, like Melville and Longfellow, paid little attention to the war, most of the others either fiercely supported it or opposed it. Whitman, a supporter, was also enamored of the violent Indian- and Mexican-killing Texas Rangers. Whitman saw the war as bolstering US self-respect and believed that a "true American" would be unable to resist "this pride in our victorious armies." Emerson opposed the war as he did all wars. His opposition to the Mexican War was based, however, not just on his pacifism but also on his belief that the Mexican "race" would poison Anglo-Americans through contact, the "heart of darkness" fear. Emerson supported territorial expansion at any cost but would have preferred it take place without war.

Most of the writers of the era were obsessed with heroism. Opposition to the Mexican War came from writers who were active abolitionists such as Thoreau, Whittier, and Lowell. They believed the war was a plot of southern slave owners to extend slavery, punishing Mexico for having outlawed slavery when it became independent from Spain. However, even the abolitionists believed in the "manifest destiny of the English race," as Lowell put it in 1859, "to occupy this whole continent and to display there that practical understanding in matters of government and colonization which no other race has given such proof of possessing since the Romans."[24]

President James K. Polk, who presided over the war, saw its significance as an example of how a democracy could carry on and win a foreign war with as much "vigor" as authoritarian governments were able to do. He believed that an elected civilian government with its volunteer people's army was even more effective than European monarchies in the quest for empire. The victory over Mexico proved to the European powers, he felt, that the United States was their equal. Standing tall through military victory over a weak country: it was not Ronald Reagan or George W. Bush who thought up that idea. The tradition is as old as the United States itself.

The US war against Mexico did more than annex half of Mexico. A debate that turned deadly ensued over whether the acquired territory would allow slavery and it brought on a civil war that produced a million casualties. The US Civil War allowed for the reorganization and modernization of the military and streamlined counterinsurgency operations—that is, ones targeting civilians. A rehearsal for this streamlining is found in the aftermath of the Mexican War in the US Army counterinsurgency against the fierce resistance of the Apaches in the portions of the territory annexed from Mexico in 1848 that later became the states of New Mexico and Arizona, as well as across the new border into what remained Mexico. The First and Second US Army Dragoons (cavalry troops) were employed for this purpose, elite mounted troops well equipped and trained for the desert terrain. During the period between the Mexican War and the Civil War, Indigenous resistance was led by Gila Apache leader Mangas Coloradas to maintain the Apaches' traditional lands and way of life. The dragoons employed the "first way of war," total war, encouraging field units to attack Apache villages and destroy crops and kill livestock, slaughtering women and children and old men left in the villages while the young men were engaged elsewhere fighting the dragoons.[25] This kind of warfare against Indigenous peoples continued throughout the Civil War and ratcheted up in the northern plains and Southwest afterward, producing the term that the US military use to this day all over the world when referring to enemy territory: "Indian Country."

EIGHT

"INDIAN COUNTRY"

*Buffalo were dark rich clouds moving upon the rolling hills
and plains of America. And then the flashing steel came
upon bone and flesh.*

—Simon J. Ortiz, *from Sand Creek*

The US Army on the eve of the Civil War was divided into seven
departments—a structure designed by John C. Calhoun during the
Monroe administration. By 1860, six of the seven departments,
comprising 183 companies, were stationed west of the Mississippi,
a colonial army fighting the Indigenous occupants of the land. In
much of the western lands, the army was the primary US government institution; the military roots to institutional development
run deep.

President Abraham Lincoln was inaugurated in March 1861, two
months after the South had seceded from the union. In April, the
Confederate States of America (CSA) seized the army base at Fort
Sumter near Charleston, South Carolina. Of more than a thousand
US Army officers, 286 left to serve the CSA, half of them being West
Point graduates, most of them Indian fighters, including Robert E.
Lee. Three of the seven army department commanders took leadership of the Confederate Army. Based on demographics alone, the
South had little chance of winning, so it is all the more remarkable
that it persisted against the Union for more than four years. The
1860 population of the United States was nearly thirty-two million, with twenty-three million in the twenty-two northern states,
and about nine million in the eleven southern states. More than a
third of the nine million Southerners were enslaved people of African heritage. Within the CSA, 76 percent of settlers owned no

slaves. Roughly 60–70 percent of those without slaves owned fewer than a hundred acres of land. Less than 1 percent owned more than a hundred slaves. Seventeen percent of settlers in the South owned one to nine slaves, and only 6.5 percent owned more than ten. Ten percent of the settlers who owned no slaves were also landless, while that many more managed to barely survive on small dirt farms. The Confederate Army reflected the same kind of percentages.[1] Those who, even today, claim that "states' rights" caused Southern secession and the Civil War use these statistics to argue that slavery was not the cause of the Civil War, but that is false. Every settler in the Southern states aspired to own land and slaves or to own *more* land and *more* slaves, as both social status and wealth depended on the extent of property owned. Even small and landless farmers relied on slavery-based rule: the local slave plantation was the market for what small farmers produced, and planters hired landless settlers as overseers and sharecroppers. Most non-slave-owning settlers supported and fought for the Confederacy.

LINCOLN'S "FREE SOIL" FOR SETTLERS

Abraham Lincoln's campaign for the presidency appealed to the vote of land-poor settlers who demanded that the government "open" Indigenous lands west of the Mississippi. They were called "free-soilers," in reference to cheap land free of slavery. New gold rushes and other incentives brought new waves of settlers to squat on Indigenous land. For this reason, some Indigenous people preferred a Confederate victory, which might divide and weaken the United States, which had grown ever more powerful. Indigenous nations in Indian Territory were more directly affected by the Civil War than anywhere else. As discussed in chapter 6, the southeastern nations— the Cherokees, Muskogees, Seminoles, Choctaws, and Chickasaws ("Five Civilized Tribes")—were forcibly removed from their homelands during the Jackson administration, but in the Indian Territory they rebuilt their townships, farms, ranches, and institutions, including newspapers, schools, and orphanages. Although a tiny elite of each nation was wealthy and owned enslaved Africans and private estates, the majority of the people continued their collective agrarian practices. All five nations signed treaties with the Confederacy, each for similar reasons. Within each nation, however, there was a clear division based on class, often misleadingly expressed as a conflict between "mixed-bloods" and "full-bloods." That is, the wealthy, assimilated, slave-owning minority that dominated politics favored the Confederacy, and the non-slave-owning poor and traditional majority wanted to stay out of the Anglo-American civil war. Historian David Chang found that Muskogee nationalism and well-founded distrust of federal power played a major role in bringing about that nation's strategic alliance with the Confederacy. Chang writes: "Was the Creek council's alliance with the South a racist defense of slavery and its class privileges, or was it a nationalist defense of Creek lands and sovereignty? The answer has to be 'both.'"[2]

John Ross, principal chief of the Cherokee Nation, at first called for neutrality, but changed his mind for reasons similar to the Muskogees and asked the Cherokee council for authority to negotiate a treaty with the CSA. Nearly seven thousand men of the five nations went into battle for the Confederacy. Stand Watie, a Cherokee, held the post of brigadier general in the Confederate Army. His First Indian Brigade of the Army of the Trans-Mississippi was among the last units in the field to surrender to the Union Army on June 23, 1865, more than two months after Lee's surrender of the Army of Northern Virginia at Appomattox Courthouse in April 1865. During the war, however, many Indigenous soldiers became disillusioned and went over to the Union forces, along with enslaved African Americans who fled to freedom.[3]

Another story is equally important, though less often told. A few months after the war broke out, some ten thousand men in Indian Territory, made up of Indigenous volunteers, along with African Americans who had freed themselves and even some Anglo-Americans, engaged in guerrilla warfare against the Confederate Army. They fought from Oklahoma into Kansas, where many of them joined unofficial Union units that had been organized by abolitionists who had trained with John Brown years earlier. This was not likely the kind of war the Lincoln administration had desired—a multiethnic volunteer Union contingent fighting pro-slavery forces in Missouri, where enslaved Africans escaped to join the Union side.[4] The self-liberation by African Americans, occurring all over the South, led to Lincoln's 1863 Emancipation Proclamation, which allowed freed Africans to serve in combat.

In Minnesota, which had become a non-slavery state in 1859, the Dakota Sioux were on the verge of starvation by 1862. When they mounted an uprising to drive out the mostly German and Scandinavian settlers, Union Army troops crushed the revolt, slaughtering Dakota civilians and rounding up several hundred men. Three hundred prisoners were sentenced to death, but upon Lincoln's orders to reduce the numbers, thirty-eight were selected at random to die in the largest mass hanging in US history. The revered leader Little Crow was not among those hanged, but was assassinated the following summer while out picking raspberries with his son; the assassin, a settler-farmer, collected a $500 bounty.[5]

One of the young Dakota survivors asked his uncle about the mysterious white people who would commit such crimes. The uncle replied:

> Certainly they are a heartless nation. They have made some of their people servants—yes, slaves. . . . The greatest object of their lives seems to be to acquire possessions—to be rich. They desire to possess the whole world. For thirty years they were trying to entice us to sell them our land. Finally the outbreak gave them all, and we have been driven away from our beautiful country.[6]

THE GENOCIDAL ARMY OF THE WEST

To free the professional soldiers posted in the West to fight against the Confederate Army in the East, Lincoln called for volunteers in the West, and settlers responded, coming from Texas, Kansas, California, Washington, Oregon, Colorado, Nebraska, Utah, and Nevada. Having few Confederates to fight, they attacked people closer to hand, Indigenous people. Land speculators in the trans-Mississippi West sought statehood for the occupied former Mexican territories in order to attract settlers and investors. Their eagerness to undertake the ethnic cleansing of the Indigenous residents to achieve the necessary population balance to attain statehood generated strong anti-Indian hysteria and violent actions. Preoccupied with the Civil War in the East, the Lincoln administration did little to prevent vicious and even genocidal actions on the part of territorial authorities consisting of volunteer Indian haters such as Kit Carson.

The mode of maintaining settler "law and order" set the pattern for postwar genocide. In the most infamous incident involving militias, the First and Third Colorado Volunteers carried out the Sand Creek Massacre. Although assigned to guard the road to Santa Fe, the units mainly engaged in raiding and looting Indigenous communities. John Chivington, an ambitious politician known as the "Fighting Parson," led the Third Colorado.[7]

By 1861, displaced and captive Cheyennes and Arapahos, under the leadership of the great peace seeker Black Kettle, were incarcerated in a US military reservation called Sand Creek, near Fort Lyon in southeastern Colorado. They camped under a white flag of truce and had federal permission to hunt buffalo to feed themselves. In early 1864, the Colorado territorial governor informed them that they could no longer leave the reservation to hunt. Despite their compliance with the order, on November 29, 1864, Chivington took seven hundred Colorado Volunteers to the reservation. Without provocation or warning, they attacked, leaving dead 105 women and children and 28 men. Even the federal commissioner of Indian affairs denounced the action, saying that the people had been "butchered in cold blood by troops in the service of the United States." In its 1865 investigation, the Congress Joint Committee on the Conduct of the War recorded testimonies and published a report that documented the aftermath of the killings, when Chivington and his volunteers burned tepees and stole horses. Worse, after the smoke had cleared, they had returned and finished off the few survivors while scalping and mutilating the corpses—women and men, young and old, children, babies. Then they decorated their weapons and caps with body parts—fetuses, penises, breasts, and vulvas— and, in the words of Acoma poet Simon Ortiz, "Stuck them / on their hats to dry / Their fingers greasy / and slick."[8] Once back in Denver, they displayed the trophies to the adoring public in Denver's

Apollo Theater and in saloons. Yet, despite the detailed report of the deeds, neither Chivington nor any of his men were reprimanded or prosecuted, signaling a free field for killing.[9]

US Army colonel James Carleton formed the Volunteer Army of the Pacific in 1861, based in California. In Nevada and Utah, a California businessman, Colonel Patrick Connor, commanded a militia of a thousand California volunteers that spent the war years massacring hundreds of unarmed Shoshone, Bannock, and Ute people in their encampments. Carleton led another contingent of militias to Arizona to suppress the Apaches, who were resisting colonization under the great leader Cochise. At the time, Cochise observed:

> When I was young I walked all over this country, east and west, and saw no other people than the Apaches. After many summers I walked again and found another race of people had come to take it. How is it? Why is it that the Apaches wait to die—that they carry their lives on their finger nails? . . . The Apaches were once a great nation; they are now but few. . . . Many have been killed in battle.[10]

Following a scorched-earth campaign against the Apaches, Carleton was promoted to the rank of brigadier general and placed in command of the Department of New Mexico. He brought in the now-seasoned killing machine of Colorado Volunteers to attack the Navajos, on whom he declared total war. He enlisted as his principal commander in the field the ubiquitous Indian killer Kit Carson.[11] With unlimited authority and answering to no one, Carleton spent the entire Civil War in the Southwest engaged in a series of search-and-destroy missions against the Navajos. The campaign culminated in March 1864 in a three-hundred-mile forced march of eight thousand Navajo civilians to a military concentration camp at Bosque Redondo in the southeastern New Mexico desert, at the army base at Fort Sumner, an ordeal recalled in Navajo oral history as the "Long Walk." One Navajo named Herrero said,

> Some of the soldiers do not treat us well. When at work, if we stop a little they kick us or do something else. . . . We do not mind if an officer punishes us, but do not like to be treated

badly by the soldiers. Our women sometimes come to the tents outside the fort and make contracts with the soldiers to stay with them for a night, and give them five dollars or something else. But in the morning they take away what they gave them and kick them off. This happens most every day.[12]

At least a fourth of the incarcerated died of starvation. Not until 1868 were the Navajos released and allowed to return to their homeland in what is today the Four Corners area. This permission to return was not based on the deadly conditions of the camp, rather that Congress determined that the incarceration was too expensive to maintain.[13] For these noble deeds, Carleton was appointed a major general in the US Army in 1865. Now he led the Fourth Cavalry in scorched-earth forays against Plains Indians.

These military campaigns against Indigenous nations constituted foreign wars fought during the US Civil War, but the end of the Civil War did not end them. They carried on unabated to the end of the century, with added killing technology and more seasoned killers, including African American cavalry units. Demobilized officers and soldiers often could not find jobs, and along with a new generation of young settlers—otherwise unemployed and often seeking violent adventure—they joined the army of the West, some of the officers accepting lower ranks in order to get career army assignments. Given that war was centered in the West and that military achievement had come to foster prestige, wealth, and political power, every West Point graduate sought to further his career by volunteering in the army. Some of their diaries echo those of combat troops in Vietnam, Afghanistan, and Iraq, who later were troubled by the atrocities they witnessed or committed. But most soldiers persevered in their ambition to succeed.

Prominent Civil War generals led the army of the West, among them Generals William Tecumseh Sherman, Philip Sheridan (to whom is ascribed the statement "The only good Indian is a dead Indian"), George Armstrong Custer, and Nelson A. Miles. The army would make effective use after 1865 of innovations made during the Civil War. The rapid-fire Gatling gun, first used in battle in 1862, would be employed during the rest of the century against Indigenous civilians. Non-technological innovations were perhaps even more important, the Civil War having fostered an extreme patriotic ideology in the Union Army that carried over into the Indian wars. Now more centralized under presidential command, US forces relied less on state contributions and were thus less subject to their control. The prestige of the Department of War rose within the federal government, so that it had far more leeway to send troops to steamroll over Indigenous peoples who challenged US dominion.

The Union Army victory over the Confederate Army transformed the South into a quasi-captive nation, a region that remains the poorest of the United States well over a century later. The situation was similar to that in South Africa two decades later when the British defeated the Boers (descendants of the original seventeenth-century Dutch settlers). As the British would later do with the Boers, the US government eventually allowed the defeated southern elite to return to their locally powerful positions, and both US southerners and Boers soon gained national political power. The powerful white supremacist southern ruling class helped further militarize the United States, the army practically becoming a southern institution. Following the effective Reconstruction experiment to empower former slaves, the US occupying army was withdrawn, and African Americans were returned to quasi-bondage and disenfranchisement through Jim Crow laws, forming a colonized population in the South.

COLONIAL POLICY PRECEDES MILITARY IMPLEMENTATION

In the midst of war, Lincoln did not forget his free-soiler settler constituency that had raised him to the presidency. During the Civil War, with the southern states unrepresented, Congress at Lincoln's behest passed the Homestead Act in 1862, as well as the Morrill Act, the latter transferring large tracts of Indigenous land to the states to establish land grant universities. The Pacific Railroad Act provided private companies with nearly two hundred million acres of Indigenous land.[14] With these land grabs, the US government broke multiple treaties with Indigenous nations. Most of the western territories, including Colorado, North and South Dakota, Montana, Washington, Idaho, Wyoming, Utah, New Mexico, and Arizona, were delayed in achieving statehood, because Indigenous nations resisted appropriation of their lands and outnumbered settlers. So the colonization plan for the West established during the Civil War was carried out over the following three decades of war and land grabs. Under the Homestead Act, 1.5 million homesteads were granted to settlers west of the Mississippi, comprising nearly three hundred million acres (a half-million square miles) taken from the Indigenous collective estates and privatized for the market.[15] This dispersal of landless settler populations from east of the Mississippi served as an "escape valve," lessening the likelihood of class conflict as the industrial revolution accelerated the use of cheap immigrant labor.

Little of the land appropriated under the Homestead Acts was distributed to actual single-family homesteaders. It was passed instead to large operators or land speculators. The land laws appeared to have been created for that result. An individual could acquire 1,120 or even more acres of land, even though homestead and pre-emption (legalized squatting) claims were limited to 160 acres.[16] A claimant could obtain a homestead and secure title after five years or pay cash within six months. Then he could acquire another 160 acres under preemption by living on another piece of land for six months and paying $1.25 per acre. While acquiring these titles, he could also be fulfilling requirements for a timber culture claim of 160 acres and a desert land claim of 640 acres, neither of which required occupancy for title. Other men within a family or other partners in an enterprise could take out additional desert land claims to increase their holdings even more. As industrialization quickened, land as a commodity, "real estate," remained the basis of the US economy and capital accumulation.[17] The federal land grants to the railroad barons, carved out of Indigenous territories, were not limited to the width of the railroad tracks, but rather formed a checkerboard of square-mile sections stretching for dozens of miles on both sides of the right of way. This was land the railroads were free to sell in parcels for their own profit. The 1863–64 federal banking acts mandated a national currency, chartered banks, and permitted the government to guarantee bonds. As war profiteers, financiers, and industrialists such as John D. Rockefeller, Andrew Carnegie, and J. P. Morgan used these laws to amass wealth in the East, Leland Stanford, Collis P. Huntington, Mark Hopkins, and Charles Crocker in the West grew rich from building railroads with eastern capital on land granted by the US government.[18]

Indigenous nations, as well as Hispanos, resisted the arrival of railroads crisscrossing their farms, hunting grounds, and homelands, bringing settlers, cattle, barbed wire fencing, and mercenary buffalo hunters in their wake. In what proved a prelude to the genocidal decades to follow, the Andrew Johnson administration in 1867–68 sent army and diplomatic representatives to negotiate peace treaties with dozens of Indigenous nations. The 371 treaties between Indigenous nations and the United States were all promulgated during the first century of US existence.[19] Congress halted formal treaty making in 1871, attaching a rider to the Indian Appropriation Act of that year stipulating "that hereafter no Indian nation or tribe within the territory of the United States shall be acknowledged or recognized as an independent nation, tribe, or power with whom the United States may contract by treaty. Provided, further, that nothing herein contained shall be construed to invalidate or impair the obligation of any treaty heretofore lawfully made and ratified with any such Indian nation or tribe."[20] This measure meant that Congress and the president could now make laws affecting an Indigenous nation with or without negotiations or consent. Nevertheless, the provision reaffirmed the sovereign legal status of those Indigenous nations that had treaties. During the period of US-Indigenous treaty making, approximately two million square miles of land passed from Indigenous nations to the United States, some of it through treaty agreements and some through breach of standing treaties.

In an effort to create Indigenous economic dependency and compliance in land transfers, the US policy directed the army to destroy the basic economic base of the Plains Nations—the buffalo. The buffalo were killed to near extinction, tens of millions dead within a few decades and only a few hundred left by the 1880s. Commercial hunters wanted only the skins, so left the rest of the animal to rot. Bones would be gathered and shipped to the East for various uses. Mainly it was the army that helped realize slaughter of the herds.[21]

Old Lady Horse of the Kiowa Nation could have been speaking for all the buffalo nations in her lament of the loss:

> Everything the Kiowas had came from the buffalo. . . . Most of all, the buffalo was part of the Kiowa religion. A white buffalo calf must be sacrificed in the Sun Dance. The priests used parts of the buffalo to make their prayers when they healed people or when they sang to the powers above.
>
> So, when the white men wanted to build railroads, or when they wanted to farm or raise cattle, the buffalo still protected the Kiowas. They tore up the railroad tracks and the gardens. They chased the cattle off the ranges. The buffalo loved their people as much as the Kiowas loved them.
>
> There was war between the buffalo and the white men. The white men built forts in the Kiowa country, and the woolly-headed buffalo soldiers shot the buffalo as fast as they could, but the buffalo kept coming on, coming on, even into the post cemetery at Fort Sill. Soldiers were not enough to hold them back.
>
> Then the white men hired hunters to do nothing but kill the buffalo. Up and down the plains those men ranged, shooting sometimes as many as a hundred buffalo a day. Behind them came the skinners with their wagons. They piled the hides and bones into the wagons until they were full, and then took their loads to the new railroad stations that were being built, to be shipped east to the market. Sometimes there would be a pile of bones as high as a man, stretching a mile along the railroad track.
>
> The buffalo saw that their day was over. They could protect their people no longer.[22]

Another aspect of US economic development that affected the Indigenous nations of the West was merchant domination. All over the world, in European colonies distant from their ruling centers, mercantile capitalists flourished alongside industrial capitalists and militaries, and together they determined the mode of colonization. Mercantile houses, usually family-owned, were organized to carry goods over long stretches of water or sparsely populated lands to their destinations. The merchants' sources of commodities in remote regions were the nearby small farmers, loggers, trappers, and specialists such as woodworkers and metalsmiths. The commodities were then sent to industrial centers for credit against which money could be drawn. Thus, in the absence of a system of indirect credit, merchants could acquire scarce currency for the purchase of foreign goods. The merchant, thereby, became the dominant source of credit for the small operator as well as for the local capitalist. Mercantile capitalism thrived in colonial areas, with many of the first merchant houses originating in the Levant among Syrians (Lebanese) and Jews. Even as mercantile capitalism waned in the twentieth century, it left its mark on Native reservations where the people relied on trading posts for credit, a market for their products, and commodities of all kinds—an opportunity for super-exploitation. Merchants and traders, often by intermarrying Indigenous women, also came to dominate Native governance on some reservations.[23]

As noted above, at the end of the Civil War the US Army hardly missed a beat before the war "to win the West" began in full force. As a far more advanced killing machine and with seasoned troops, the army began the slaughter of people, buffalo, and the land itself, destroying the natural tall grasses of the plains and planting short grasses for cattle, eventually leading to the loss of the topsoil four decades later. William Tecumseh Sherman came out of the Civil War a major general and soon commanded the US Army, replacing war hero Ulysses S. Grant when Grant became president in 1869. As commanding general through 1883, Sherman was responsible for the genocidal wars against the resistant Indigenous nations of the West.

Sherman's family was among the first generation of settlers who rushed to the Ohio Valley region after the total war that drove the people of the Shawnee Nation out of their homes, towns, and farms. Sherman's father gave his son the trophy name Tecumseh after the Shawnee leader who was killed by the US Army. The general had been a successful lawyer and banker in San Francisco and New York before he turned to a military career. During the Civil War, most famously in the siege of Atlanta, he made his mark as a proponent and practitioner of total war, scorched-earth campaigns against civilians, particularly targeting their food supplies. This had long been the colonial and US American way of war against the Indigenous peoples east of the Mississippi. Sherman sent an army commission to England to study English colonial campaigns worldwide, looking to employ successful English tactics for the US wars against Indigenous peoples. In Washington, Sherman had to contend with the upper echelons of the military that were under the sway of Carl von Clausewitz's book *On War*, which dealt with conflict between European nation-states with standing armies. This dichotomy of training the US military for standard European warfare but also training it in colonial counterinsurgency methods continues in the twenty-first century. Although a man of war, Sherman, like most in the US ruling class, was an entrepreneur at heart, and his mandate as head of the army and his passion were to protect the Anglo conquest of the West. Sherman regarded railroads a top priority. In a letter to Grant in 1867 he wrote, "We are not going to let a few thieving, ragged Indians stop the progress of [the railroads]."[24]

An alliance of the Sioux, Cheyenne, and Arapaho Nations was blocking the "Bozeman Trail," over which thousands of crazed gold seekers crashed through Indigenous territories in the Dakotas and Wyoming in 1866 to reach newly discovered goldfields in Montana. The army arrived to protect them, and in preparation for constructing Fort Phil Kearny, Lieutenant Colonel William Fetterman led eighty soldiers out to clear the trail in December 1866. The Indigenous alliance defeated them in battle. Strangely, this being war, the defeat of the US Army in the battle has come down in historical annals as "the Fetterman Massacre." Following this event, General Sherman wrote to Grant, who was still army commander: "We must act with vindictive earnestness against the Sioux, even to their extermination, men, women, and children." Sherman made it clear that "during an assault, the soldiers can not pause to distinguish between male and female, or even discriminate as to age."[25]

In adopting total war in the West, Sherman brought in its most notorious avatar, George Armstrong Custer, who proved his mettle right away by leading an attack on unarmed civilians on November 27, 1868, at the Southern Cheyenne reservation at Washita Creek in Indian Territory. Earlier, at the Colorado Volunteers' 1864

Sand Creek Massacre, the Cheyenne leader Black Kettle had escaped death. He and other Cheyenne survivors were then forced to leave Colorado Territory for a reservation in Indian Territory. Some young Cheyenne men, determined to resist reservation confinement and hunger, decided to hunt and to fight back with guerrilla tactics. Since the army was rarely able to capture them, Custer resorted to total war, murdering the incarcerated mothers, wives, children, and elders. When Black Kettle received word from Indigenous spies within the army ranks that the mounted troops of the Seventh Cavalry were leaving their fort and headed for the Washita reservation, he and his wife rode out at dawn in a snowstorm, unarmed, to attempt to talk with Custer and assure him that no resisters were present on the reservation. Upon Black Kettle's approaching the troops with a hoisted white flag, Custer ordered the soldiers to fire, and a moment later Black Kettle and his wife lay dead. All told, the Seventh Cavalry murdered over a hundred Cheyenne women and children that day, taking ghoulish trophies afterward.[26]

COLONIAL SOLDIERS

Many of the intensive genocidal campaigns against Indigenous civilians took place during the administration of President Grant, 1869–77. In 1866, two years before Grant's election, Congress had created two all–African American cavalry regiments that came to be called the buffalo soldiers. Some four million formerly enslaved Africans were free citizens in 1865, thanks to the Emancipation Proclamation, which took effect in January 1863. The legislation was intended to have a demoralizing effect on the CSA, but it gave belated official recognition to what was already fact: many African Americans, especially young men, had freed themselves by fleeing servitude and joining Union forces.[27] Up to 1862, Africans had been barred from serving in their own capacity in the army. Now the Union Army incorporated them but at lower pay and in segregated units under white officers. The War Department created the federal Bureau of Colored Troops, and one hundred thousand armed Africans served in the unit. Their courage and commitment made them the best and most effective fighters, although they had the highest mortality rate. At the end of the Civil War, 186,000 Black soldiers had fought and 38,000 had died (in combat and from disease), a higher death toll than that of any individual state. The state with the highest casualty count was New York, with troops comprising mostly poor white immigrant soldiers, largely Irish. After the war many Black soldiers, like their poor white counterparts, remained in the army and were assigned to segregated regiments sent west to crush Indigenous resistance.

This reality strikes many as tragic, as if oppressed former slaves and Indigenous peoples being subjected to genocidal warfare should magically be unified against their common enemy, "the white man." In fact, this is precisely how colonialism in general and colonial warfare in particular work. It is not unique to the United States, but rather a part of the tradition of European colonialism since the Roman legions. The British organized whole armies of ethnic troops in South and Southwestern Asia, the most famous being the Gurkhas from Nepal, who fought as recently as Margaret Thatcher's war against Argentina in 1983.[28] The buffalo soldiers were such a specially organized colonial military unit. As Stanford L. Davis, a descendant of a buffalo soldier, writes:

> Slaves and the black soldiers, who couldn't read or write, had no idea of the historical deprivations and the frequent genocidal intent of the U.S. government toward Native Americans. Free blacks, whether they could read and write, generally had no access to first-hand or second-hand unbiased information on the relationship. Most whites who had access often didn't really care about the situation. It was business as usual in the name of "Manifest Destiny." Most Americans viewed the Indians as incorrigible and non-reformable savages. Those closest to the warring factions or who were threatened by it, naturally wanted government protection at any cost.[29]

Many Black men opted for army service for survival reasons, as it gave them food and shelter, pay and a pension, and even some glory. The United States had its own motives for assigning Black troops to the West. Southerners and the eastern population did not want thousands of armed Black soldiers in their communities. There was also fear that if they demobilized, the labor market would be flooded. For US authorities, it was a good way of getting rid of the Black soldiers *and* the Indians.

The Civil War also set the template for the rapid "Americanization" of immigrants. Jewish immigrants fought on both sides in the war, and as individuals they earned a level of freedom from US bigotry they had never experienced before.

Indian scouts and soldiers were essential to the army as well, both as individuals and as nations making war on other Indigenous nations. Many decades later, Native Americans have continued to volunteer in US wars in percentages far beyond their populations. Wichita Nation citizen Stan Holder appeared in a 1974 documentary film on the Vietnam War, *Hearts and Minds*, in which he explained his volunteering for service. While growing up he had heard the older people's stories about Wichita warriors, and, looking around, the only warriors he could identify were marines, so he enlisted in what he considered a warrior society. It is no accident that the US Marine Corps evokes that image in angry young men. As with Black men who volunteered in the Indian wars and enlisted and served in other wars, Native men seized the security and potential glory of the colonialist army.

The explicit purpose of the buffalo soldiers and the army of the West as a whole was to invade Indigenous lands and ethnically cleanse them for Anglo settlement and commerce. As Native historian Jace Weaver has written: "The Indian Wars were not fought by the blindingly white American cavalry of John Ford westerns but by African Americans and Irish and German immigrants."[30] The haunting Bob Marley song "Buffalo Soldier" captures the colonial experience in the United States: "Said he was a buffalo soldier / Win the war for America."[31]

The army of the West was a colonial army with all the problems of colonial armies and foreign occupation, principally being hated by the people living under occupation. It's no surprise that the US military uses the term "Indian Country" to refer to what it considers enemy territory. Much as in the Vietnam War, the 1980s covert wars in Central America, and the wars of the early twenty-first century in Muslim countries, counterinsurgent army volunteers in the late-nineteenth-century US West had to rely heavily on intelligence from those native to the land, informers and scouts. Many of these were double agents, reporting back to their own people, having joined the US Army for that purpose. Failing to find guerrilla fighters, the army resorted to scorched-earth campaigns, starvation, attacks on and removals of civilian populations—the weapons of counterinsurgency warfare. During the Soviet counterinsurgency in Afghanistan in the 1980s, the UN High Commissioner for Refugees called the effect "migratory genocide"—an apt term to apply retrospectively to the nineteenth-century US counterinsurgency against Indigenous peoples.[32]

ANNIHILATION UNTO TOTAL SURRENDER

The US Army's search-and-destroy missions and forced relocations (ethnic cleansing) in the West are well documented but perhaps not normally considered in the light of counterinsurgency.

Mari Sandoz recorded one such story in her 1953 best-selling work of nonfiction *Cheyenne Autumn*, on which John Ford based a 1964 film.[33] In 1878, the great Cheyenne resistance leaders Little Wolf and Dull Knife led more than three hundred Cheyenne civilians from a military reservation in Indian Territory, where they had been forcibly confined, to their original homeland in what is today Wyoming and Montana. They were eventually intercepted by the military, but only following a dramatic chase covered by newspaper reporters. So much sympathy was aroused in eastern cities that the Cheyennes were provided a reservation in a part of their original homeland. A similar feat was that of the Nimi'ipuu (Nez Perce) under Chief Joseph, who tried to lead his people out of military incarceration in Idaho to exile in Canada. In 1877, pursued by two thousand soldiers of the US cavalry led by Nelson Miles, Nimi'ipuu led eight hundred civilians toward the Canadian border. They held out for nearly four months, evading the soldiers as well as fighting hit-and-run battles, while covering seventeen hundred miles. Some were rounded up and placed in Pauls Valley, Oklahoma, but they soon left on their own and returned to their Idaho homeland, eventually securing a small reservation there.

The longest military counterinsurgency in US history was the war on the Apache Nation, 1850–86. Goyathlay, known as Geronimo, famously led the final decade of Apache resistance. The Apaches and their Diné relatives, the Navajos, did not miss a beat in continuing resistance to colonial domination when the United States annexed their territory as a part of the half of Mexico taken in 1848. The Treaty of Guadalupe Hidalgo between the United States and Mexico, which sealed the transfer of territory, even stipulated that both parties were required to fight the "savage" Apaches. By 1877 the army had forced most Apaches into inhospitable desert reservations. Led by Geronimo, Chiricahua Apaches resisted incarceration in the San Carlos reservation designated for them in Arizona. When Geronimo finally surrendered—he was never captured—the group numbered only thirty-eight, most of those women and children, with five thousand soldiers in pursuit, which meant that the insurgents had wide support both north and south of the recently drawn US-Mexico border. Guerrilla warfare persists only if it has deep roots in the people being represented, the reason it is sometimes called "people's war." Obviously, the Apache resistance was not a military threat to the United States but rather a symbol of resistance and freedom. Herein lies the essence of counterinsurgent colonialist warfare: no resistance can be tolerated. Historian William Appleman Williams aptly described the US imperative as "annihilation unto total surrender."[34]

Geronimo and three hundred other Chiricahuas who were not even part of the fighting force were rounded up and transported by train under military guard to Fort Marion, in St. Augustine, Florida, to join hundreds of other Plains Indian fighters already incarcerated there. Remarkably, Geronimo negotiated an agreement with the United States so that he and his band would surrender as prisoners of war, rather than as common criminals as the Texas Rangers desired, which would have meant executions by civil authorities. The POW status validated Apache sovereignty and made the captives eligible for treatment according to the international laws of war. Geronimo and his people were transferred again, to the army base at Fort Sill in Indian Territory, and lived out their lives there. The US government had not yet created the term "unlawful combatant," which it would do in the early twenty-first century, depriving legitimate prisoners of war fair treatment under international law.

During the Grant administration, the United States began experimenting with new colonial institutions, the most pernicious of which were the boarding schools, modeled on Fort Marion prison. In 1875, Captain Richard Henry Pratt was in charge of transporting seventy-two captive Cheyenne and other Plains Indian warriors from the West to Fort Marion, an old Spanish fortress, dark and dank. After the captives were left shackled for a period in a dungeon, Pratt took their clothes away, had their hair cut, dressed them in army uniforms, and drilled them like soldiers. "Kill the Indian and save the man" was Pratt's motto. This "successful" experiment led Pratt to establish the Carlisle Indian Industrial School in Pennsylvania in 1879, the prototype for the many militaristic federal boarding schools set up across the continent soon after, augmented by dozens of Christian missionary boarding schools. The decision to establish Carlisle and other off-reservation boarding schools was made by the US Office of Indian Affairs, later renamed the Bureau of Indian Affairs (BIA). The stated goal of the project was assimilation. Indigenous children were prohibited from speaking their mother tongues or practicing their religions, while being indoctrinated in Christianity. As in the Spanish missions in California, in the US boarding schools the children were beaten for speaking their own languages, among other infractions that expressed their humanity. Although stripped of the languages and skills of their communities, what they learned in boarding school was useless for the purposes of effective assimilation, creating multiple lost generations of traumatized individuals.[35]

Just before the centennial of US independence, in late June 1876, then–Lieutenant Colonel Custer, commanding 225 soldiers of the Seventh Cavalry, prepared to launch a military assault on the civilians living in a cluster of Sioux and Cheyenne villages that lay along the Little Bighorn River. Led by Crazy Horse and Sitting Bull, the Sioux and Cheyenne warriors were ready for the assault and wiped out the assailants, including Custer, who after death was promoted to general. The proud author of multiple massacres of Indigenous civilians, starting during the Civil War with his assault on unarmed and reservation-incarcerated Cheyennes on the Washita in Indian Territory, Custer "died for your [colonialist] sins," in the words of Vine Deloria Jr.[36] A year later, Crazy Horse was captured and imprisoned, then killed trying to escape. He was thirty-five years old.

Crazy Horse was a new kind of leader to emerge after the Civil War, at the beginning of the army's wars of annihilation in the northern plains and the Southwest. Born in 1842 in the shadow of the sacred Paha Sapa (Black Hills), he was considered special, a quiet and brooding child. Already the effects of colonialism were present among his people, particularly alcoholism and missionary influence. Crazy Horse became a part of the Akicita, a traditional Sioux society that kept order in villages and during migrations. It also had authority to make certain that the hereditary chiefs were doing their duty and dealt harshly with those who did not. Increasingly during Crazy Horse's youth, the primary concern was the immigrant defilement of the Sioux territory. A steady stream of Euro-American migrants clotted the trail to Oregon Territory. Young militant Sioux wished to drive them away, but the Sioux were now dependent on the trail for supplies. In 1849, the army arrived and planted a base, Fort Laramie, in Sioux territory. Sporadic fighting broke out, leading to treaty meetings and agreements, most of which were bogus army documents signed by unauthorized individuals. Crazy Horse was a natural in guerrilla warfare, becoming legendary among his people. Although Crazy Horse and other militants did not approve of the 1868 US treaty with the Sioux, some stability held until Custer's soldiers found gold in the Black Hills. Then a gold rush was on, with hordes of prospectors from all over converging and running rampant over the Sioux. The treaty had ostensibly been a guarantee that such would not occur. Soon after, the Battle of the Little Bighorn put an end to Custer but not to the invasion.

Indigenous peoples in the West continued to resist, and the soldiers kept hunting them down, incarcerating them, massacring civilians, removing them, and stealing their children to haul off to faraway boarding schools. The Apache, Kiowa, Sioux, Ute, Kickapoo, Comanche, Cheyenne, and other nations were attacked, leaving community after community decimated. By the 1890s, although some military assaults on Indigenous communities and valiant Indigenous armed resistance continued, most of the surviving Indigenous refugees were confined to federal reservations, their children transported to distant boarding schools to unlearn their Indigenousness.

GHOST DANCING

Disarmed, held in concentration camps, their children taken away, half starved, the Indigenous peoples of the West found a form of resistance that spread like wildfire in all directions from its source, thanks to a Paiute holy man, Wovoka, in Nevada. Pilgrims journeyed to hear his message and to receive directions on how to perform the Ghost Dance, which promised to restore the Indigenous world as it was before colonialism, making the invaders disappear and the buffalo return. It was a simple dance performed by everyone, requiring only a specific kind of shirt that was to protect the dancers from gunfire. In the twentieth century Sioux anthropologist Ella Deloria interviewed a sixty-year-old Sioux man who remembered the Ghost Dance he had witnessed fifty years before as a boy:

> Some fifty of us, little boys about eight to ten, started out across country over hills and valleys, running all night. I know now that we ran almost thirty miles. There on the Porcupine Creek thousands of Dakota people were in camp, all hurrying about very purposefully. In a long sweat lodge with openings at both ends, people were being purified in great companies for the holy dance, men by themselves and women by themselves, of course. . . .
>
> The people, wearing the sacred shirts and feathers, now formed a ring. We were in it. All joined hands. Everyone was respectful and quiet, expecting something wonderful to happen. It was not a glad time, though. All wailed cautiously and in awe, feeling their dead were close at hand.

The leaders beat time and sang as the people danced, going round to the left in a sidewise step. They danced without rest, on and on, and they got out of breath but still they kept going as long as possible. Occasionally someone thoroughly exhausted and dizzy fell unconscious into the center and lay there "dead." Quickly those on each side of him closed the gap and went right on. After a while, many lay about in that condition. They were now "dead" and seeing their dear ones. As each one came to, she, or he, slowing sat up and looked about, bewildered, and then began wailing inconsolably. . . .

Waking to the drab and wretched present after such a glowing vision, it was little wonder that they wailed as if their poor hearts would break in two with disillusionment. But at least they had seen! The people went on and on and could not stop, day or night, hoping perhaps to get a vision of their own dead, or at least to hear the visions of others. They preferred that to rest or food or sleep. And so I suppose the authorities did think they were crazy—but they weren't. They were only terribly unhappy.[37]

When the dancing began among the Sioux in 1890, reservation officials reported it as disturbing and unstoppable. They believed that it had been instigated by Hunkpapa Teton Sioux leader Tatanka Yotanka (Sitting Bull), who had returned with his people in 1881 from exile in Canada. He was put under arrest and imprisoned in his home, closely guarded by Indian police. Sitting Bull was killed by one of his captors on December 15, 1890.

All Indigenous individuals and groups living outside designated federal reservations were considered "fomenters of disturbance," as the War Department put it. Following Sitting Bull's death, military warrants of arrest were issued for leaders such as Big Foot, who was responsible for several hundred civilian refugees who had not yet turned themselves in to the designated Pine Ridge Reservation. When Big Foot heard of Sitting Bull's death and that the army was looking for him and his people—350 Lakotas, 230 of them women and children—he decided to lead them through the subzero weather to Pine Ridge to surrender. En route on foot, they encountered US troops. The commander ordered that they be taken to the army camp at Wounded Knee Creek, where armed soldiers surrounded them. Two Hotchkiss machine guns were mounted on the hillside, enough firepower to wipe out the whole group. During the night, Colonel James Forsyth and the Seventh Cavalry, Custer's old regiment, arrived and took charge. These soldiers had not forgotten that Lakota relatives of these starving, unarmed refugees had killed Custer and decimated his troops at the Little Bighorn fourteen years earlier. With orders to transport the refugees to a military stockade in Omaha, Forsyth added two more Hotchkiss guns trained on the camp, then issued whiskey to his officers. The following morning, December 29, 1890, the soldiers brought the captive men out from their campsites and called for all weapons to be turned in. Searching tents, soldiers confiscated tools, such as axes and knives. Still not satisfied, the officers ordered skin searches. A Winchester rifle turned up. Its young owner did not want to part with his beloved rifle, and, when the soldiers grabbed him, the rifle fired a shot into the air. The killing began immediately. The Hotchkiss guns began firing a shell a second, mowing down everyone except a few who were able to run fast enough. Three hundred Sioux lay dead. Twenty-five soldiers were killed in "friendly fire."[38] Bleeding survivors were dragged into a nearby church. Being Christmastime, the sanctuary was candlelit and decked with greenery. In the front, a banner read: PEACE ON EARTH AND GOOD WILL TO MEN.

The Seventh Cavalry attack on a group of unarmed and starving Lakota refugees attempting to reach Pine Ridge to accept reservation incarceration in the frozen days of December 1890 symbolizes the end of Indigenous armed resistance in the United States. The slaughter is called a battle in US military annals. Congressional Medals of Honor were bestowed on twenty of the soldiers involved. A monument was built at Fort Riley, Kansas, to honor the soldiers killed by friendly fire. A battle streamer was created to honor the event and added to other streamers that are displayed at the Pentagon, West Point, and army bases throughout the world. L. Frank Baum, a Dakota Territory settler later famous for writing *The Wonderful Wizard of Oz*, edited the *Aberdeen Saturday Pioneer* at the time. Five days after the sickening event at Wounded Knee, on

January 3, 1891, he wrote, "The Pioneer [*sic*] has before declared that our only safety depends upon the total extermination of the Indians. Having wronged them for centuries we had better, in order to protect our civilization, follow it up by one more wrong and wipe these untamed and untamable creatures from the face of the earth."[39]

Three weeks before the massacre, General Sherman had made clear that he regretted nothing of his three decades of carrying out genocide. In a press conference he held in New York City, he said, "Injins must either work or starve. They never have worked; they won't work now, and they will never work." A reporter asked, "But should not the government supply them with enough to keep them from starvation?" "Why," Sherman asked in reply, "should the government support 260,000 able-bodied campers? No government that the world has ever seen has done such a thing."[40]

The reaction of one young man to Wounded Knee is representative but also extraordinary. Plenty Horses attended the Carlisle school from 1883 to 1888, returning home stripped of his language, facing the dire reality of the genocide of his people, with no traditional or modern means to make a living. He said, "There was no chance to get employment, nothing for me to do whereby I could earn my board and clothes, no opportunity to learn more and remain with the whites. It disheartened me and I went back to live as I had before going to school."[41] Historian Philip Deloria notes: "The greatest threat to the reservation program . . . was the disciplined Indian who refused the gift of civilization and went 'back to the blanket,' as Plenty Horses tried."[42] But it wasn't simple for Plenty Horses to find his place. As Deloria points out, he had missed the essential period of Lakota education, which takes place between the ages of fourteen and nineteen. Due to his absence and Euro-American influence, he was suspect among his own people, and even that world was disrupted by colonialist chaos and violence. Still, Plenty Horses returned to traditional dress, grew his hair long, and participated in the Ghost Dance. He also joined a band of armed resisters, and they were present at Pine Ridge on December 29, 1890, when the bloody bodies were brought in from the Wounded Knee Massacre. A week later, he went out with forty other mounted warriors who accompanied Sioux leaders to meet Lieutenant Edward Casey for possible negotiations. The young warriors were angry, none more than Plenty Horses, who pulled out from the group and got behind Casey and shot him in the back of his head.

Army officials had to think twice about charging Plenty Horses with murder. They were faced with the corollary of the recent army massacre at Wounded Knee, in which the soldiers received Congressional Medals of Honor for their deeds. At trial, Plenty Horses was acquitted due to the state of war that existed. Acknowledging a state of war was essential in order to give legal cover to the massacre.

As a late manifestation of military action against Indigenous peoples, Wounded Knee stands out. Deloria notes that in the preceding years, the Indian warrior imagery so prevalent in US American society was being replaced with "docile, pacified Indians started out on the road to civilization."

> Luther Standing Bear, for example, recounts numerous occasions on which the Carlisle Indian Industrial School students were displayed as docile and educable Indians. The Carlisle band played at the opening of the Brooklyn Bridge in 1883 and then toured several churches. Students were carted around East Coast cities. Standing Bear himself was placed on display in Wanamaker's Philadelphia department store, locked in a glass cell in the center of the store and set to sorting and pricing jewelry.[43]

GREED IS GOOD

During the final phase of military conquest of the continent, surviving Indigenous refugees were deposited in Indian Territory, piled on top of each other in smaller and smaller reservations. In 1883, the first of several conferences were held in Mohonk, New York, of a group of influential and wealthy advocates of the "manifest destiny" policy. These self-styled "friends of the Indians" developed a policy of assimilation soon formulated into an act of Congress written by one of their members, Senator Henry Dawes: the General Allotment Act of 1887. Arguing for allotment of collectively held Indigenous lands, Dawes said: "The defect of the [reservation] system was apparent. It is [socialist] Henry George's system and under that there is no enterprise to make your home any better than that of your neighbors. There is no selfishness, which is at the bottom of civilization. Till this people will consent to give up their lands, and divide among their citizens so that each can own the land he cultivates they will not make much more progress." Although allotment did not create the desired selfishness, it did reduce the overall Indigenous land base by half and furthered both Indigenous impoverishment and US control. In 1889, a part of Indian Territory the federal government called the Unassigned Lands, left over after allotment, was opened to settler homesteading, triggering the "Oklahoma Run."

Oil had been discovered in Indian Territory, but the Dawes Allotment Act could not be applied to the five Indigenous nations removed from the South, because their territories were not technically reservations, rather sovereign nations. In contradiction to the terms of the removal treaties, Congress passed the Curtis Act in 1898, which unilaterally deposed the sovereignty of those nations and mandated allotment of their lands. Indigenous territories were larger than the sum of 160-acre allotments, so the remaining land after distribution was declared surplus and opened to homesteading.

Allotment did not proceed in Indian Territory without fierce resistance. Cherokee traditionalist Redbird Smith rallied his brethren to revive the Keetoowah secret society. Besides direct action, they also sent lawyers to argue before Congress. When they were overridden, they formed a community in the Cookson Hills, refusing to participate in privatization. Similarly, the Muskogee Creeks resisted, led by Chitto Harjo, who was lovingly nicknamed Crazy Snake. He led in the founding of an alternate government, with its capital a settlement they called Hickory Ground. More than five thousand Muskogees were involved. Captured and jailed, when freed Harjo led his people into the woods and carried on the fight for another decade. He was shot by federal troops in 1912, but the legacy of the Crazy Snake resistance remains a strong force in eastern Oklahoma. Muskogee historian Donald Fixico describes a contemporary enclave: "There is a small Creek town in Oklahoma which lies within the Creek Nation. The name of this town is Thlopthlocco. Thlopthlocco is a small independent community which operates almost independently. They are not very much dependent on the federal government, nor are they dependent on the Creek Nation. So they're kind of a renegade group."[44]

In 1907, Indian Territory was dissolved and the state of Oklahoma entered the Union. Under the Dawes and Curtis Acts, privatization of Indigenous territories was imposed on half of all federal reservations, with a loss of three-fourths of the Indigenous land base that still existed after decades of army attacks and wanton land grabs. Allotment continued until 1934, when it was halted by the Indian Reorganization Act, but the land taken was never restored and its former owners were never compensated for their losses, leaving all the Indigenous people of Oklahoma (except the Osage Nation) without effective collective territories and many families with no land at all.[45]

The Hopi Nation resisted allotment with partial success. In 1894, they petitioned the federal government with a letter signed by every leader and chief of the Hopi villages:

> To the Washington Chiefs:
>
> During the last two years strangers have looked over our land with spy-glasses and made marks upon it, and we know but little of what it means. As we believe that you have no wish to disturb our Possessions we want to tell you something about this Hopi land.
>
> None of us were asked that it should be measured into separate lots, and given to individuals for they would cause confusion.
>
> The family, the dwelling house and the field are inseparable, because the woman is the heart of these, and they rest with her. Among us the family traces its kin from the mother, hence all its possessions are hers. The man builds the house but the woman is the owner, because she repairs and preserves it; the man cultivates the field, but he renders its harvest into the woman's keeping, because upon her it rests to prepare the food, and the surplus of stores for barter depends upon her thrift.

A man plants the fields of his wife, and the fields assigned to the children she bears, and informally he calls them his, although in fact they are not. Even of the field which he inherits from his mother, its harvests he may dispose of at will, but the field itself he may not.[46]

The petition continues, explaining the matriarchal communal society and why dividing it up for private ownership would be unthinkable. Washington authorities never replied and the government continued to carve up the lands, finally giving up because of Hopi resistance. In the heart of New Mexico, the nineteen Indigenous city-states of the Pueblo Indians organized resistance under US occupation using the legal system as a means of survival, as they had under Spanish colonialism and in their relationship with the republic of Mexico. In the decades after they had lost their autonomous political status under Mexico and were counted as former Mexican citizens under US law, both Hispanos and Anglo squatters encroached upon the Pueblos' ancestral lands. The only avenue for the Pueblos was to use the US court of private land claims. The following report reflects their status in the eyes of the Anglo-American judiciary:

Occasionally the court room at Santa Fe would be enlivened by a squad of Indians who had journeyed thither from their distant Pueblos as witnesses for their grant. These delegations were usually headed by the governor of their tribe, who exhibited great pride in striding up to the witness stand and being sworn on the holy cross; wearing a badge on his breast, a broad red sash round his waist, and clad in a white shirt, the full tail of which hung about his Antarctic zone like the skirt of a ballet dancer, and underneath which depended his baggy white muslin trousers, a la Chinese washee-washee. The grave and imperturbable bow which the governor gave to the judges on the bench, in recognition of their equality with himself as official dignitaries, arrayed in that grotesque fashion, was enough to evoke a hilarious bray from a dead burro.[47]

Without redress for their collective land rights under the claims court, the Pueblos had no choice but to seek federal Indian trust status. After they lost in their first attempt, finally in 1913 the US Supreme Court reversed the earlier decision and declared the Pueblos wards of the federal government with protected trust status, stating: "They are essentially a simple, uninformed, inferior people."[48]

At the beginning of the twentieth century, sculptor James Earle Fraser unveiled the monumental and iconic sculpture *The End of the Trail*, which he had created exclusively for the triumphal 1915 Panama-Pacific International Exposition in San Francisco, California. The image of the near naked, exhausted, dying Indian mounted on his equally exhausted horse proclaimed the final solution, the elimination of the Indigenous peoples of the continent. The following year, Ishi, the California Yani who had been held captive for five years by anthropologists who studied him, died and was proclaimed "the last Indian." Dozens of other popular images of "the vanishing Indian" were displayed during this period. The film industry soon kicked in, and Indians were killed over and over on screens viewed by millions of children, including Indian girls and boys.

With utter military triumph on the continent, the United States then set out to dominate the world, but the Indigenous peoples remained and persisted as the "American Century" proceeded.

NINE

US TRIUMPHALISM
AND PEACETIME COLONIALISM

There is one feature in the expansion of the peoples of white, or European, blood during the past four centuries which should never be lost sight of, especially by those who denounce such expansion on moral grounds. On the whole, the movement has been fraught with lasting benefit to most of the peoples already dwelling in the lands over which the expansion took place.

—Theodore Roosevelt, "The Expansion of the White Races," 1909

And the trademark they had in Black Hills,
they had carved George Washington, them others there.
Them people didn't own that piece of land,
but they make some carving over there.
Anybody could realize
you have to go to Washington
Europe
and carve my face over there.

—Henry Crow Dog

Although US imperialism abroad might seem at first to fall outside the scope of this book, it's important to recognize that the same methods and strategies that were employed with the Indigenous peoples on the continent were mirrored abroad. While the Indigenous Americans were being brutally colonized, eliminated, relocated, and killed, the United States from its beginning was also pursuing overseas dominance. Between 1798 and 1827, the United States intervened militarily twenty-three times from Cuba to Tripoli (Libya) to Greece. There were seventy-one overseas interventions between

1831 and 1896, on all continents, and the United States dominated most of Latin America economically, some countries militarily. The forty interventions and occupations between 1898 and 1919 were conducted with even more military heft but using the same methods and sometimes the same personnel.

CONNECTIONS

US colonies established during 1898–1919 include Hawai'i (formerly called the Sandwich Islands), Alaska, Puerto Rico, the Virgin Islands, Guam, American Samoa, the Marshall Islands, and Northern Mariana. Most of these, and dozens more islands depopulated in the Pacific and Indian Oceans and the Caribbean for military bases and bomb testing, remain colonies (called "territories" and "commonwealths") in the twenty-first century.[1]

One of the first outspoken proponents of transoceanic imperialism was former abolitionist William H. Seward who was Lincoln's secretary of state and who considered it the destiny of the United States to dominate the Pacific Ocean. Seward did everything possible to fulfill that perceived destiny, including arranging the purchase of Alaska in 1867. In early 1874, the United States began military control of Hawai'i, and in 1898 it annexed the islands after overthrowing the Hawai'ian queen, Liliuokalani. Following post–World War II ascendancy to statehood, Indigenous Hawai'ians and Alaskan Natives were brought under similar US colonial rule as Native Americans.[2]

Overseas ventures gained increasingly exuberant public support in the late nineteenth century. In the best-selling book *Our Country* (1885) the Reverend Josiah Strong of the American Home Missionary Society argued that the United States had inherited the mantle of Anglo-Saxonism and, as a superior race, had a divine responsibility to control the world. By 1914 there were six thousand US Protestant missionaries in China and thousands of others in every other part of the non-European world, and they remained, as from the early seventeenth century, ensconced in Native American communities.

The United States built the naval "Great White Fleet" and expanded the army from twenty-five thousand to nearly three hundred thousand men by the time it invaded and occupied Cuba, undermining the ongoing independence movement against Spain there. While US troops were headed to Havana Harbor in 1898, Admiral George Dewey led the US Navy to intervene in the Philippines—purportedly to assist a force of thirty thousand indigenous Filipino rebels who had won and declared their independence from Spain. Dewey referred to the Filipinos as "the Indians" and vowed to "enter the city [Manila] and keep the Indians out."[3] It took the United States three more years to crush the Filipino "Indian" resistance to US occupation, the army using counterinsurgency techniques practiced against the Indigenous nations of the North American continent, including new forms of torture such as water-boarding, and under many of the same army commanders. Twenty-six of the thirty US generals in the Philippines had been officers in the "Indian wars."[4] Major General Nelson A. Miles, who had commanded the army in campaigns against Indigenous peoples, was put in general command of the army in the Philippines war.

The continuity between invading and occupying sovereign Indigenous nations in order to achieve continental control in North America and employing the same tactics overseas to achieve global control is key to understanding the future of the United States in the world. The military provided that continuity. As a colonel in the 1870s, Nelson Miles had been in charge of pursuing every last Sioux and herding them onto reservations guarded by troops or recently trained Indian police. The reservations were not safe havens for the incarcerated. Struck By the Ree told of multiple horrors of daily life on the Yankton Sioux Reservation, which was not out of the ordinary:

> Another time when General Sully came up he passed through the middle of our field, turned all his cattle and stock into our corn and destroyed the whole of it. . . . The soldiers set fire to the prairie and burnt up four of our lodges and all there was in them. . . . The soldiers are very drunken and come to our place—they have arms and guns; they run after our women and fire into our houses and lodges; one soldier came along

and wanted one of our young men to drink, but he would not, and turned to go away, and the soldier shot at him. Before the soldiers came along we had good health; but once the soldiers come along they go to my squaws and want to sleep with them, and the squaws being hungry will sleep with them in order to get something to eat, and will get a bad disease, and then the squaws turn to their husbands and give them the bad disease.[5]

As related in chapter 8, Miles had also led the army's pursuit of Chief Joseph and the Nez Perce as they sought to escape to Canada, and in 1886 Miles took charge of the War Department's efforts to capture Geronimo, commanding five thousand soldiers, a third of the army's combat force, along with five hundred Apache scouts forced into service and thousands of volunteer settler militiamen. In 1898, now general in chief of the army, Miles personally commanded the army forces that seized Puerto Rico. Miles's second in command, General Wesley E. Merritt, was assigned to head the military invasion of the Philippines. He had served under Custer, fighting Sioux and Cheyenne resistance. Commanding the army occupation of the Philippines was General Henry W. Lawton, to whom Geronimo had turned himself in, making Lawton an instant hero for "capturing" Geronimo. Lawton had led troops in Cuba before going to the Philippines. Ironically, Filipino insurgents under the leadership of a man named Geronimo killed Lawton in an attack. What these US officers had learned in counterinsurgency warfare in North America they applied against the Filipinos. Younger officers would apply lessons learned in the Philippines to future imperial ventures, or in at least one case, pass them to a son. General Arthur MacArthur, father of World War II general Douglas MacArthur, chased Filipino guerrilla leader Emilio Aguinaldo, finally capturing him.[6]

By this time, Theodore Roosevelt was president. His corporate-friendly militarism, particularly his rapid development of the navy and his carefully staged performance as leader of the Rough Riders militia in Cuba, brought him to the presidency. He was popular with both settlers and big business. Roosevelt referred to Aguinaldo as a "renegade Pawnee" and observed that Filipinos did not have the right to govern their country just because they happened to occupy it. Two hundred thousand US soldiers fought in the Philippines, suffering seven thousand casualties (3.5 percent). Twenty percent of the Philippine population died, mostly civilians, as a result of the US Army's scorched-earth strategy (food deprivation, targeting civilians for killing, and so on) and displacement.[7] In 1904 Roosevelt pronounced what has come to be known as the Roosevelt Corollary to the Monroe Doctrine. It mandated that any nation engaged in "chronic wrong-doing"—that is, did anything to threaten perceived US economic or political interests—would be disciplined militarily by the United States, which was to serve as an "international police power."[8]

As the US economy rapidly industrialized, the army also intervened frequently on the side of big business in domestic conflicts between corporations and workers. Troops were used for this purpose in the Great Railroad Strike of 1877—the first nationwide work stoppage—begun by railroad workers protesting wage cuts. Begun in West Virginia, the strike soon spread along rail lines from ocean to ocean and from north to south. General Philip Sheridan and his troops were called in from the Great Plains, where they had been campaigning against the Sioux, to halt the strike in Chicago.

Industrialization affected farming as machinery replaced farmers' hands and cash crops came to prevail. Large operators moved in and banks foreclosed on small farmers, leaving them landless. Farmers' movements, most of them socialist-leaning and anti-imperialist, opposed military conscription and US entry into World War I—the "rich man's war," as they called it. Tens of thousands protested and carried out acts of civil disobedience. In August 1917, white, Black, and Muskogee tenant farmers and sharecroppers in several eastern and southern Oklahoma counties took up arms to stop conscription, with a larger stated goal of overthrowing the US government to establish a socialist commonwealth. These more radically minded grassroots socialists had organized their own Working Class Union (WCU), with Anglo-American, African American, and Indigenous Muskogee farmers forming a kind of rainbow alliance. Their plan was to march to Washington, DC, motivating millions of working people to arm themselves and to join them along the way. After a day of dynamiting oil pipelines and bridges in southeastern Oklahoma, the men and their families created a liberated zone where they ate, sang hymns, and rested. By the following day, heavily armed posses supported by police and militias stopped the revolt, which became known as the Green Corn Rebellion. Those who didn't get away were arrested and received prison sentences. The rebellion is today considered as the waning voice of the people pushed off the land, but it also reflects the crisis induced by the forced allotment of Indigenous territories and the reality of a multiethnic resistance movement, a rare occurrence in US colonialist history.[9]

At the same time, landless Indigenous farmers were launching a revolution in Mexico. Before President Wilson put General John J. Pershing at the head of the American Expeditionary Forces in Europe in 1917, the president had sent him to lead troops, mainly buffalo soldiers, inside Mexico for nearly a year to stop the revolution in the north led by Francisco "Pancho" Villa. The military intervention did not go well. Even the Mexican federal troops fighting Villa resented the presence of US soldiers. About the only notable success for the US military expedition was the killing of Villa's second-in-command by a young lieutenant named George Patton.[10]

MARKETS KILL

The extension of US military power into the Pacific and Caribbean was not militarism for its own sake. Rather, it was all about securing markets and natural resources, developing imperialist power to protect and extend corporate wealth. Indigenous peoples in the United States were severely affected by US industrialization and the development of corporations. In a study of corporations in Indian Territory, historian H. Craig Miner defines the corporation as "an organization legally authorized by charter to act as a single individual, characterized by the issuance of stock and the limitation of liability of its stockholders to the amount of their respective investment . . . an artificial person that could not be held accountable in a manner familiar to the American Indian way of thinking. Individual responsibility could be masked in corporate personality . . . a legal abstraction."[11]

The burgeoning of the corporation brought about a new era of attacks on Indigenous governments, lands, and resources. After the military power and resistance of Indigenous nations and communities were stifled by the growing US military machine following the Civil War, compliance on the part of Indigenous leaders became necessary for survival. Miner argues that "industrial civilization" diminishes the relevance of persons or communities in its way and also notes that industrial civilization is not exactly the same as "industrialization," that it is something quite different and more pervasive. Industrial civilization justified exploitation and destruction of whole societies and expansion without regard for the sovereignty of peoples; it promoted individualism, competition, and selfishness as righteous character traits.[12] The means by which the US government assured corporate freedom to intrude in Indigenous territories was federal trusteeship, the very instrument that was mandated to protect them.

Beginning at the end of the Civil War, government funds from Indigenous land sales or royalties were not distributed to reservation citizens or held by their governments; rather they were held in trust and managed in Washington. The Bureau of Indian Affairs, without Indigenous peoples' consent, invested Indigenous funds in railroad companies and various municipal and state bonds. For instance, the Cherokee national fund and the Muskogee Creek Orphan Fund were so invested. Indigenous leaders were well aware of these practices but were powerless to stop them. They certainly did protest, as evidenced by a petition filed by the Chickasaw Nation: "The Indians did not lend this money; the United States lent it, to increase the value of its multiple states. . . . But now the attempt is made to force the Indian to contribute his pittance to the growth of all this prosperity and power; and this, too, when the United States, triumphant over the perils that once surrounded it, is more than ever able to be liberal, although nothing more is asked of it than to be just."[13]

Cherokee official Lewis Downing, writing in 1869 that rules would have to be agreed on and adhered to, noted the differences between Indigenous values and those of American businessmen, "in that industry, habit, and energy of character which is the result of the development of the idea of accumulation." Free development without restraint of consensual policy would not do, Downing declared: "To us, it appears that once cut loose from our treaty moorings, we will roll and tumble upon the tempestuous ocean of American politics and congressional legislation, and shipwreck [will] be our inevitable destination."[14]

Entering the 1920s, Indigenous peoples were at their lowest point—both in population and possibility for survival after decades of violent military operations during and following the Civil War, along with federal theft of Indigenous treaty-guaranteed funds and then two decades of allotment of Indigenous lands. Then the US government imposed unsolicited citizenship on American Indians with the Indian Citizenship Act of 1924, gesturing toward assimilation and dissolving the nations. It was a boom time for the national economy, but life threatening for Native Americans everywhere. Robert Spott of the Yurok Nation in Northern California, also an army veteran of World War I, described his community's situation, which could have been applied to every Native community. Speaking before the Commonwealth Club of San Francisco in 1926, he said:

There are many Indian women that are almost blind, and they only have one meal a day, because there is no one to look after them. Most of these people used to live on fish, which they cannot get, and on acorns, and they are starving. They hardly have any clothing to cover them. Many children up along the Klamath River have passed away with disease. Most of them from tuberculosis. There is no road into there where the Indians are. The only road they have got is the Klamath River.

To reach doctors they have to take their children down the Klamath River to the mouth of the Klamath. It is 24 miles to Crescent City, where we have to go for doctors. It costs us $25.00. Where are the poor Indians to get this money from to get a doctor for their children? They go from place to place to borrow money. If they cannot get it, the poor child dies without aid. Inside of four or five years more there will be hardly any Indians left upon the Klamath River.

I came here to notify you that something has to be done.

We must have a doctor, and we must have a school to educate our children, and we must have a road upon the Klamath River besides the bank of the river. . . .

My father was an Indian chief, and we used to own everything there. When the land was allotted they allotted him only ten acres, a little farm of land which is mostly gravel and rock, with little scrubby trees and redwood. . . .

Often we see a car go past. It is the Indian Service. Do you suppose the man driving that car would stop? Always he has no time for the Indians, and the car with some one from the U.S.A. Indian Service goes past just like a tourist.[15]

Natives joined African Americans, Mexican Americans, and Chinese immigrants as targets of individual racial discrimination between the end of Reconstruction in the South in the 1880s to the mid-twentieth century. Jim Crow segregation reigned in the South, where more than five thousand African Americans were lynched.[16] As Black people fled terror and impoverishment in the South, their populations grew in northern and midwestern cities where they still faced discrimination and violence. Chicago, Tulsa, and dozens of other cities were marred by deadly "race riots" against African Americans.[17] The virulent and organized racism of the 1920s spilled over to other peoples of darker hue. The pseudoscience of eugenics and racial purity was more robust in the United States than in Europe, further solidifying the ideology of white supremacy. For Indigenous peoples, this was manifest in development of US government policy measuring "blood quantum" in order to qualify for Indigenousness, replacing culture (especially language) and self-identification. While African Americans were classified as such by the measure of "one drop of blood," Indigenous people were increasingly called to prove their degree of ancestry as a significant fraction.

NEW DEAL TO TERMINATION

Some relief for Indigenous nations came with the 1930s New Deal. The Roosevelt administration's programs to combat economic collapse included an acknowledgment of Indigenous self-determination. Roosevelt appointed anthropologist and self-identified socialist John Collier as US commissioner of Indian affairs in 1933.[18] As a young activist scholar in 1922, Collier had been hired by the General Federation of Women's Clubs to assist the Pueblo Indians of New Mexico in their land-claims struggle, a project that culminated in success when Congress passed the 1924 Pueblo Lands Act. Having lived at Taos Pueblo, whose residents practiced traditional lifeways, Collier had developed respect for the communal social relations he observed in Indigenous communities and had confidence that these peoples could govern themselves successfully and even influence a move toward socialism in the United States. He understood and agreed with Indigenous opposition to assimilation as individuals into the general society—what the ongoing allotment in severalty of Native collective estates and the Indian Citizenship Act of 1924 sought to institutionalize.

As commissioner for Indian affairs, in consultation with Native communities, Collier drafted and successfully lobbied for passage of the Wheeler-Howard bill, which became the Indian Reorganization Act (IRA) of 1934. One of its provisions was to end further allotment of Indigenous territories, which was immediately implemented, although already allotted land was not restored. Another provision committed the federal government to purchase available land contiguous to reservations in order to restore lands to relevant Native nations. The IRA's main provision was more controversial with Indigenous peoples, calling for the formation of "tribal governments." In a gesture toward self-determination, the IRA did not require any Indigenous nation to accept the law's terms, and several, including the Navajo Nation, declined. The IRA was limited in that it did not apply to the relocated Native nations in Oklahoma; separate legislation was later drawn up for their unique circumstances.[19]

The Navajo Nation, with the largest land base and population among Indigenous peoples in the United States, soundly rejected signing off on the IRA. The Great Depression of the 1930s was, in the words of postwar Navajo chairman Sam Ankeah, "the most devastating experience in [Navajo] history since the imprisonment at Fort Sumner from 1864–1868."[20] When Collier became commissioner in 1933, he pushed for reduction of Navajo sheep and goats as part of a larger New Deal conservation scheme to stem stock overgrazing. He badgered the twelve Navajo Council members into accepting the reduction, promising unlikely new jobs under the Civilian Conservation Corps to replace lost income. Collier suggested, without basis, that soil erosion in the Navajo Reservation was responsible for the silting up of the Boulder Dam site. His action likely was influenced by agribusinesses that wanted to get rid of all small producers in order to create an advantage to Anglo settler ranchers in New Mexico and Arizona.[21] The process is still bitterly remembered by Navajos. With traumatized Navajos watching, government agents shot sheep and goats and left them to rot or cremated them after dousing them with gasoline. At one site alone, thirty-five goats were shot and left to rot. One hundred fifty thousand goats and fifty thousand sheep were killed in this manner. Oral history interviews tell of the pressure tactics on the Navajos, including arrests of those who resisted, and express bitterness over the destruction of their livestock. As Navajo Council member Howard Gorman said:

> All of these incidents broke a lot of hearts of the Navajo people and left them mourning for years. They didn't like it that the sheep were killed; it was a total waste. That is what the people said. To many of them livestock was a necessity and meant survival. Some people consider livestock as sacred because it is life's necessity. They think of livestock as their mother. The cruel way our stock was handled is something that should never have happened.[22]

In addition to the trauma experienced by the Navajos, the effect of the reductions was to impoverish the owners of small herds.

For those Native nations, the majority, that did accept the Indian Reorganization Act, a negative consequence was that English-speaking Native elites, often aligned with Christian denominations, signed on to the law and formed authoritarian governments that enriched a few families and undermined communal traditions and traditional forms of governance, a problem that persists. However, the IRA did end allotment and set a precedent for acknowledging Indigenous self-determination and recognizing collective and cultural rights, a legal reality that made it difficult for those who sought to undo the incipient empowerment of Indigenous peoples in the 1950s.

The Truman administration pushed out John Collier, among many other progressive Roosevelt appointees. Following the end of World War II, attitudes among the ruling class and Congress regarding Indigenous nations turned from supporting autonomy to their elimination as peoples with a new regimen of individual assimilation. In 1946 Congress established the Indian Claims Commission and the Indian Claims Court to legitimize the prior illegal federal taking of Indigenous treaty lands. Between 1946 and 1952—the cutoff date for filing claims—370 petitions representing 850 claims were filed on behalf of Indigenous nations. Although the government's stated purpose was to clear title for lands illegally taken, the claims mechanism barred restitution of lands taken illegally or acquiring new ones to replace the loss. Settlement was limited to monetary compensation based on the property's value at the time of the taking, and without interest. Adding insult to injury, any expenditure made by the federal government on behalf of the Indigenous nations making claims was subtracted from the overall award, thereby penalizing the Indigenous people for services they had not requested. The average interval between filing a claim and receiving an award was fifteen years.

In creating the Indian Claims Commission, Congress was acknowledging the fact that the federal government had illegally seized Indigenous lands guaranteed by treaties. That validation became useful in Indigenous strategies for strengthening sovereignty and pursuing restitution of the land rather than monetary compensation. On the other hand, the process became a stepping-stone to ending federal acknowledgment of Indigenous nations altogether. The Eisenhower administration lost no time in collaborating with Congress to weaken federal trust responsibility, transferring Indian education to the states and moving Indian health care from the Bureau of Indian Affairs to the Department of Health.

This policy trend toward assimilation culminated in the Termination Act (House Concurrent Resolution 108) in 1953, which provided—in Orwellian language—that Congress should, "as quickly as possible, move to free those tribes listed from Federal supervision and control and from all disabilities and limitations specially applicable to Indians." Under termination, the federal trust protection and transfer payments guaranteed by treaties and agreements would end. Dillon S. Myer, who had headed the War Relocation Authority that administered the concentration camps for US citizens of Japanese descent, was, significantly, the Eisenhower administration's commissioner of Indian affairs to implement termination.[23] Commissioner Myer noted that Indigenous consent was immaterial, saying, "We must proceed even though Indian cooperation may be lacking in certain cases."[24] In the same year, Congress imposed Public Law 280 that transferred police power on reservations from the federal government to the states.

Despite the piecemeal eating away of Indigenous landholdings and sovereignty and federal trust responsibility based on treaties, the US government had no constitutional or other legal authority to deprive federally recognized Native nations of their inherent sovereignty or territorial boundaries. It could only make it nearly impossible for them to exercise that sovereignty, or, alternatively, eliminate Indigenous identity entirely through assimilation, a form of genocide. The latter was the goal of the 1956 Indian Relocation Act (Public Law 949). With BIA funding, any Indigenous individual or family could relocate to designated urban industrial areas—the San Francisco Bay Area, Los Angeles, Phoenix, Dallas, Denver, Cleveland—where BIA offices were established to make housing and job training and placement available. This project gave rise to large Native urban populations scattered among already poor and struggling minority working-class communities, holding low-skilled jobs or dealing with long-term unemployment. Yet many of these mostly young migrants were influenced by the civil rights movement emerging in cities in the 1950s and 1960s and began their own distinct intertribal movements organized around the urban American Indian centers they established. In one of the largest of the relocation destinations, the San Francisco Bay Area, this would culminate in the eighteen-month occupation of Alcatraz in the late 1960s.

CIVIL RIGHTS ERA BEGINS

The founding of the National Congress of American Indians (NCAI) in 1944 had marked a surge of Indigenous resistance. An extraordinary group of Native leaders emerged in the 1950s, including D'Arcy McNickle (Flathead), Edward Dozier (Santa Clara Pueblo), Helen Peterson (Northern Cheyenne/Lakota), and dozens of others from diverse nations. Without their efforts, the termination period would have been more damaging than it was, possibly ending Indigenous status altogether. As a result of their organizing, the government ceased enforcing termination in 1961, though the legislation remained on the books until its repeal in 1988.[25] However, by 1960, more than a hundred Indigenous nations had been terminated. A few were later able to regain federal trusteeship through protracted court battles and demonstrations, which took decades and financial hardship. Indigenous leaders such as Ada Deer and James White of the terminated Menominee Nation played key roles in the struggle to have Indigenous cases heard by Congress and by the Supreme Court in suits and appeals. The restitution movement attracted publicity through community organizing and direct action.[26] Postwar Indigenous resistance operated in relation to a United States far wealthier and more powerful than before, but also within the era of decolonization and human rights inaugurated with establishment of the United Nations and adoption of its Universal Declaration of Human Rights as well as the Convention on the Prevention and Punishment of the Crime of Genocide in 1948. Native leaders paid attention and were inspired.

Native organizing, like the organization of the African American desegregation and voting rights movement, developed within the context of a nationalistic anticommunist ideology that intensified with the Cold War and nuclear arms race in the 1950s. This second great Red Scare (the first had been in the wake of World War I) targeted the labor movement under the guise of combating the "communist threat" from the Soviet Union.[27] It also attacked the civil rights and self-determination movements of the period, and racism broadened and flourished. The wars against Japan and then Korea, along with the successful Chinese communist revolution, revived the early-twentieth-century racist fear of a "yellow peril." Mexican migrant workers largely replaced the Asian agricultural workers displaced by the Japanese American internment, but in 1953 "Operation Wetback," as the federal program was called, forced the deportation of more than a million Mexican workers, in the process subjecting millions of US citizens of Mexican heritage to illegal search and arrest. Native Americans continued to experience brutality, including rape and detention in the border towns on the edges of reservation lands, at the hands of citizens as well as law enforcement officials. The situation of African Americans was one of continued legalized segregation in the South, and extralegal but open discrimination elsewhere. Then, thanks to the long and hard work of the National Association for the Advancement of Colored People (NAACP) in 1954, the US Supreme Court ordered desegregation of public schools. Years of persistent and little-publicized civil rights organizing, particularly in the South, burst into public view with the bus boycott in Montgomery, Alabama, the following year. The white response was murderous: a well-funded campaign by White Citizens' Councils that formed all over the country, accusing civil rights activists of communist influence and infiltration. When white vigilantes bombed and burned Black churches, it was said that "the communists" were doing it to gain sympathy for integration.

As national liberation movements surged in European colonies in Africa and Asia, the United States responded with counterinsurgency. The US Central Intelligence Agency (CIA) was formed in 1947 and expanded in size and global reach during the Eisenhower administration under director Allen Dulles, brother of Eisenhower's secretary of state, John Foster Dulles. The CIA instrumentalized the overthrow of the democratically elected governments of Iran in 1953 and Guatemala in 1954.[28] Guatemala had been the leading light in developing the Inter-American Indian Institute, a 1940 treaty-based initiative that Dave Warren and D'Arcy McNickle were involved with. Following the coup, the institute headquarters relocated from Guatemala City to Mexico City, but there it no longer had the same clout. Covert action came to be the primary means of counterinsurgency, while military invasion remained an option as in Vietnam following a decade of covert counterinsurgency there. In the buildup to the US war in Vietnam, the CIA set the stage with its "secret war" in Laos, organizing the indigenous Hmong as a CIA-sponsored army. After Iran and Guatemala, the CIA engineered coups in Indonesia, the Congo, Greece, and Chile, while attempting assassinations or coups that failed in Cuba, Iraq, Laos, and other countries.

Two years before John F. Kennedy took office as president of the United States, the Cuban people, after decades of struggle and years of urban and rural organizing and guerrilla war, deposed the corrupt and despised dictator Batista, who had been financed and supported by the United States to the bitter end. The CIA spent the next several years trying to assassinate revolutionary leader Fidel Castro and made many attempts to invade, the most infamous of which was the 1961 Bay of Pigs fiasco. Many Cubans who left Cuba for the United States after the revolution were recruited as CIA operatives. The revolution in Cuba, just ninety miles off the Florida coast, would be a touchstone for increasingly radicalized young people in the United States, but even more so for the Indigenous peoples of Latin America, which resonated with Native American activists seeking self-determination to their north.

TEN

GHOST DANCE PROPHECY

A NATION IS COMING

The whole world is coming,
A nation is coming, a nation is coming,
The Eagle has brought the message to the tribe.

—from the Lakota Ghost Dance song, "Maka' Sito'maniyañ"

Little Wounded Knee is turned into a giant world.

—Wallace Black Elk, 1973

THE NEW FRONTIER

Seventy years after the Wounded Knee Massacre, when the conquest of the continent was said to have been complete, and with Hawai'i and Alaska made into states, rounding out the fifty stars on today's flag, the myth of an exceptional US American people destined to bring order out of chaos, to stimulate economic growth, and to replace savagery with civilization—not just in North America but throughout the world—proved to have enormous staying power.

A key to John F. Kennedy's political success was that he revived the "frontier" as a trope of populist imperialism openly based on the drama and popular myth of "settling" the continent, of "taming" a different sort of "wilderness." In Kennedy's acceptance speech at the 1960 Democratic National Convention in Los Angeles, historian Richard Slotkin writes, the presidential nominee "asked his audience to see him as a new kind of frontiersman confronting a different sort of wilderness: 'I stand tonight facing west on what was once the last frontier. From the lands that stretch 3000 miles behind me, the pioneers of old gave up their safety, their comfort and sometimes their lives to build a new world here in the West. . . . We stand today on the edge of a new frontier . . . a frontier of unknown opportunities and paths, a frontier of unfulfilled hopes and threats.'"[1]

Kennedy's use of "new frontier" to encapsulate his campaign echoed debates about US history that had begun more than six decades earlier. In 1894, historian Frederick Jackson Turner had presented his history-making "frontier thesis," claiming that the crisis of that era was the result of the closing of the frontier and that a new frontier was needed to fill the ideological and spiritual vacuum created by the completion of settler colonialism. The "Turner Thesis" served as a dominant school of the history of the US West through most of the twentieth century. The frontier metaphor described Kennedy's plan for employing political power to make the world the new frontier of the United States. Central to this vision was the Cold War, what Slotkin calls "a *heroic* engagement in the 'long twilight struggle'" against communism, to which the nation was summoned, as Kennedy characterized it in his inaugural address. Soon after he took office, that struggle took the form of a counterinsurgency program in Vietnam. "Seven years after Kennedy's nomination," Slotkin reminds us, "American troops would be describing Vietnam as 'Indian Country' and search-and-destroy missions as a game of 'Cowboys and Indians'; and Kennedy's ambassador to Vietnam would justify a massive military escalation by citing the necessity of moving the 'Indians' away from the 'fort' so that the 'settlers' could plant 'corn.'"[2]

The movement of Indigenous peoples to undo what generations of "frontier" expansionists had wrought continued during the Vietnam War era and won some major victories but more importantly a shift in consensus, will, and vision toward self-determination and land restitution, which prevails today. Activists' efforts to end termination and secure restoration of land, particularly sacred sites, included Taos Pueblo's sixty-four-year struggle with the US government to reclaim their sacred Blue Lake in the Sangre de Cristo Mountains of New Mexico. In the first land restitution to any Indigenous nation, President Richard M. Nixon signed into effect Public

Law 91-550 on December 15, 1970, which had been approved with bipartisan majorities in Congress. President Nixon stated, "This is a bill that represents justice, because in 1906 an injustice was done in which land involved in this bill—48,000 acres—was taken from the Taos Pueblo Indians. The Congress of the United States now returns that land to whom it belongs."[3]

In hearings held in the preceding years by the Senate Subcommittee on Indian Affairs, members expressed fear of establishing a precedent in awarding land—based on ancient use, treaties, or aboriginal ownership—rather than monetary payment. As one witness testifying in opposition to the return of Taos lands said, "The history of the land squabbles in New Mexico among various groups of people, including Indian-Americans and Spanish Americans, is well known. Substantially every acre of our public domain, be it national forest, state parks, or wilderness areas is threatened by claims from various groups who say they have some ancestral right to the land to the exclusion of all other persons . . . which can only be fostered and encouraged by the present legislation if passed."[4]

Although the Senate subcommittee members finally agreed to the Taos claim by satisfying themselves that it was unique, it did in fact set a precedent.[5] The return of Blue Lake as a sacred site begs the question of whether other Indigenous sacred sites remaining as national or state parks or as US Forest Service or Bureau of Land Management lands and waterways should also be returned. Administration of the Grand Canyon National Park has been partially restored to its ancestral caretakers, the Havasupai Nation, but other federal lands have not. A few sites, such as the volcanic El Malpais, a sacred site for the Pueblo Indians, have been designated as national monuments by executive order rather than restored as Indigenous territory. The most prominent struggle has been the Lakota Sioux's attempt to restore the Paha Sapa, or Black Hills, where the odious Mount Rushmore carvings have scarred the sacred site. Called the "Shrine of Democracy" by the federal government, it is anything but that; rather it is a shrine of in-your-face illegal occupation and colonialism.

RESURGENCE

The return of Taos Blue Lake was not a gift from above. In addition to the six-decade struggle of Taos Pueblo, the restitution took place in the midst of a renewed powerful and growing Native American struggle for self-determination. The movement's energy was evident when twenty-six young Native activists and students founded the National Indian Youth Council (NIYC) in 1961, based in Albuquerque, New Mexico. From twenty-one different Native nations, some from reservations or small towns and others from relocated families far from home, the founders included Gloria Emerson and Herb Blatchford (both Navajo), Clyde Warrior (Ponca from Oklahoma), Mel Thom (Paiute from Nevada), and Shirley Hill Witt (Mohawk). Cherokee anthropologist Robert K. Thomas mentored the militant young activists. Although primarily committed to local struggles, their vision was international. As Shirley Hill Witt put it: "At a time when new nations all over the globe are emerging from colonial control, their right to choose their own course places a vast burden of responsibility upon the most powerful nations to honor and protect those rights. . . . The Indians of the United States may well present the test case of American liberalism."[6]

In 1964, the NIYC organized support for the ongoing Indigenous struggle to protect treaty-guaranteed fishing rights in Washington State. Actor Marlon Brando took an interest and provided financial support and publicity. The "fish-in" movement soon put the tiny community at Frank's Landing in the headlines. Sid Mills was arrested there on October 13, 1968. Eloquently, he explained his actions:

> I am a Yakima and Cherokee Indian, and a man. For two years and four months, I've been a soldier in the United States Army. I served in combat in Vietnam—until critically wounded. . . . I hereby renounce further obligation in service or duty to the United States Army.
>
> My first obligation now lies with the Indian People fighting for the lawful Treaty to fish in usual and accustomed water of the Nisqually, Columbia and other rivers of the Pacific

Northwest, and in serving them in this fight in any way possible. . . .

Just three years ago today, on October 13, 1965, 19 women and children were brutalized by more than 45 armed agents of the State of Washington at Frank's Landing on the Nisqually river in a vicious, unwarranted attack. . . .

Interestingly, the oldest human skeletal remains ever found in the Western Hemisphere were recently uncovered on the banks of the Columbia River—the remains of Indian fishermen. What kind of government or society would spend millions of dollars to pick upon our bones, restore our ancestral life patterns, and protect our ancient remains from damage—while at the same time eating upon the flesh of our living People?

We will fight for our rights.[7]

Hank Adams with other local leaders founded the Survival of American Indians Association, which was composed of the Swinomish, Nisqually, Yakama, Puyallup, Stilaguamish, and other Indigenous peoples of the Pacific Northwest to carry on the fishing-rights struggle.[8] The backlash from Anglo sport fishers was swift and violent, but in 1973 fourteen of the fishing nations sued Washington State, and, in a reflection of changed times, the following year US District Court Judge George Boldt found in their favor. He validated their right to 50 percent of fish taken "in the usual and accustomed places" that were designated in the 1850s treaties, even where those places were not under tribal control. This was a landmark decision for historical Indigenous sovereignty over territories outside designated reservation boundaries.

The NIYC saw itself as an engine for igniting local organizing, marshaling community organizing projects with access to funds from the Johnson administration's "War on Poverty," the mandate of which was to implement the principles of economic and social equality intended by authors of the Civil Rights Act of 1964. Interethnic alliances, including a significant representation of Native peoples, developed during the mid-1960s. These culminated in the 1968 Poor People's Campaign spearheaded by the Reverend Martin Luther King Jr., which consisted of community organizing and leading marches across the country. In the final month of campaign planning, Dr. King was assassinated on April 4, 1968. Thousands of marchers arrived in Washington, DC, in the next month and gathered in a tent city, then remained there for six weeks.[9]

While local actions multiplied in Native communities and nations, the spectacular November 1969 seizure and eighteen-month occupation of Alcatraz Island in San Francisco Bay grabbed wide media attention. An alliance known as Indians of All Tribes was initiated by Native American students and community members living in the Bay Area. They built a thriving village on the island that drew Native pilgrimages from all over the continent, radicalizing thousands, especially Native youth. Indigenous women leaders were particularly impressive, among them Madonna Thunderhawk, LaNada Means War Jack, Rayna Ramirez, and many others who continued organizing into the twenty-first century. The Proclamation of the Indians of All Tribes expressed the level of Indigenous solidarity that was attained and the joyful good humor that ruled:

We, the Native Americans, reclaim the land known as Alcatraz Island in the name of all American Indians by right of discovery.

We wish to be fair and honorable in our dealings with the Caucasian inhabitants of this land, and hereby offer the following treaty:

We will purchase said Alcatraz Island for twenty-four dollars (24) in glass beads and red cloth, a precedent set by the white man's purchase of a similar island about 300 years ago.

We will give to the inhabitants of this island a portion of the land for their own to be held in trust by the American Indians Government and by the bureau of Caucasian Affairs to hold in perpetuity—for as long as the sun shall rise and the rivers go down to the sea. We will further guide the inhabitants in the proper way of living. We will offer them our religion, our education, our life-ways, in order to help them achieve our level of civilization and thus raise them and all their white brothers up from their savage and unhappy state. . . .

Further, it would be fitting and symbolic that ships from all over the world, entering the Golden Gate, would first see Indian land, and thus be reminded of the true history of this nation. This tiny island would be a symbol of the great lands once ruled by free and noble Indians.[10]

Despite the satirical riff on the history of US colonialism, the group made serious demands for five institutions to be established on Alcatraz: a Center for Native American Studies; an American Indian Spiritual Center; an Indian Center of Ecology that would do scientific research on reversing pollution of water and air; a Great Indian Training School that would run a restaurant, provide job training, market Indigenous arts, and teach "the noble and tragic events of Indian history, including the Trail of Tears, and the Massacre of Wounded Knee"; and a memorial, a reminder that the island had been established as a prison initially to incarcerate and execute California Indian resisters to US assault on their nations.[11]

Under orders from the Nixon White House, the Indigenous residents remaining on Alcatraz were forced to evacuate in June 1971. Indigenous professors Jack Forbes and David Risling, who were in the process of establishing a Native American studies program at the University of California, Davis, negotiated a grant from the federal government of unused land near Davis, where the institutions demanded by Alcatraz occupants could be established. A two-year Native-American–Chicano college and movement center, D-Q (Deganawidah-Quetzalcoatl) University, was founded, while UC Davis became the first US university to offer a doctorate in Native American studies.

During this period of intense protest and activism, alliances among Indigenous governments—including the National Congress of American Indians (NCAI) led by young Sioux attorney Vine Deloria Jr.—turned militant demands into legislation. A year before the seizure of Alcatraz, Ojibwe activists Dennis Banks and Clyde Bellecourt founded the American Indian Movement (AIM), which initially patrolled the streets around Indigenous housing projects in Minneapolis.[12] Going national, AIM became involved at Alcatraz. With the rather bitter end of the island occupation, as Paul Smith and

Robert Warrior write: "The future of Indian activism would belong to people far angrier than the student brigades of Alcatraz. Urban Indians who managed a life beyond the bottles of cheap wine cruelly named Thunderbird would continue down the protest road."[13]

With the Vietnam War still raging and the reelection of Richard Nixon in November 1972 imminent, a coalition of eight Indigenous organizations—AIM, the National Indian Brotherhood of Canada (later renamed Assembly of First Nations), the Native American Rights Fund, the National Indian Youth Council, the National American Indian Council, the National Council on Indian Work, National Indian Leadership Training, and the American Indian Committee on Alcohol and Drug Abuse—organized "The Trail of Broken Treaties." Armed with a "20-Point Position Paper" that focused on the federal government's responsibility to implement Indigenous treaties and sovereignty, caravans set out in the fall of 1972. The vehicles and numbers of participants multiplied at each stop, converging in Washington, DC, one week before the presidential election. Hanging a banner from the front of the Bureau of Indian Affairs building that proclaimed it to be the "Native American Embassy," hundreds of protesters hailing from seventy-five Indigenous nations entered the building to sit in. BIA personnel, at the time largely non-Indigenous, fled, and the capitol police chain-locked the doors announcing that the Indigenous protesters were illegally occupying the building. The protesters stayed for six days, enough time for them to read damning federal documents that revealed gross mismanagement of the federal trust responsibility, which they boxed up and took with them. The Trail of Broken Treaties solidified Indigenous alliances, and the "20-Point Position Paper,"[14] the work mainly of Hank Adams, provided a template for the affinity of hundreds of Native organizations. Five years later, in 1977, the document would be presented to the United Nations, forming the basis for the 2007 UN Declaration on the Rights of Indigenous Peoples.

Three months after the BIA building takeover, Oglala Lakota traditional people at the Pine Ridge Sioux Reservation in South Dakota invited the American Indian Movement to assist them in halting collusion between their tribal government, formed under the terms of the Indian Reorganization Act, and the federal government that had crushed the people and further impoverished them. The people opposed the increasingly authoritarian reign of the elected tribal chairman, Richard Wilson. They invited AIM to send a delegation to support them. On February 27, 1973, long deliberations took place in the Pine Ridge Calico Hall between the local people and AIM leaders, led by Russell Means, a citizen of Pine Ridge. The AIM activists were well known following the Trail of Broken Treaties Caravan, and upon AIM's arrival, the FBI, tribal police, and the chairman's armed special unit, the Guardians of the Oglala Nation (they called themselves "the GOON squad"), mobilized. The meeting ended with a consensus decision to go to Wounded Knee in a caravan to protest the chairman's misdeeds and the violence of his GOONs. The law enforcement contingent followed and circled the protesters. Over the following days, hundreds of more armed men surrounded Wounded Knee, and so began a two-and-a-half-month siege of protesters at the 1890 massacre site. The late-twentieth-century hamlet of Wounded Knee was made up of little more than a trading post, a Catholic church, and the mass grave of the hundreds of Lakotas slaughtered in 1890. Now armed personnel carriers, Huey helicopters, and military snipers surrounded the site, while supply teams of mostly Lakota women made their way through the military lines and back out again through dark of night.

WOUNDED KNEE 1890 AND 1973

The period between the "closing of the frontier," marked by the 1890 Wounded Knee Massacre, and the 1973 siege of Wounded Knee, which marks the beginning of Indigenous decolonization in North America, is illuminated by following the historical experience of the Sioux. The first international relationship between the Sioux Nation and the US government was established in 1805 with a treaty of peace and friendship two years after the United States acquired the Louisiana Territory, which included the Sioux Nation among many other Indigenous nations. Other such treaties followed in 1815 and 1825. These peace treaties had no immediate effect on Sioux political autonomy or territory. By 1834, competition in the fur trade, with the market dominated by the Rocky Mountain Fur Company, led the Oglala Sioux to move away from the Upper Missouri to the Upper Platte near Fort Laramie. By 1846, seven thousand Sioux had moved south. Thomas Fitzpatrick, the Indian agent in 1846, recommended that the United States purchase land to establish a fort, which became Fort Laramie. "My opinion," Fitzpatrick wrote, "is that a post at, or in the vicinity of Laramie is much wanted, it would be nearly in the center of the buffalo range, where all the formidable Indian tribes are fast approaching, and near where there will eventually be a struggle for the ascendancy [in the fur trade]."[15] Fitzpatrick believed that a garrison of at least three hundred soldiers would be necessary to keep the Indians under control.

Although the Sioux and the United States redefined their relationship in the Fort Laramie Treaty of 1851, this was followed by a decade of war between the two parties, ending with the Peace Treaty of Fort Laramie in 1868. Both of these treaties, though not reducing Sioux political sovereignty, ceded large parts of Sioux territory by establishing mutually recognized boundaries, and the Sioux granted concessions to the United States that gave legal color to the Sioux's increasing economic dependency on the United States and its economy. During the half century before the 1851 treaty, the Sioux had been gradually enveloped in the fur trade and had become dependent on horses and European-manufactured guns, ammunition, iron cookware, tools, textiles, and other items of trade that replaced their traditional crafts. On the plains the Sioux gradually abandoned farming and turned entirely to bison hunting for their subsistence and for trade. This increased dependency on the buffalo in turn brought deeper dependency on guns and ammunition that had to be purchased with more hides, creating the vicious circle that characterized modern colonialism. With the balance of power tipped by mid-century, US traders and the military exerted pressure on the Sioux for land cessions and rights of way as the buffalo population decreased. The hardships for the Sioux caused by constant attacks on their villages, forced movement, and resultant disease and starvation took a toll on their strength to resist domination. They entered into the 1868 treaty with the United States on strong terms from a military standpoint—the Sioux remained an effective guerrilla fighting force through the 1880s, never defeated by the US army—but their dependency on buffalo and on trade allowed for escalated federal control when buffalo were purposely exterminated by the army between 1870 and 1876. After that the Sioux were fighting for survival.

Economic dependency on buffalo and trade was replaced with survival dependency on the US government for rations and commodities guaranteed in the 1868 treaty. The agreement stipulated that "no treaty for the cession of any portion or part of the reservation herein described which may be held in common shall be of any validation or force against the said Indians, unless executed and signed by at least three fourths of all the adult male Indians." Nevertheless, in 1876, with no such validation, and with the discovery of gold by Custer's Seventh Cavalry, the US government seized the Black Hills—Paha Sapa—a large, resource-rich portion of the treaty-guaranteed Sioux territory, the center of the great Sioux Nation, a religious shrine and sanctuary. When the Sioux surrendered after the wars of 1876–77, they lost not only the Black Hills but also the Powder River country. The next US move was to change the western boundary of the Sioux Nation, whose territory, though atrophied from its original, was a contiguous block. By 1877, after the army drove the Sioux out of Nebraska, all that was left was a block between the 103rd meridian and the Missouri, thirty-five thousand square miles of land the United States had designated as Dakota Territory (the next step toward statehood, in this case the states of North and South Dakota). The first of several waves of northern European immigrants now poured into eastern Dakota Territory, pressing against the Missouri River boundary of the Sioux. At the Anglo-American settlement of Bismarck on the Missouri, the westward-pushing Northern Pacific Railroad was blocked by the reservation. Settlers bound for Montana and the Pacific Northwest called for trails to be blazed and defended across the reservation. Promoters who wanted cheap land to sell at high prices to immigrants schemed to break up the reservation. Except for the Sioux units that continued to fight, the majority of the Sioux people were unarmed, had no horses, and were unable even to feed and clothe themselves, dependent upon government rations.

Next came allotment. Before the Dawes Act was even implemented, a government commission arrived in Sioux territory from Washington, DC, in 1888 with a proposal to reduce the Sioux Nation to six small reservations, a scheme that would leave nine million acres open for Euro-American settlement. The commission found it impossible to obtain signatures of the required three-fourths of the nation as required under the 1868 treaty, and so returned to Washington with a recommendation that the government ignore the treaty and take the land without Sioux consent. The only means to accomplish that goal was legislation, Congress having relieved the government of the obligation to negotiate a treaty. Congress commissioned General George Crook to head a delegation to try again, this time with an offer of $1.50 per acre. In a series of manipulations and dealings with leaders whose people were now starving, the commission garnered the needed signatures. The great Sioux Nation was broken into small islands soon surrounded on all sides by European immigrants, with much of the reservation land a checkerboard with settlers on allotments or leased land.[16] Creating these isolated reservations broke the historical relationships between clans and communities of the Sioux Nation and opened areas where Europeans settled. It also allowed the Bureau of Indian Affairs to exercise tighter control, buttressed by the bureau's boarding school system. The Sun Dance, the annual ceremony that had brought Sioux together and reinforced national unity, was outlawed, along with other religious ceremonies. Despite the Sioux people's weak position under late-nineteenth-century colonial domination, they managed to begin building a modest cattle-ranching business to replace their former bison-hunting economy. In 1903, the US Supreme Court ruled, in *Lone Wolf v. Hitchcock*, that a March 3, 1871, appropriations rider was constitutional and that Congress had "plenary" power to manage Indian property. The Office of Indian Affairs could thus dispose of Indian lands and resources regardless of the terms of previous treaty provisions. Legislation followed that opened the reservations to settlement through leasing and even sale of allotments taken out of trust. Nearly all prime grazing lands came to be occupied by non-Indian ranchers by the 1920s.

By the time of the New Deal–Collier era and nullification of

Indian land allotment under the Indian Reorganization Act, non-Indians outnumbered Indians on the Sioux reservations three to one. However, the drought of the mid- to late-1930s drove many settler ranchers off Sioux land, and the Sioux purchased some of that land, which had been theirs. However, "tribal governments" imposed in the wake of the Indian Reorganization Act proved particularly harmful and divisive for the Sioux.[17] Concerning this measure, the late Mathew King, elder traditional historian of the Oglala Sioux (Pine Ridge), observed: "The Bureau of Indian Affairs drew up the constitution and by-laws of this organization with the Indian Reorganization Act of 1934. This was the introduction of home rule. . . . The traditional people still hang on to their Treaty, for we are a sovereign nation. We have our own government."[18] "Home rule," or neocolonialism, proved a short-lived policy, however, for in the early 1950s the United States developed its termination policy, with legislation ordering gradual eradication of every reservation and even the tribal governments.[19] At the time of termination and relocation, per capita annual income on the Sioux reservations stood at $355, while that in nearby South Dakota towns was $2,500. Despite these circumstances, in pursuing its termination policy, the Bureau of Indian Affairs advocated the reduction of services and introduced its program to relocate Indians to urban industrial centers, with a high percentage of Sioux moving to San Francisco and Denver in search of jobs.[20]

Mathew King has described the United States throughout its history as alternating between a "peace" policy and a "war" policy in its relations with Indigenous nations and communities, saying that these pendulum swings coincided with the strength and weakness of Native resistance. Between the alternatives of extermination and termination (war policies) and preservation (peace policy), King argued, were interim periods characterized by benign neglect and assimilation. With organized Indigenous resistance to war programs and policies, concessions are granted. When pressure lightens, new schemes are developed to separate Indians from their land, resources, and cultures. Scholars, politicians, policymakers, and the media rarely term US policy toward Indigenous peoples as colonialism. King, however, believed that his people's country had been a colony of the United States since 1890.

The logical progression of modern colonialism begins with economic penetration and graduates to a sphere of influence, then to protectorate status or indirect control, military occupation, and finally annexation. This corresponds to the process experienced by the Sioux people in relation to the United States. The economic penetration of fur traders brought the Sioux within the US sphere of influence. The transformation of Fort Laramie from a trading post, the center of Sioux trade, to a US Army outpost in the mid-nineteenth century indicates the integral relationship between trade and colonial control. Growing protectorate status established through treaties culminated in the 1868 Sioux treaty, followed by military occupation achieved by extreme exemplary violence, such as at Wounded Knee in 1890, and finally dependency. Annexation by the United States is marked symbolically by the imposition of US citizenship on the Sioux (and most other Indians) in 1924. Mathew King and other traditional Sioux saw the siege of Wounded Knee in 1973 as a turning point, although the violent backlash that followed was harsh.

Two decades of collective Indigenous resistance culminating at Wounded Knee in 1973 defeated the 1950s federal termination policy. Yet proponents of the disappearance of Indigenous nations seem never to tire of trying. Another move toward termination developed in 1977 with dozens of congressional bills to abrogate all Indian treaties and terminate all Indian governments and trust territories. Indigenous resistance defeated those initiatives as well, with another caravan across the country. Like colonized peoples elsewhere in the world, the Sioux have been involved in decolonization efforts since the mid-twentieth century. Wounded Knee in 1973 was part of this struggle, as was their involvement in UN committees and international forums.[21] However, in the early twenty-first century, free-market fundamentalist economists and politicians identified the communally owned Indigenous reservation lands as an asset to be exploited and, under the guise of helping to end Indigenous poverty on those reservations, call for doing away with them—a new extermination and termination initiative.

"INDIAN WARS" AS A TEMPLATE FOR
THE UNITED STATES IN THE WORLD

The integral link between Wounded Knee in 1890 and Wounded Knee in 1973 suggests a long-overdue reinterpretation of Indigenous-US relations as a template for US imperialism and counterinsurgency wars. As Vietnam veteran and author Michael Herr observed, we "might as well say that Vietnam was where the Trail of Tears was headed all along, the turnaround point where it would touch and come back to form a containing perimeter."[22] Seminole Nation Vietnam War veteran Evan Haney made the comparison in testifying at the Winter Soldier Investigations: "The same massacres happened to the Indians. . . . I got to know the Vietnamese people and I learned they were just like us. . . . I have grown up with racism all my life. When I was a child, watching cowboys and Indians on TV, I would root for the cavalry, not the Indians. It was that bad. I was that far toward my own destruction."[23]

As it happened, the fifth anniversary of the My Lai massacre in Vietnam occurred at the time of the 1973 siege of Wounded Knee. It was difficult to miss the analogy between the 1890 Wounded Knee massacre and My Lai, 1968. Alongside the front-page news and photographs of the Wounded Knee siege that was taking place in real time were features with photos of the scene of mutilation and death at My Lai. Lieutenant William "Rusty" Calley was then serving his twenty-year sentence under house arrest in luxurious officers' quarters at Fort Benning, Georgia, near his hometown. Yet he remained a national hero who received hundreds of support letters weekly, who was lauded by some as a POW being held by the US military. One of Calley's most ardent defenders was Jimmy Carter, then governor of Georgia. In 1974, President Richard Nixon would pardon Calley. One of the documented acts, among many, that Calley committed and ordered others to carry out at My Lai took place when he saw a baby crawling from a ditch filled with mutilated, bloody bodies. He picked the baby up by a leg, threw the infant back into the pit, and then shot the baby point-blank. My Lai was one of thousands of such slaughters led by officers just like Calley, who a few weeks before My Lai had been observed throwing a stooped old man down a well and firing his automatic rifle down the shaft.

The ongoing siege at Wounded Knee in 1973 elicited some rare journalistic probing into the 1890 army massacre. In 1970, university librarian Dee Brown had written the book *Bury My Heart at Wounded Knee*, which documented and told the 1890 Wounded Knee story, among many other such nineteenth-century anti-Indian crimes and tragedies. The book was a surprise best seller, so the name Wounded Knee resonated with a broad public by 1973. On the front page of one newspaper, editors placed two photographs side by side, each of a pile of bloody, mutilated bodies in a ditch. One was from My Lai in 1968, the other from the Wounded Knee army massacre of the Lakota in 1890. Had they not been captioned, it would have been impossible to tell the difference in time and place.

During the first US military invasion of Iraq, a gesture intended to obliterate the "Vietnam Syndrome," on February 19, 1991, Brigadier General Richard Neal, briefing reporters in Riyadh, Saudi Arabia, stated that the US military wanted to ensure a speedy victory once it committed land forces to "Indian Country." The following day, in a little-publicized statement of protest, the National Congress of American Indians pointed out that fifteen thousand Native Americans were serving as combat troops in the Persian Gulf. As we have seen, the term "Indian Country" is not merely an insensitive racial slur to indicate the enemy, tastelessly employed by accident. Neither Neal nor any other military authority apologized for the statement, and it continues to be used by the military and the media, usually in its shortened form, "In Country," which originated in the Vietnam War. "Indian Country" and "In Country" are military terms of trade, like other euphemisms such as "collateral damage" (killing civilians) and "ordnance" (bombs) that appear in military training manuals and are used regularly. "Indian Country" and "In Country" mean "behind enemy lines." Its current use should serve to remind us of the origins and development of the US military, as well as the nature of our political and social history: annihilation unto unconditional surrender.

When the redundant "ground war," more appropriately tagged a "turkey shoot," was launched, at the front of the miles of killing machines were armored scouting vehicles of the Second Armored Calvary Regiment (ACR), a self-contained elite unit that won fame during World War II when it headed General Patton's Third Army crossing Europe. In the Gulf War, the Second ACR played the role of chief scouts for the US Seventh Corps. A retired ACR commander proudly told a television interviewer that the Second ACR had been formed in the 1830s to fight the Seminoles, and that it had its first great victory when it finally defeated those Indians in the Florida Everglades in 1836. The Second ACR in the vanguard of the ground assault on Iraq thus symbolized the continuity of US war victories and the source of the nation's militarism: the Iraq War was just another Indian war in the US military tradition. After weeks of high-tech bombing in Iraq followed by a caravan of armored tanks shooting everything that moved, the US Special Forces entered Iraqi officers' quarters in Kuwait City. There they found carrier pigeons in cages and notes in Arabic strewn over a desk, which they interpreted to mean that the Iraqi commanders were communicating with their troops, and even with Baghdad, using the carrier pigeons. High-tech soldiers had been fighting an army that communicated by carrier pigeon—as Shawnees and Muskogees had done two centuries earlier.

Twelve years after the Gulf War, a US military force of three hundred thousand invaded Iraq again. A little-read report from Associated Press correspondent Ellen Knickmeyer illustrates the symbolic power of Indian wars as a source of US military memory and practice. Once again we find the armored scouting vehicles and their troops retracing historical bloody footprints as they perform their "Seminole Indian war dance":

> Capt. Phillip Wolford's men leaped into the air and waved empty rifles in an impromptu desert war dance. . . .
>
> With thousands of M1A1 Abrams tanks, Bradley fighting vehicles, Humvees and trucks, the mechanized infantry unit known as the "Iron Fist" would be the only U.S. armored division in the fight, and would likely meet any Iraqi defenses head on.
>
> "We will be entering Iraq as an army of liberation, not

domination," said Wolford, of Marysville, Ohio, directing the men of his 4th Battalion, 64th Armor Regiment to take down the U.S. flags fluttering from their sand-colored tanks.

After a brief prayer, Wolford leaped into an impromptu desert war dance. Camouflaged soldiers joined him, jumping up and down in the sand, chanting and brandishing rifles carefully emptied of their rounds.[24]

HISTORY NOT PAST

In April 2007, all the news seemed to be coming from Virginia and was about murder—the murder of Indigenous farmers that commenced four hundred years before with the founding of Jamestown and the rampage at nearby Virginia Tech University on April 16, 2007. Yet no one commented in the media on the juxtaposition of these bookends of colonialism. Jamestown was famously the first permanent settlement that gave birth to the Commonwealth of Virginia, the colonial epicenter of what became the United States of America nearly two centuries later, the colony out of which was carved the US capital, Washington, on the river whose mouth lay up the coast. A few years after Jamestown was established, the more familiar and revered colony of Plymouth was planted by English religious dissidents, under the auspices of private investors with royal approval, as with Jamestown, and the same mercenary activities personified by Captain John Smith. This was the beginning of British overseas colonialism, after the conquest and colonization of Scotland, Wales, and Ireland turned England into Great Britain. The Virginia Tech killings were described in 2007 as the worst "mass killing," the "worst massacre," in US history. Descendants of massacred Indigenous ancestors took exception to that designation. It was curious with the media circus surrounding the Jamestown celebration, and with Queen Elizabeth and President Bush presiding, that journalists failed to compare the colonial massacres of Powhatans four centuries earlier and the single, disturbed individual's shootings of his classmates. The shooter himself was a child of colonial war, the US war in Korea.

Meditating on the five major US wars since World War II—in Korea, Vietnam, Iraq (1991), Afghanistan, and Iraq (2003)—with flashes of historical memory of Jamestown, the Ohio Valley, and Wounded Knee, brings us to the essence of US history. A red thread of blood connects the first white settlement in North America with today and the future. As military historian John Grenier puts it:

> U.S. people are taught that their military culture does not approve of or encourage targeting and killing civilians and know little or nothing about the nearly three centuries of warfare—before and after the founding of the U.S.—that reduced the Indigenous peoples of the continent to a few reservations by burning their towns and fields and killing civilians, driving the refugees out—step by step—across the continent. . . . [V]iolence directed systematically against noncombatants through irregular means, from the start, has been a central part of Americans' way of war.[25]

ELEVEN

THE DOCTRINE OF DISCOVERY

The whip covers the fault.

—D'Arcy McNickle, *The Surrounded*

Native liberty, natural reason, and survivance
are concepts that originate in narratives,
not in the mandates of monarchies, papacies,
severe traditions, or federal policies.

—Gerald Vizenor, *The White Earth Nation*

In 1982, the government of Spain and the Holy See (the Vatican, which is a nonvoting state member of the United Nations) proposed to the UN General Assembly that the year 1992 be celebrated in the United Nations as an "encounter" between Europe and the peoples of the Americas, with Europeans bearing the gifts of civilization and Christianity to the Indigenous peoples. To the shock of the North Atlantic states that supported Spain's resolution (including the United States and Canada), the entire African delegation walked out of the meeting and returned with an impassioned statement condemning a proposal to celebrate colonialism in the United Nations, which was established for the purpose of ending colonialism.[1]

The "Doctrine of Discovery" had reared its head in the wrong place. The resolution was dead, but it was not the end of efforts by Spain, the Vatican, and others in the West to make the Quincentennial a cause for celebration.

Only five years before the debacle in the UN General Assembly, the Indigenous Peoples of the Americas conference at the UN's Geneva headquarters had proposed that 1992 be made the UN "year of mourning" for the onset of colonialism, African slavery, and genocide against the Indigenous peoples of the Americas, and that October 12 be designated as the UN International Day of the World's Indigenous Peoples. As the time drew near to the Quincentennial, Spain took the lead in fighting the Indigenous proposals. Spain and the Vatican also spent years and huge sums of money preparing for their own celebration of Columbus, enlisting the help of all of the countries of Latin America except Cuba, which refused (and paid for this in withdrawn Spanish financial investments). In the United States, the George H. W. Bush administration cooperated with the project and produced its own series of events. In the end, compromise won at the United Nations: Indigenous peoples garnered a Decade for the World's Indigenous Peoples, which officially began in 1994 but was inaugurated at UN headquarters in New York in December 1992. August 9, not October 12, was designated as the annual UN International Day for the World's Indigenous Peoples, and the Nobel Peace Prize went to Guatemalan Mayan leader Rigoberta Menchú, announced in Oslo on October 12, 1992, a decision that infuriated the Spanish government and the Vatican. The organized celebrations of Columbus flopped, thanks to multiple, highly visible protests by Indigenous peoples and their allies. Particularly, support grew for the work of Indigenous peoples at the United Nations to develop new international law standards.

According to the centuries-old Doctrine of Discovery, European nations acquired title to the lands they "discovered," and Indigenous inhabitants lost their natural right to that land after Europeans had arrived and claimed it.[2] Under this legal cover for theft, Euro-American wars of conquest and settler colonialism devastated Indigenous nations and communities, ripping their territories away from them and transforming the land into private property, real estate. Most of that land ended up in the hands of land speculators and agribusiness operators, many of which, up to the mid-nineteenth century, were plantations worked by another form of private property, enslaved Africans. Arcane as it may seem, the doctrine remains the basis for federal laws still in effect that control Indigenous peoples' lives and destinies, even their histories by distorting them.

THE WHIP OF COLONIALISM

From the mid-fifteenth century to the mid-twentieth century, most of the non-European world was colonized under the Doctrine of Discovery, one of the first principles of international law Christian European monarchies promulgated to legitimize investigating, mapping, and claiming lands belonging to peoples outside Europe. It originated in a papal bull issued in 1455 that permitted the Portuguese monarchy to seize West Africa. Following Columbus's infamous exploratory voyage in 1492, sponsored by the king and queen of the infant Spanish state, another papal bull extended similar permission to Spain. Disputes between the Portuguese and Spanish monarchies led to the papal-initiated Treaty of Tordesillas (1494), which, besides dividing the globe equally between the two Iberian empires, clarified that only non-Christian lands fell under the discovery doctrine.[3] This doctrine on which all European states relied thus originated with the arbitrary and unilateral establishment of the Iberian monarchies' exclusive rights under Christian canon law to colonize foreign peoples, and this right was later seized by other European monarchical colonizing projects. The French Republic used this legalistic instrument for its nineteenth- and twentieth-century settler colonialist projects, as did the newly independent United States when it continued the colonization of North America begun by the British.

In 1792, not long after the US founding, Secretary of State Thomas Jefferson claimed that the Doctrine of Discovery developed by European states was international law applicable to the new US government as well. In 1823 the US Supreme Court issued its decision in *Johnson v. McIntosh*. Writing for the majority, Chief Justice John Marshall held that the Doctrine of Discovery had been an established principle of European law and of English law in effect in Britain's North American colonies and was also the law of the United States. The Court defined the exclusive property rights that a European country acquired by dint of discovery: "Discovery gave title to the government, by whose subjects, or by whose authority, it was made, against all other European governments, which title might be consummated by possession." Therefore, European and Euro-American "discoverers" had gained real-property rights in the lands of Indigenous peoples by merely planting a flag. Indigenous rights were, in the Court's words, "in no instance, entirely disregarded; but were necessarily, to a considerable extent, impaired." The Court further held that Indigenous "rights to complete sovereignty, as independent nations, were necessarily diminished." Indigenous people could continue to live on the land, but title resided with the discovering power, the United States. A later decision concluded that Native nations were "domestic, dependent nations."

The Doctrine of Discovery is so taken for granted that it is rarely mentioned in historical or legal texts published in the Americas. The UN Permanent Forum on Indigenous Peoples, which meets annually for two weeks, devoted its entire 2012 session to the doctrine.[4] Three decades earlier, as Indigenous peoples of the Americas began asserting their presence in the UN human rights system, they had proposed such a conference and study. The World Council of Churches, the Unitarian Universalist Church, the Episcopal Church, and other Protestant religious institutions, responding to demands from Indigenous peoples, have made statements disassociating themselves from the Doctrine of Discovery. The New York Society of Friends (Quakers), in denying the legitimacy of the doctrine, asserted in 2012 that it clearly "still has the force of law today" and is not simply a medieval relic. The Quakers pointed out that the United States rationalizes its claims to sovereignty over Native nations, for instance in the 2005 US Supreme Court case, *City of Sherrill v. Oneida Nation of Indians*. The statement asserts: "We cannot accept that the Doctrine of Discovery was ever a true authority for the forced takings of lands and the enslavement or extermination of peoples."[5] The Unitarian Universalist Association (UUA) resolution regarding this is particularly powerful and an excellent model. The UUA "repudiate(s) the Doctrine of Discovery as a relic of colonialism, feudalism, and religious, cultural, and racial biases having no place in the modern day treatment of indigenous peoples." The Unitarians resolved to "expose the historical reality and impact of the Doctrine of Discovery and eliminate its presence in the contemporary policies, programs, theologies, and structures of Unitarian Universalism; and . . . invite indigenous partners to a process of Honor and Healing (often called Truth and Reconciliation)." They additionally encouraged "other religious bodies to reject the use of the Doctrine of Discovery to dominate indigenous peoples" and resolved to collaborate with groups "to propose a specific Congressional Resolution to repudiate this doctrine . . . and call upon the United States to fully implement the standards of the U.N. Declaration on the Rights of Indigenous Peoples in the U.S. law and policy without qualifications."[6]

TANGLED CONTRADICTIONS

US officials get tangled in the contradictions inherent in the attempt to legitimize empire building through the Doctrine of Discovery and the origin story of making a clear break from the British empire. The rhetoric is often baffling, particularly when it references US American cultural memory of the wars against Native nations, as it did following the declaration of the "War on Terror" after the terrorist attacks of September 11, 2001.

In early 2011, a Yemeni citizen, Ali Hamza al Bahlul, was serving a life sentence at Guantánamo as an "enemy combatant," a military tribunal having convicted him of crimes associated with his service to al-Qaeda as Osama bin Laden's media secretary. The Center for Constitutional Rights (CCR) issued a statement prior to the hearing in the appeal of Bahlul's conviction. In arguing that Bahlul's conviction be upheld, a Pentagon lawyer, navy captain Edward S. White, relied on a precedent from an 1818 tribunal. In his thirty-seven-page military commissions brief, Captain White wrote: "Not only was the Seminole belligerency unlawful, but, much like modern-day al Qaeda, the very way in which the Seminoles waged war against U.S. targets itself violate the customs and usages of war." The CCR objected to this passage in the government's brief. "The court should . . . reject the government's notable reliance on the 'Seminole Wars' of the 1800s, a genocide that led to the Trail of Tears," the CCR declared. "The government's characterization of Native American resistance to the United States as 'much like modern-day al Qaeda' is not only factually wrong but overtly racist, and cannot present any legitimate legal basis to uphold Mr. Bahlul's conviction."[7] In response, the Pentagon's general counsel issued a letter stating that the US government stood by its precedent.

"WE WISH TO CONTINUE TO EXIST"

The question of self-determination of peoples is a recent historical phenomenon integral both to the formation of modern European nation-states and to the gradual formation of an imperialist world system eventually led by the United States. National integration and state formation occurred first in western Europe as its states established colonies and colonial regimes in Africa, Asia, the Pacific, the Americas, and the Caribbean, and as the United States established itself as an independent state. These conquests afforded European states and the United States access to vast resources and labor that in turn allowed them to industrialize and to create efficient bureaucratic structures and political republicanism. At the end of this process, with decolonization of European holdings in the twentieth century, self-determination became a major global issue eventually incorporating all human beings as citizens of nation-states. The creation of nation-states and the redrawing of national boundaries that this often entailed inevitably raised the questions of which national, ethnic, religious, and linguistic communities were included and whether their consent or participation would be required. There are peoples and nations without their own states, locked under a state authority that may or may not be willing to respond to their demands for autonomy within the existing state. If the state is not willing, the peoples or nations may choose to insist on independence. That is the work of self-determination.

In the United States, Indigenous nations that seek political autonomy or even independence engage in nation building—that is, developing Indigenous governance and an economic base. For decades, Native activists and organizers in North America have worked tirelessly to establish the validity of treaties and to foster and protect the self-determination and sovereignty of Indigenous nations. The nations seek control of their social and political institutions without compromising what they consider unique and essential cultural values. The central concern for Indigenous peoples in the United States is prevailing upon the federal government to honor hundreds of treaties and other agreements concluded between the United States and Indigenous nations as between two sovereign states. Demands to have treaties and agreements upheld have never abated, and they have accelerated since the end of the termination era. However, the Indigenous concept of nation and sovereignty is quite distinct from the Western model of the state as the final arbiter of decision making, based on police enforcement. Rather, as Indigenous lawyer and activist Sharon Venne has put it, "We know the laws given to us by the Creator. It is an obligation. It is a duty. It is the future of our [children's] children. We cannot like the non-indigenous people who make rules and regulations and change them when they don't like the rule or regulation. We were given the laws by the Creator. We have to live the laws. This is sovereignty of Indigenous Peoples."[8]

Following the 1973 standoff at Wounded Knee, the American Indian Movement brought together more than five thousand Indigenous representatives, including ones from Latin America and the Pacific, in a ten-day gathering that founded the International Indian Treaty Council (IITC), which then applied for and received UN nongovernmental consultative status in 1975. The IITC proceeded to organize the first conference to be held at the United Nations on Indigenous Peoples of the Americas in 1977. At this conference, Northern Cheyenne tribal judge Marie Sanchez opened the proceedings:

> Members of this conference, delegates, and my brothers and sisters who are present here today.
>
> We are the target for the total final extermination of us as people.
>
> The question I would like to bring forth to this conference, to the delegates from other countries here present, is why have you not recognized us as sovereign people before? Why did we have to travel this distance to come to you? Had you not thought that the United States Government in its deliberate and systematic attempt to suppress us, had you not thought

that that was the reason they did not want to recognize us as sovereign people? The only positive thing that I feel should come out of this conference, if you are going to include us as part of the international family is for you to recognize us, for you to give us this recognition. Only with that can we continue to live as completely sovereign people.

And you also, because you are part of the family of this world, you should also be very concerned, because the common enemy is your enemy too, and that enemy dictates policy to your governments also. I warn you not to be so dependent on the country that we are under, on the government that we are under. We have demonstrated to you how many hundreds of years we have survived.

We wish to continue to exist.[9]

This international work at the United Nations grew slowly at first, but by the mid-1980s it was attracting grassroots Indigenous representatives from around the world and constructing important initiatives.

The global Indigenous cause reached a major milestone in 2007 when the UN General Assembly passed the Declaration on the Rights of Indigenous Peoples. Only four members of the assembly voted in opposition, all of them Anglo settler-states—the United States, Canada, New Zealand, and Australia. All four, with some embarrassment, later changed their votes to approval.[10] Leo Killsback reflects the perceptions of most Native people that the declaration might "bring western cultures out of their old world of savagery and closer to humanity," noting the example of the end of World War II:

> After the fall of Nazi Germany, its leaders were publicly ostracized, tried, convicted, and executed for war crimes at the Nuremburg trials. This led to the Genocide Convention and the Universal Declaration of Human Rights. Nazi society members affirmed that the Holocaust occurred and some were forced to visit concentration camps only feet from their place of residence. Under truth and reconciliation German society

began to rebuild itself, and with the end of their savage world, they and numerous other countries adopted Holocaust-denial laws. This is exactly how a society moved from one reality to another.[11]

For Indigenous peoples in North America an important action within the UN human rights framework was the 1987 mandate given to a UN special rapporteur, Miguel Alfonso Martínez, to investigate the status of treaties and agreements between Indigenous nations and the original colonial powers and the national governments that now claim authority over Indigenous nations by virtue of those treaties. The UN Study on Treaties, completed in 1999, is a useful tool for Indigenous peoples in the United States in their continuing struggles for land restoration and sovereignty. The investigation concluded that Indigenous treaty rights in the United States have contemporary effective status. The special rapporteur based this finding largely on the US Constitution, which in Article VI provides that "all treaties made, or which shall be made, under the Authority of the United States, shall be the supreme Law of the Land; and the Judges in every State shall be bound thereby, any Thing in the Constitution or Laws of any State to the Contrary notwithstanding." Article I, Section 8, of the Constitution explicitly includes relations with Indigenous nations as among the powers of Congress: "To regulate Commerce with foreign Nations, and among the several States, and with the Indian Tribes."[12]

LAND CLAIMS

With a large part of Indigenous nations' territories and resources in what is now the United States taken through aggressive war, outright theft, and legislative appropriations, Native peoples have vast claims to reparations and restitution. Indigenous nations negotiated numerous treaties with the United States that included land transfers and monetary compensation, but the remaining Indigenous territories have steadily shrunk due to direct federal appropriation by various means as well as through government failure to meet its obligation to protect Indigenous landholdings as required under treaties. The US government has acknowledged some of these claims and has offered monetary compensation. However, since the upsurge of Indian rights movements in the 1960s, Indigenous nations have demanded restoration of treaty-guaranteed land rather than monetary compensation.

Native Americans, including those who are legal scholars, ordinarily do not use the term "reparations" in reference to their land claims and treaty rights. Rather, they demand restoration, restitution, or repatriation of lands acquired by the United States outside valid treaties. These demands for return of lands and water and other resource rights illegally taken certainly could be termed "reparations," but they have no parallel in the monetary reparations owed, for example, to Japanese Americans for forced incarceration or to descendants of enslaved African Americans. No monetary amount can compensate for lands illegally seized, particularly those sacred lands necessary for Indigenous peoples to regain social coherence. One form of Native claim does seek monetary compensation and might provide a template for other classes. Of the hundreds of lawsuits for federal trust mismanagement that Indigenous groups have filed, most since the 1960s, the largest and best known is the *Cobell v. Salazar* class-action suit, initially filed in 1996 and settled in 2011. The individual Indigenous litigants, from many Native nations, claimed that the US Department of the Interior, as trustee of Indigenous assets, had lost, squandered, stolen, and otherwise wasted hundreds of millions of dollars dating back to the forced land allotment beginning in the late 1880s. By the end of 2009, it was clear that the case was headed for a decision favoring the Indigenous groups when the lead plaintiffs, representing nearly a half-million Indigenous individuals, accepted a $3.4-billion settlement proposed by the Obama administration. The amount of the settlement was greater than the half-billion dollars that the court would likely have awarded. However, what was sacrificed in the settlement was a detailed accounting of the federal government's misfeasance. As one reporter lamented: "The result will see some involved with the case, especially lawyers, become quite rich, while many Indians—the majority, in all likelihood—will receive about a third of what it takes to feed a family of four for just one year."[13]

Another important form of reparations is the repatriation of remains of dead ancestors and burial items. After considerable struggle on the part of Indigenous religious practitioners, Congress enacted the Native American Graves Protection and Repatriation Act of 1990 (NAGPRA), which requires that museums return human remains and burial items to the appropriate Indigenous communities. It is fitting that Congress used the term "repatriation" in the act. Before NAGPRA, the federal government had used "repatriation" to describe the return of remains of prisoners of war to foreign nations. Native American nations are sovereign as well, and Congress correctly characterized the returns as repatriations.[14]

Although compensation for federal trust mismanagement and repatriation of ancestral remains represent important victories, land claims and treaty rights are most central to Indigenous peoples' fight for reparations in the United States. The case of the great Sioux Nation exemplifies the persistence among Indigenous nations and communities to protect their sovereignty and cultures. The Sioux have never accepted the validity of the US confiscation of Paha Sapa, the Black Hills. Mount Rushmore is controversial among Native Americans because it is located in the Black Hills. Members of the American Indian Movement led occupations of the monument beginning in 1971. Return of the Black Hills was the major Sioux demand in the 1973 occupation of Wounded Knee.[15] Due to a decade of intense protests and occupations by the Sioux, on July 23, 1980, in *United States v. Sioux Nation of Indians*, the US Supreme Court ruled that the Black Hills had been taken illegally and that remuneration equal to the initial offering price plus interest—nearly $106 million—be paid. The Sioux refused the award and continued to demand return of the Black Hills. The money remained in an interest-bearing account, which by 2010, amounted to more than $757 million. The Sioux believe that accepting the money would validate the US theft of their most sacred land. The Sioux Nation's determination to repatriate the Black Hills attracted renewed media attention in 2011. A segment of the PBS *NewsHour* titled "For Great Sioux Nation, Black Hills Can't Be Bought for $1.3 Billion" aired on August 24. The reporter described a Sioux reservation as one of the most difficult places in which to live in the United States:

Few people in the Western Hemisphere have shorter life expectancies. Males, on average, live to just 48 years old, females to 52. Almost half of all people above the age of 40 have diabetes.

And the economic realities are even worse. Unemployment rates are consistently above 80 percent. In Shannon County, inside the Pine Ridge Reservation, half the children live in poverty, and the average income is $8,000 a year.

But there are funds available, a federal pot now worth more than a billion dollars. That sits here in the U.S. Treasury Department waiting to be collected by nine Sioux tribes. The money stems from a 1980 Supreme Court ruling that set aside $105 million to compensate the Sioux for the taking of the Black Hills in 1877, an isolated mountain range rich in minerals that stretched from South Dakota to Wyoming. The only problem: The Sioux never wanted the money because the land was never for sale.[16]

That one of the most impoverished communities in the Americas would refuse a billion dollars demonstrates the relevance and significance of the land to the Sioux, not as an economic resource but as a relationship between people and place, a profound feature of the resilience of the Indigenous peoples of the Americas.

ECONOMIC SELF-DETERMINATION

The relationship of economic development and Indigenous peoples in the United States is not a twentieth-century phenomenon. The collusion of business and government in the theft and exploitation of Indigenous lands and resources is the core element of colonization and forms the basis of US wealth and power. By the end of the nineteenth century, Indigenous communities had little control over their resources or their economic situations, receiving only royalties for mining and leasing, funds held in trust in Washington. During the Johnson administration's War on Poverty, most reservation economic development was spurred by funding and grants from the

Economic Development Administration, the Office of Economic Opportunity, and other government agencies. The Bureau of Indian Affairs began a program to woo industrial plants to reservations, promising cheap labor and infrastructure investment. The largest such experiment was that of the giant electronics company Fairchild's assembly plant in the Navajo Nation.

Established at the town of Shiprock (in the northeastern part of the reservation, in New Mexico) in 1969, the plant became the single largest industrial employer in New Mexico by 1975. Twelve hundred Navajos made up the initial workforce. By 1974, the numbers had lessened to a thousand, but still Navajos were 95 percent of the workforce. Then, during 1974–75, the Navajo workforce shrunk to six hundred. Fairchild's Mountain View, California, headquarters claimed that Navajos were quitting, something very common in the electronics assembly industry. Non-Indians were being hired to replace Navajos. What actually had been happening were layoffs, not resignations. The federal government subsidized the wages for the six-month training period on the job, for which little training is required, and Fairchild was laying off those workers whom they would have to pay and hiring new trainees at no cost. Local Navajo activists and former Fairchild employees, along with help from American Indian Movement leaders, organized a protest at the plant, which led to the workers occupying it. Fairchild decommissioned the plant and moved it overseas. Documents recovered by protesters revealed that Fairchild was seeking a pretext to break its lease. The Navajo Nation had built the plant to Fairchild's specifications at a cost of three and a half million dollars.[17]

The Indian Self-Determination Act of 1975 validated Indigenous control over their own social and economic development with continuation of federal financial obligations under treaties and agreements. Acting upon the new mandate, a number of Indigenous nations with mineral resources formed the Council of Energy Resource Tribes (CERT). Patterned after the federation of oil-producing states, OPEC (Organization of the Petroleum Exporting Countries), CERT sought to renegotiate mineral leases that the BIA had practically given away to energy companies. Native lands west of the Mississippi held considerable resources: 30 percent of the low-sulfur coal in the United States, 5 percent of the oil, 10 percent of the natural gas, and 80 percent of the uranium. CERT was able to establish a center of information and action in Denver to serve its members with technical and legal assistance. The Jicarilla Apache Nation slapped a severance tax on the oil and gas taken from their lands. A corporate legal challenge to this wound up in the Supreme Court, which found that Native nations had the right to tax corporations that operated in their boundaries.

Navajo chairman Peter MacDonald was the force behind the founding of CERT and was its first director. But he quickly found his scheme of mining as the basis for economic development challenged by young Navajos who perceived the downside of ecological destruction. Strip-mining of coal and uranium in the Navajo Nation was bad enough, but then a coal-gasification plant was established to feed into the Navajo electricity-generating plant that sent power to Phoenix and Los Angeles but provided Navajos with little or none. Navajo activist John Redhouse, who became director of the National Indian Youth Council, led decades of struggle against unrestricted mining, with new generations continuing the fight.[18]

Like many de-industrializing US cities and states in the 1980s, some Native nations turned to gaming for revenue. In 1986, they formed the National Indian Gaming Association for the purpose of lobbying state and federal governments and to represent the interests of its members. But in 1988 Congress passed the Indian Gaming Regulatory Act, which gave the states some control over gaming, a dangerous surrender of sovereignty for those Native nations operating casinos. Indigenous gaming operations now constitute a $26 billion industry annually that employs three hundred thousand people, with about half the 564 federally recognized nations operating casinos of various sizes. Profits have been used in myriad ways, some for per capita payments, others earmarked for educational and linguistic development, housing, hospitals, and even investing in larger projects such as the Smithsonian Institution's National Museum of the American Indian. A good portion of profits go to lobbying politicians of state and federal governments. The Indian gaming lobby in California, for instance, is second only to the prison guards union in the state.[19]

THE NARRATIVE OF DYSFUNCTION

The mainstream media and books regularly expose and denounce the poverty and social dysfunction found in Indigenous communities. Rates of alcoholism and suicide are far higher than national averages, and higher even than in other communities living in poverty. In a book of case studies of poverty and neglected sites of deterioration in the United States, journalist Chris Hedges offered an impassioned account of the Pine Ridge Reservation.[20]

As well-meaning and accurate as such portrayals are, however, they miss the specific circumstances that reproduce Indigenous poverty and social scarring—namely, the colonial condition. As Vine Deloria Jr. and other Native American activists and scholars have emphasized, there is a direct link between the suppression of Indigenous sovereignty and the powerlessness manifest in depressed social conditions. Deloria Jr. explained that for the Sioux, everyone has responsibility and rituals to perform that involve a particular geography. In their case, this means sites in the Black Hills: "Some of the holy men up there will say that a lot of the social problems with the Sioux are the result of losing the Black Hills, so you couldn't perform your duties and become a contributor to the ongoing creation. And consequently, people began to fall away and they started to suffer and they started to fight among themselves."[21] In continuing to disregard treaty rights and deny restitution of sacred lands such as the Black Hills, the federal government prevents Indigenous communities from performing their most elemental responsibilities as inscribed in their cultural and religious teachings. In other words, sovereignty equates to survival—nationhood instead of genocide. Ethnographer Nancy Oestreich Lurie provocatively described Indian drinking as "the world's oldest on-going protest demonstration."[22] The effects of continued colonization form similar patterns among Indigenous communities throughout the Americas, as well as among the Maori of New Zealand and the Australian Aborigines.[23]

The experience of generations of Native Americans in on- and off-reservation boarding schools, run by the federal government or Christian missions, contributed significantly to the family and social dysfunction still found in Native communities. Generations of child abuse, including sexual abuse—from the founding of the first schools by missionaries in the 1830s and the federal government in 1875 until most were closed and the remaining ones reformed in the 1970s—traumatized survivors and their progeny.[24] In 2002, a coalition of Indigenous groups started the Boarding School Healing Project, which documented through research and oral history the extensive abuses that go beyond individual casualties to disruption of Indigenous life at every level. Sun Elk was the first child from the very traditional Taos Pueblo to attend the Carlisle Indian Industrial School, spending seven years there beginning in 1883. After a harsh reentry into Taos society, he told his story:

> They told us that Indian ways were bad. They said we must get civilized. I remember that word too. It means "be like the white man." I am willing to be like the white man, but I did not believe Indians' ways were wrong. But they kept teaching us for seven years. And the books told how bad the Indians had been to the white men—burning their towns and killing their women and children. But I had seen white men do that to Indians. We all wore white man's clothes and ate white man's food and went to white man's churches and spoke white man's talk. And so after a while we also began to say Indians were bad. We laughed at our own people and their blankets and cooking pots and sacred societies and dances.[25]

Corporal punishment was unknown in Indigenous families but was routine in the boarding schools. Often punishment was inflicted for being "too Indian"—the darker the child, the more often and severe the beatings. The children were made to feel that it was criminal to be Indian.[26] A woman whose mother experienced boarding school related the results:

> Probably my mother and . . . her brothers and sisters were the first in our family to go to boarding school. . . . And the stories she told . . . were horrendous. There were beatings. There

[was] a very young classmate—I don't know how old they were, probably preschool or grade school—who lost a hand in having to clean this machine that baked bread or cut dough or something, and having to kneel for hours on cold basement floors as punishment. . . . My mother lived with a rage all her life, and I think the fact that they were taken away so young was part of this rage and how it—the fallout—was on us as a family.[27]

Ponca historian Roger Buffalohead verifies that testimony:

The idea of corporal punishment, so foreign to traditional Indian cultures, became a way of life for those students returning from their educational experience.

Yet you find by the thirties and forties in most Native communities, where large numbers of young people had, in the previous years, attended boarding schools, an increasing number of parents who utilized corporal punishment in the raising of their children, so that although you can't prove a direct connection, I think you can certainly see that boarding school experiences, where corporal punishment was the name of the game, had [their] impact on the next generations of native people.[28]

Sexual abuse of both girls and boys was also rampant. One woman remembers: "We had many different teachers during those years; some got the girls pregnant and had to leave. . . . [One teacher] would put his arms around and fondle this girl, sometimes taking her on his lap. . . . When I got there, Mr. M put his arm around me and rubbed my arm all the way down. He rubbed his face against mine." At one mission school, a priest was known for his sexual advances. "Anyway, I ended up beside him [the priest] . . . and all of a sudden he started to feel my legs. . . . I was getting really uncomfortable and he started trying to put his hands in my pants."[29] Nuns also participated in sexual abuse: "A nun was sponge bathing me and proceeded to go a little too far with her sponge bathing. So I pushed her hand away. She held my legs apart while she strapped the insides of my thighs. I never stopped her again."[30]

Much documentation and testimony attest to the never-ending resistance by children in boarding schools. Running away was the most common way to resist, but there were also acts of nonparticipation and sabotage, secretly speaking their languages and practicing ceremonies. This surely accounts for their survival, but the damage is nearly incomprehensible. Mohawk historian Taiaiake Alfred asks, "What is the legacy of colonialism? Dispossession, disempowerment, and disease inflicted by the white man, to be sure. . . . Yet the enemy is in plain view: residential schools, racism, expropriation, extinguishment, warship, welfare."[31]

Indigenous women, in particular, have continued to bear the brunt of sexual violence, both within families and by settler predators. Incidence of rape on reservations has long been astronomical. The colonialist restrictions on Indigenous policing authority on reservations—yet another legacy of the Doctrine of Discovery and the impairment of Indigenous sovereignty—opened the door to perpetrators of sexual violence who knew there would be no consequences for their actions.[32] Under the US colonial system, jurisdiction for crimes committed on Native lands falls to federal and state authorities because Native justice can be applied only to reservation residents, and then only for misdemeanors. One in three Native American women has been raped or experienced attempted rape, and the rate of sexual assault on Native American women is more than twice the national average. For five years after publication of a scathing 2007 report by Amnesty International, Native American and women's organizations, including the National Organization for Women (NOW), lobbied Congress to add a new section to the 1994 Violence Against Women Act (VAWA) addressing the special situation of Native American women living on reservations.[33] The added provision would allow Native nations' courts jurisdiction to arrest and prosecute non-Native men who enter reservations and commit rape. At the end of 2012, the Republican-dominated US Congress denied reauthorization of the VAWA, because it included the provision. In March 2013, however, that opposition was overcome, and President Barack Obama signed the amended act back into law—a small step forward for Native sovereignty.

INDIGENOUS GOVERNANCE

For generations, Native nations, occasionally with the help of federal or state government, treated the symptoms of colonialism. But with the powerful Indigenous self-determination movements of the second half of the twentieth century, those nations participated in drafting and instituting new international law that supports their aspirations, and they began working on shoring up their sovereignty through governance. Through this work, US Indigenous peoples have reconceptualized their current forms of government based on new constitutions that reflect their specific cultures. Navajo thinking on a future constitution expresses that desire. Like some other Native nations, the Navajo, the most populous and the one holding the largest land base in the United States, has never had a constitution. But others do have constitutions similar to that of the United States. Nearly sixty Native nations adopted constitutions before 1934. Following the Indian Reorganization Act of that year, another 130 nations wrote constitutions according to federal guidelines but without significant participation of their citizenry.[34] The movement to create, revise, or rewrite constitutions has seen notable success in two instances during the first decade of the twenty-first century.

From 2004 to 2006 the Osage Nation, located in northeastern Oklahoma, engaged in a contentious process of reform that produced a new constitution. The preamble reflects the extraordinary context and content of the new law:

> We the Wah-zha-zhe, known as the Osage People, having formed as Clans in the far distant past, have been a People and as a People have walked this earth and enjoyed the blessing of Wah-kon-tah for more centuries than we truly know.
>
> Having resolved to live in harmony, we now come together so that we may once more unite as a Nation and as a People, calling upon the fundamental values that we hold sacred: Justice, Fairness, Compassion, Respect for and Protection of Child, Elder, All Fellow Beings, and Self.
>
> Paying homage to generations of Osage leaders of the past

and present, we give thanks for their wisdom and courage. Acknowledging our ancient tribal order as the foundation of our present government, first reformed in the 1881 Constitution of the Osage Nation, we continue our legacy by again reorganizing our government.

This Constitution, created by the Osage People, hereby grants to every Osage citizen a vote that is equal to all others and form a government that is accountable to the citizens of the Osage Nation.

We, the Osage People, based on centuries of being a People, now strengthen our government in order to preserve and perpetuate a full and abundant Osage way of life that benefits all Osages, living and as yet unborn.[35]

Similarly, in 2009, the White Earth Nation of the Anishinaabeg (Ojibwe people) adopted a new constitution. White Earth is located in central Minnesota and is one of a number of Anishinaabe reservations in Minnesota, with others in Wisconsin, South Dakota, and Canada. The preamble to the White Earth constitution is revealing:

The Anishinaabeg of the White Earth Nation are the ancestors of a great tradition of continental liberty, a native constitution of families, totemic associations. The Anishinaabeg create stories of natural reason, of courage, loyalty, humor, spiritual inspiration, survivance, reciprocal altruism, and native cultural sovereignty.

We the Anishinaabeg of the White Earth Nation in order to secure an inherent and essential sovereignty, to promote traditions of liberty, justice, and peace, and reserve common resources, and to ensure the inalienable rights of native governance for our posterity, do constitute, ordain, and establish this Constitution of the White Earth Nation.[36]

Gerald Vizenor, a citizen of the White Earth Nation, best-selling author, and leading intellectual, participated in the writing of this constitution. Explaining the concept of "survivance," a term he coined, he stresses that it originates in Indigenous narratives: "The conventions of survivance create a sense of Native presence over nihility and victory. Survivance is an active presence: it is not absence, deracination, or ethnographic oblivion, and survivance is the continuance of narratives, not a mere reaction, however pertinent. Survivance stories are renunciations of dominance, the unbearable sentiments of tragedy, and the legacy of victimry."[37]

The Doctrine of Discovery is dissolving in light of these profound acts of sovereignty. But neither arcane colonial laws nor the historical trauma of genocide simply disappear with time, certainly not when conditions of life and consciousness perpetuate them. The Indigenous self-determination and sovereignty movement is not only transforming the continent's Indigenous communities and nations but also, inevitably, the United States. The ways it is doing that are explored in the concluding chapter.

THE FUTURE OF THE UNITED STATES

That the continued colonization of American Indian nations, peoples, and lands provides the United States the economic and material resources needed to cast its imperialist gaze globally is a fact that is simultaneously obvious within— and yet continually obscured by—what is essentially a settler colony's national construction of itself as an ever more perfect multicultural, multiracial democracy. . . . [T]he status of American Indians as sovereign nations colonized by the United States continues to haunt and inflect its raison d'etre.

—Jodi Byrd

The conventional narrative of US history routinely segregates the "Indian wars" as a subspecialization within the dubious category "the West." Then there are the westerns, those cheap novels, movies, and television shows that nearly every US American imbibed with mother's milk and that by the mid-twentieth century were popular in every corner of the world.[1] The architecture of US world dominance was designed and tested by this period of continental US militarism, which built on the previous hundred years and generated its own innovations in total war. The opening of the twenty-first century saw a new, even more brazen form of US militarism and imperialism explode on the world scene when the election of George W. Bush turned over control of US foreign policy to a long-gestating neoconservative and warmongering faction of the Pentagon and its civilian hawks. Their subsequent eight years of political control included two major military invasions and hundreds of small wars employing US Special Forces around the globe, establishing a template that continued after their political power waned.

"INJUN COUNTRY"

One highly regarded military analyst stepped forward to make the connections between the "Indian wars" and what he considered the country's bright imperialist past and future. Robert D. Kaplan, in his 2005 book *Imperial Grunts*, presented several case studies that he considered highly successful operations: Yemen, Colombia, Mongolia, and the Philippines, in addition to ongoing complex projects in the Horn of Africa, Afghanistan, and Iraq.[2] While US citizens and many of their elected representatives called for ending the US military interventions they *knew* about—including Iraq and Afghanistan—Kaplan hailed protracted counterinsurgencies in Africa, Asia, the Middle East, Latin America, and the Pacific. He presented a guide for the US controlling those areas of the world based on its having achieved continental dominance in North America by means of counterinsurgency and employing total and unlimited war.

Kaplan, a meticulous researcher and influential writer born in 1952 in New York City, wrote for major newspapers and magazines before serving as "chief geopolitical strategist" for the private security think tank Stratfor. Among other prestigious posts, he has been a senior fellow at the Center for a New American Security in Washington, DC, and a member of the Defense Policy Board, a federal advisory committee to the US Department of Defense. In 2011, *Foreign Policy* magazine named Kaplan as one of the world's "top 100 global thinkers." Author of numerous best-selling books, including *Balkan Ghosts* and *Surrender or Starve*, Kaplan became one of the principal intellectual boosters for US power in the world through the tried-and-true "American way of war." This is the way of war dating to the British-colonial period that military historian John Grenier called a combination of "unlimited war and irregular war," a military tradition "that accepted, legitimized, and encouraged attacks upon and the destruction of noncombatants, villages and agricultural resources . . . in shockingly violent campaigns to achieve their goals of conquest."[3]

Kaplan sums up his thesis in the prologue to *Imperial Grunts*, which he subtitles "Injun Country":

By the turn of the twenty-first century the United States military had already appropriated the entire earth, and was ready to flood the most obscure areas of it with troops at a moment's notice.

The Pentagon divided the planet into five area commands—similar to the way that the Indian Country of the American West had been divided in the mid-nineteenth century by the U.S. Army. . . . [A]ccording to the soldiers and marines I met on the ground in far-flung corners of the earth, the comparison with the nineteenth century was . . . apt. "Welcome to Injun Country" was the refrain I heard from troops from Colombia to the Philippines, including Afghanistan and Iraq. To be sure, the problem for the American military was less [Islamic] fundamentalism than anarchy. The War on Terrorism was really about taming the frontier.[4]

Kaplan goes on to ridicule "elites in New York and Washington" who debate imperialism in "grand, historical terms," while individuals from all the armed services interpret policy according to the particular circumstances they face and are indifferent to or unaware of the fact that they are part of an imperialist project. This book shows how colonialism and imperialism work.

Kaplan challenges the concept of manifest destiny, arguing that "it was not inevitable that the United States should have an empire in the western part of the continent." Rather, he argues, western empire was brought about by "small groups of frontiersmen, separated from each other by great distances." Here Kaplan refers to what Grenier calls settler "rangers," destroying Indigenous towns and fields and food supplies. Although Kaplan downplays the role of the US Army compared to the settler vigilantes, which he equates to the modern Special Forces, he acknowledges that the regular army provided lethal backup for settler counterinsurgency in slaughtering the buffalo, the food supply of Plains peoples, as well as making continuous raids on settlements to kill or confine the families of the Indigenous fighters.[5] Kaplan summarizes the genealogy of US militarism today:

Whereas the average American at the dawn of the new millennium found patriotic inspiration in the legacies of the Civil War and World War II, when the evils of slavery and fascism were confronted and vanquished, for many commissioned and noncommissioned officers the U.S. Army's defining moment was fighting the "Indians."

The legacy of the Indian wars was palpable in the numerous military bases spread across the South, the Middle West, and particularly the Great Plains: that vast desert and steppe comprising the Army's historical "heartland," punctuated by such storied outposts as Forts Hays, Kearney, Leavenworth, Riley, and Sill. Leavenworth, where the Oregon and Santa Fe trails separated, was now the home of the Army's Command and General Staff College; Riley, the base of George Armstrong Custer's 7th Cavalry, now that of the 1st Infantry Division; and Sill, where Geronimo lived out the last years of his life, the headquarters of the U.S. Artillery. . . .

While microscopic in size, it was the fast and irregular military actions against the Indians, memorialized in bronze and oil by Remington, that shaped the nature of American nationalism.[6]

Although Kaplan relies principally on the late-nineteenth-century source of US counterinsurgency, in a footnote he reports what he learned at the Airborne Special Operations Museum in Fayetteville, North Carolina: "It is a small but interesting fact that members of the 101st Airborne Division, in preparation for their parachute drop on D-Day, shaved themselves in Mohawk style and applied war paint on their faces."[7] This takes us back to the pre-independence colonial wars and then through US independence and the myth popularized by *The Last of the Mohicans.*

Kaplan debunks the argument that the attacks on the World Trade Center and the Pentagon on September 11, 2001, brought the United States into a new era of warfare and prompted it to establish military bases around the world. Prior to 2001, Kaplan rightly observes, the US Army's Special Operations Command had been carrying out maneuvers since the 1980s in "170 countries per year, with an average of nine 'quiet professionals' on each mission. America's reach was long; its involvement in the obscurest states protean. Rather than the conscript army of citizen soldiers that fought World War II, there was now a professional military that, true to other imperial forces throughout history, enjoyed the soldiering life for its own sake."[8]

On October 13, 2011, testifying before the Armed Services Committee of the US House of Representatives, General Martin Dempsey stated: "I didn't become the chairman of the Joint Chiefs to oversee the decline of the Armed Forces of the United States, and an end state that would have this nation and its military not be a global power. . . . That is not who we are as a nation."

THE RETURN OF LEGALIZED TORTURE

Bodies—tortured bodies, sexually violated bodies, imprisoned bodies, dead bodies—arose as a primary topic in the first years of the George W. Bush administration following the September 2001 attacks with a war of revenge against Afghanistan and the overthrow of the government of Iraq. Afghans resisting US forces and others who happened to be in the wrong place at the wrong time were taken into custody, and most of them were sent to a hastily constructed prison facility on the US military base at Guantánamo Bay, Cuba, on land the United States appropriated in its 1898 war against Cuba. Rather than bestowing the status of prisoner of war on the detainees, which would have given them certain rights under the Geneva Conventions, they were designated as "unlawful combatants," a status previously unknown in the annals of Western warfare. As such, the detainees were subjected to torture by US interrogators and shamelessly monitored by civilian psychologists and medical personnel.

In response to questions and condemnations from around the globe, a University of California international law professor, John C. Yoo, on leave to serve as assistant US attorney general in the Justice Department's Office of Legal Counsel, penned in March 2003 what became the infamous "Torture Memo." Not much was made at the time of one of the precedents Yoo used to defend the designation "unlawful combatant," the US Supreme Court's 1873 opinion in *Modoc Indian Prisoners.*

In 1872, a group of Modoc men led by Kintpuash, also known as Captain Jack, attempted to return to their own country in Northern California after the US Army had rounded them up and forced them to share a reservation in Oregon. The insurgent group of fifty-three was surrounded by US troops and Oregon militiamen and forced to take refuge in the barren and rugged lava beds around Lassen Peak, a dormant volcano, a part of their ancestral homeland that they knew every inch of. More than a thousand troops commanded by General Edward R. S. Canby, a former Civil War general, attempted to capture the resisters, but had no success as the Modocs engaged in effective guerrilla warfare. Before the Civil War, Canby had built his military career fighting in the Second Seminole War and later in the invasion of Mexico. Posted to Utah on the eve of the Civil War, he had led attacks against the Navajos, and then began his Civil War service in New Mexico. Therefore, Canby was a seasoned Indian killer. In a negotiating meeting between the general and Kintpuash, the Modoc leader killed the general and the other commissioners when they would allow only for surrender. In response, the United States sent another former Civil War general in with more than a thousand additional soldiers as reinforcements, and in April 1873 these troops attacked the Modoc stronghold, this time forcing the Indigenous fighters to flee. After four months of fighting that cost the United States almost $500,000—equal to nearly $10 million currently—and the lives of more than four hundred of its soldiers and a general, the nationwide backlash against the Modocs was vengeful.[9] Kintpuash and several other captured Modocs were imprisoned and then hanged at Alcatraz, and the Modoc families were scattered and incarcerated on reservations. Kintpuash's corpse was embalmed and exhibited at circuses around the country. The commander of the army's Pacific Military Division at the time, Lieutenant General John M. Schofield, wrote of the Modoc

War in his memoir, *Forty-Six Years in the Army*: "If the innocent could be separated from the guilty, plague, pestilence, and famine would not be an unjust punishment for the crimes committed in this country against the original occupants of the soil."[10]

Drawing a legal analogy between the Modoc prisoners and the Guantánamo detainees, Assistant US Attorney General Yoo employed the legal category of *homo sacer*: in Roman law, a person banned from society, excluded from its legal protections but still subject to the sovereign's power.[11] Anyone may kill a *homo sacer* without it being considered murder. As Jodi Byrd notes, "One begins to understand why John C. Yoo's infamous March 14, 2003, torture memos cited the 1865 *Military Commissions* and the 1873 *The Modoc Indian Prisoners* legal opinions in order to articulate executive power in declaring the state of exception, particularly when *The Modoc Indian Prisoners* opinion explicitly marks the Indian combatant as *homo sacer* to the United States."[12] To buttress his claim, Yoo quoted from the 1873 *Modoc Indian Prisoners* opinion:

It cannot be pretended that a United States soldier is guilty of murder if he kills a public enemy in battle, which would be the case if the municipal law were in force and applicable to an act committed under such circumstances. All the laws and customs of civilized warfare may not be applicable to an armed conflict with the Indian tribes upon our western frontier; but the circumstances attending the assassination of Canby [Army general] and Thomas [U.S. peace commissioner] are such as to make their murder as much a violation of the laws of savage as of civilized warfare, and the Indians concerned in it fully understood the baseness and treachery of their act.[13]

Byrd points out that, according to this line of thinking, anyone who could be defined as "Indian" could thus be killed legally, and they also could be held responsible for crimes they committed against any US soldier. "As a result, citizens of American Indian nations become in this moment the origin of the stateless terrorist combatant within U.S. enunciations of sovereignty."[14]

RAMPED-UP MILITARIZATION

The Chagos Archipelago comprises more than sixty small coral islands isolated in the Indian Ocean halfway between Africa and Indonesia, a thousand miles south of the nearest continent, India. Between 1968 and 1973, the United States and Britain, the latter the colonial administrator, forcibly removed the indigenous inhabitants of the islands, the Chagossians. Most of the two thousand deportees ended up more than a thousand miles away in Mauritius and the Seychelles, where they were thrown into lives of poverty and forgotten. The purpose of this expulsion was to create a major US military base on one of the Chagossian islands, Diego Garcia. As if being rounded up and removed from their homelands in the name of global security were not cruel enough, before being deported the Chagossians had to watch as British agents and US troops herded their pet dogs into sealed sheds where they were gassed and burned. As David Vine writes in his chronicle of this tragedy:

> The base on Diego Garcia has become one of the most secretive and powerful US military facilities in the world, helping to launch the invasions of Afghanistan and Iraq (twice), threatening Iran, China, Russia, and nations from southern Africa to southeast Asia, host to a secret CIA detention center for high-profile terrorist suspects, and home to thousands of U.S. military personnel and billions of dollars in deadly weaponry.[15]

The Chagossians are not the only indigenous people around the world that the US military has displaced. The military established a pattern during and after the Vietnam War of forcibly removing indigenous peoples from sites deemed strategic for the placement of military bases. The peoples of the Bikini Atoll in the South Pacific and Puerto Rico's Vieques Island are perhaps the best-known examples, but there were also the Inughuit of Thule, Greenland, and the thousands of Okinawans and Indigenous peoples of Micronesia. During the harsh deportation of the Micronesians in the 1970s, the press took some notice. In response to one reporter's question,

Secretary of State Henry Kissinger said of the Micronesians: "There are only ninety thousand people out there. Who gives a damn?"[16] This is a statement of permissive genocide.

By the beginning of the twenty-first century, the United States operated more than 900 military bases around the world, including 287 in Germany, 130 in Japan, 106 in South Korea, 89 in Italy, 57 in the British Isles, 21 in Portugal, and 19 in Turkey. The number also comprised additional bases or installations located in Aruba, Australia, Djibouti, Egypt, Israel, Singapore, Thailand, Kyrgyzstan, Kuwait, Qatar, Bahrain, the United Arab Emirates, Crete, Sicily, Iceland, Romania, Bulgaria, Honduras, Colombia, and Cuba (Guantánamo Bay), among many other locations in some 150 countries, along with those recently added in Iraq and Afghanistan.[17]

In her book *The Militarization of Indian Country*, Anishinaabe activist and writer Winona LaDuke analyzes the continuing negative effects of the military on Native Americans, considering the consequences wrought on Native economy, land, future, and people, especially Native combat veterans and their families. Indigenous territories in New Mexico bristle with nuclear weapons storage, and Shoshone and Paiute territories in Nevada are scarred by decades of aboveground and underground nuclear weapons testing. The Navajo Nation and some New Mexico Pueblos have experienced decades of uranium strip mining, the pollution of water, and subsequent deadly health effects. "I am awed by the impact of the military on the world and on Native America," LaDuke writes. "It is pervasive."[18]

Political scientist Cynthia Enloe, who specializes in US foreign policy and the military, observes that US culture has become even more militarized since the attacks on the World Trade Center and the Pentagon. Her analysis of this trend draws on a feminist perspective:

Militarization . . . [is] happening at the individual level, when a woman who has a son is persuaded that the best way she can be a good mother is to allow the military recruiter to recruit her son so her son will get off the couch. When she is persuaded to let him go, even if reluctantly, she's being militarized. She's not as militarized as somebody who is a Special Forces soldier, but she's being militarized all the same. Somebody who gets excited because a jet bomber flies over the football stadium to open the football season and is glad that he or she is in the stadium to see it, is being militarized. So militarization is not just about the question "do you think the military is the most important part of the state?" (although obviously that matters). It's not just "do you think that the use of collective violence is the most effective way to solve social problems?"—which is also a part of militarization. But it's also about ordinary, daily culture, certainly in the United States.[19]

As John Grenier notes, however, the cultural aspects of militarization are not new; they have deep historical roots, reaching into the nation's British-colonial past and continuing through unrelenting wars of conquest and ethnic cleansing over three centuries.

Beyond its sheer military utility, Americans also found a use for the first way of war in the construction of an "American identity." . . . [T]he enduring appeal of the romanticized myth of the "settlement" (not the conquest) of the frontier, either by "actual" men such as Robert Rogers or Daniel Boone or fictitious ones like Nathaniel Bumppo of James Fenimore Cooper's creation, points to what D. H. Lawrence called the "myth of the essential white American."[20]

The astronomical number of firearms owned by US civilians, with the Second Amendment as a sacred mandate, is also intricately related to militaristic culture. Everyday life and the culture in general are damaged by ramped-up militarization, and this includes academia, particularly the social sciences, with psychologists and anthropologists being recruited as advisors to the military. Anthropologist David H. Price, in his indispensable book *Weaponizing Anthropology*, remarks that "anthropology has always fed between the lines of war." Anthropology was born of European and US colonial wars. Price, like Enloe, sees an accelerated pace of militarization in the early twenty-first century: "Today's weaponization of anthropology and other social sciences has been a long time coming, and post-9/11 America's climate of fear coupled with reductions in traditional academic funding provided the conditions of a sort of perfect storm for the militarization of the discipline and the academy as a whole."[21]

In their ten-part cable television documentary series and seven-hundred-page companion book *The Untold History of the United States*, filmmaker Oliver Stone and historian Peter Kuznick ask: "Why does our country have military bases in every region of the globe, totaling more than a thousand by some counts? Why does the United States spend as much money on its military as the rest of the world combined? Why does it still possess thousands of nuclear weapons, many on hair-trigger alert, even though no nation poses an imminent threat?"[22] These are key questions. Stone and Kuznick condemn the situation but do not answer the questions. The authors see the post–World War II development of the United States into the world's sole superpower as a sharp divergence from the founders' original intent and historical development prior to the mid-twentieth century. They quote an Independence Day speech by President John Quincy Adams in which he condemned British colonialism and claimed that the United States "goes not abroad, in search of monsters to destroy." Stone and Kuznick fail to mention that the United States at the time was invading, subjecting, colonizing, and removing the Indigenous farmers from their land, as it had since its founding and as it would through the nineteenth century. In ignoring that fundamental basis for US development as an imperialist power, they do not see that overseas empire was the logical outcome of the course the United States chose at its founding.

NORTH AMERICA IS A CRIME SCENE

Jodi Byrd writes: "The story of the new world is horror, the story of America a crime." It is necessary, she argues, to start with the origin of the United States as a settler-state and its explicit intention to occupy the continent. These origins contain the historical seeds of genocide. Any true history of the United States must focus on what has happened to (and with) Indigenous peoples—and what still happens.[23] It's not just past colonialist actions but also "the continued colonization of American Indian nations, peoples, and lands" that allows the United States "to cast its imperialist gaze globally" with "what is essentially a settler colony's national construction of itself as an ever more perfect multicultural, multiracial democracy," while "the status of American Indians as sovereign nations colonized by the United States continues to haunt and inflect its raison d'etre." Here Byrd quotes Lakota scholar Elizabeth Cook-Lynn, who spells out the connection between the "Indian wars" and the Iraq War:

> The current mission of the United States to become the center of political enlightenment to be taught to the rest of the world began with the Indian wars and has become the dangerous provocation of this nation's historical intent. The historical connection between the Little Big Horn event and the "uprising" in Baghdad must become part of the political dialogue of America if the fiction of decolonization is to happen and the hoped-for deconstruction of the colonial story is to come about.[24]

A "race to innocence" is what occurs when individuals assume that they are innocent of complicity in structures of domination and oppression.[25] This concept captures the understandable assumption made by new immigrants or children of recent immigrants to any country. They cannot be responsible, they assume, for what occurred in their adopted country's past. Neither are those who are already citizens guilty, even if they are descendants of slave owners, Indian killers, or Andrew Jackson himself. Yet, in a settler society that has not come to terms with its past, whatever historical trauma was entailed in settling the land affects the assumptions and behavior of living generations at any given time, including immigrants and the children of recent immigrants.

In the United States the legacy of settler colonialism can be seen in the endless wars of aggression and occupations; the trillions spent on war machinery, military bases, and personnel instead of social services and quality public education; the gross profits of corporations, each of which has greater resources and funds than more than half the countries in the world yet pay minimal taxes and provide few jobs for US citizens; the repression of generation after generation of activists who seek to change the system; the incarceration of the poor, particularly descendants of enslaved Africans; the individualism, carefully inculcated, that on the one hand produces self-blame for personal failure and on the other exalts ruthless dog-eat-dog competition for possible success, even though it rarely results; and high rates of suicide, drug abuse, alcoholism, sexual violence against women and children, homelessness, dropping out of school, and gun violence.

These are symptoms, and there are many more, of a deeply troubled society, and they are not new. The large and influential civil rights, student, labor, and women's movements of the 1950s through the 1970s exposed the structural inequalities in the economy and the historical effects of more than two centuries of slavery and brutal genocidal wars waged against Indigenous peoples. For a time, US society verged on a process of truth seeking regarding past atrocities, making demands to end aggressive wars and to end poverty, witnessed by the huge peace movement of the 1970s and the War on Poverty, affirmative action, school busing, prison reform, women's equity and reproductive rights, promotion of the arts and humanities, public media, the Indian Self-Determination Act, and many other initiatives.[26]

A more sophisticated version of the race to innocence that helps perpetuate settler colonialism began to develop in social movement theory in the 1990s, popularized in the work of Michael Hardt and Antonio Negri. *Commonwealth*, the third volume in a trilogy, is one of a number of books in an academic fad of the early twenty-first century seeking to revive the Medieval European concept of the commons as an aspiration for contemporary social movements.[27] Most writings about the commons barely mention the fate of Indigenous peoples in relation to the call for all land to be shared. Two Canadian scholar-activists, Nandita Sharma and Cynthia Wright, for example, do not mince words in rejecting Native land claims and sovereignty, characterizing them as xenophobic elitism. They see Indigenous claims as "regressive neo-racism in light of the global diasporas arising from oppression around the world."[28]

Cree scholar Lorraine Le Camp calls this kind of erasure of Indigenous peoples in North America "terranullism," harking back to the characterization, under the Doctrine of Discovery, of purportedly vacant lands as *terra nullis*.[29] This is a kind of no-fault history. From the theory of a liberated future of no borders and nations, of a vague commons for all, the theorists obliterate the present and presence of Indigenous nations struggling for their liberation from states of colonialism. Thereby, Indigenous rhetoric and programs for decolonization, nationhood, and sovereignty are, according to this project, rendered invalid and futile.[30] From the Indigenous perspective, as Jodi Byrd writes, "any notion of the commons that speaks for and as indigenous as it advocates transforming indigenous governance or incorporating indigenous peoples into a multitude that might then reside on those lands forcibly taken from indigenous peoples does nothing to disrupt the genocidal and colonialist intent of the initial and now repeated historical process."[31]

BODY PARTS

Another aspect of the demand for US public dominion appears under the guise of science. Despite the passage in 1990 of the Native American Graves Protection and Repatriation Act (NAGPRA), some researchers under the cloak of science have fought tooth and nail not to release the remains and burial offerings of some two million Indigenous people held in storage, much of it uncataloged, in the Smithsonian Institution and other museums and by universities, state historical societies, National Park Service offices, warehouses, and curio shops. Until the 1990s, archaeologists and physical anthropologists claimed to need the remains—which they labeled "resources" or "data," but rarely as "human remains"—for "scientific" experimentation, but most were randomly stored in boxes.[32]

In doing so, they also challenge the definition of "Native American" and the claimants' right to sovereignty. They even accuse Native Americans of being anti-science for seeking to repatriate the remains of their relatives.[33] However, since anthropologist Franz Boas in 1911 discredited the theories of racial superiority and inferiority upon which such research was premised, little actual examination of the Indigenous body parts has taken place. When

Ishi—identified by Anglos in 1911 as the last of the Yahi people of Northern California—died in 1916, the University of California at Berkeley anthropologist who had studied him and his culture, Arthur Kroeber, insisted on an Indigenous traditional burial and no autopsy, according to Ishi's wishes. When asked about the cause of science, Kroeber said: "If there is any talk about the interest of science, say for me that science can go to hell. . . . Besides I cannot believe that any scientific value is materially involved. We have hundreds of Indian skeletons that nobody ever comes to study."[34]

Despite Kroeber's stance, Ishi's brain was removed and preserved and sent to the Smithsonian Institution in Washington. As anthropologist Erik Davis observes, the bodies have never had scientific value. Rather, they have become a fetish, "a marker of value, the power of which derives specifically from the obscuring of the referent to which it originally referred. It is my claim that Indian identity, and its material form, the dead Native body, has functioned for a very long time, and with increasing power, as a fetish marking the possession of land by those who have conquered it already."[35]

The "Kennewick Man" phenomenon of the 1990s revealed much about the pathology Davis references. In 1996, a nearly complete skeleton and skull were found on a riverbank on traditional land of the Umatilla Nation near Kennewick, Washington. The county coroner determined that the bones were ancient—at least nine thousand years old—and therefore Native American. Under NAGRA they should be handed over to the Umatilla authorities. But a local archaeologist, James C. Chatters, asked to examine the remains. Several weeks later Chatters called a press conference at which he proclaimed the remains to be "Caucasoid" and with a story to tell. Up to that moment, little attention had been paid to the find, but with Chatters's claims it became a public sensation fueled by headlines such as "Europeans Invade America: 20,000 BC" (*Discover*), "Was Someone Here before the Native Americans?" (*New Yorker*), "America before the Indians" (*US News and World Report*), and "Hunt for the First Americans" (*National Geographic*). The archaeologist had made a series of logical conclusions from a bogus premise: the remains were ancient; the skeleton and skull were said not to resemble those of living Natives, and might be more akin to those of modern Europeans, therefore, Europeans were the "first Americans." The Archaeological Institute of America dismissed such claims, denouncing the already discredited "science" of determining racial characteristics projected back in time. Yet the claims stuck in the public mind and media bias.

Clearly the controversy was not about science, but rather about Native claims of antiquity, sovereignty, and rights, and settler resentment. Chatters made this clear when he was interviewed on the CBS program *60 Minutes*: "The tribe's fight against further testing of Kennewick Man is based largely on fear, fear that if someone was here before they were, their status as sovereign nations, and all that goes with it—treaty rights, and lucrative casinos . . . could be at risk." The white supremacist group Asutru Folk Assembly made a similar assessment: "Kennewick Man is our kin. . . . Native American groups have strongly contested this idea, perceiving that they have much to lose if their status as the 'First Americans' is overturned. We will not let our heritage be hidden by those who seek to obscure it."[36]

Chatters claimed that Kennewick Man "has so many stories to tell. . . . When you work with these individuals you develop an empathy, it's like you know another individual intimately."[37] Erik Davis, calling this identification with the remains a scientist studies "pathological ventriloquism," points out that even the judge who sided with Chatters in the dispute with the Umatilla Nation got into the act, saying that the remains were "a book that they can read, a history written in bone instead of on paper, just as the history of a region may be 'read' by observing layers of rock or ice, or the rings of a tree."[38] Forty-five years ago, archaeologist Robert Silverberg wrote about the appeal of "lost tribes" to Anglo-Americans: "The dream of a lost prehistoric race in the American heartland was profoundly satisfying, and if the vanished ones had been giants, or white men, or Israelites, or Danes, or Toltecs, or great white Jewish Toltec Vikings, so much the better."[39] Anything but Indians, for that would provide evidence reminding Anglo settlers' descendants that the continent was stolen, genocide committed, and the land repopulated by settlers who seek authenticity but never find it because of the lie they live with, suspecting the truth and fearing it.

GHOSTS AND DEMONS TO HIDE FROM

A living symbol of the genocidal history of the United States, as well as a kind of general subconscious knowledge of it, is the "Winchester Mystery House," a tourist site in the Santa Clara (Silicon) Valley of Northern California. Fifty miles south of San Francisco, it is billed as a ghost house on billboards that start appearing in Oregon to the north and San Diego to the south. Sarah L. Winchester, the wealthy widow of William Wirt Winchester, built the Victorian mansion to avoid and elude ghosts, although there is no record of any ghosts ever having found their way into her home. It could be said, perhaps, that Mrs. Winchester's project from 1884 to her death in 1922 was a success. She likely was well aware of the widely publicized Ghost Dance in 1890, which led to the killing of Sitting Bull and the Wounded Knee massacre. The dancers believed that the dance would bring back their dead warriors.

It makes sense that Mrs. Winchester felt the need to guard herself from the ghosts of those killed by the Winchester repeating rifle, which her late husband's father had invented and produced in 1866, with later models being even more lethal. Mrs. Winchester inherited the fortune accumulated by her husband's family through sales of the rifle. There was one major purchaser: the US Department of War. The chief reason for the War Department's purchases of the rifle in great quantities: to kill Indians. The rifle was a technological innovation designed especially for the US Army's campaigns against the Plains Indians following the Civil War.

The Winchester house amazes all who tour it. There are five floors, more or less, since they are staggered. Each room in itself appears normal, decorated in the late-nineteenth-century Victorian mode. But there is more than meets the eye in getting from parlors to bedrooms to kitchen to closets and from floor to floor. Numerous stairways dead-end, and secret trapdoors hide the actual stairways. Closet doors open to walls, and pieces of furniture are really doors to closets. Huge bookcases serve as entrances to adjoining rooms. Part of the house was unfinished when the widow died, as she had construction workers building every day from dawn to dusk, adding rooms and traps until her death. Visitors trekking through the widow's home are astounded, and perhaps saddened, by the evidence all around them of the fears and anguish of an obviously mentally disturbed person. Yet there is another possibility: a sense of the scaffolding that supports US society, a kind of hologram in the minds of each and every person on the continent.

Mrs. Winchester might have been more aware of the truth than most people and therefore fearful of its consequences. Regardless, in continuing to find or invent enemies across the globe, expand what is already the largest military force in the world, and add to an elaborate global network of military bases, all in the name of national or global "security," does not the United States today resemble Mrs. Winchester constantly trying to foil her ghosts? The guilt harbored by most is buried and expressed in other ways, on a larger scale, as "regeneration through violence," in Richard Slotkin's phrasing.

THE FUTURE

How then can US society come to terms with its past? How can it acknowledge responsibility? The late Native historian Jack Forbes always stressed that while living persons are not responsible for what their ancestors did, they are responsible for the society they live in, which is a product of that past. Assuming this responsibility provides a means of survival and liberation. Everyone and everything in the world is affected, for the most part negatively, by US dominance and intervention, often violently through direct military means or through proxies. It is an urgent concern. Historian and teacher Juan Gómez-Quiñones writes, "American Indian ancestries and heritages ought to be integral to K–12 curriculums and university explorations and graduate expositions . . . [with] full integration of Native American histories and cultures into academic curriculums." Gómez-Quiñones coins a measure of intelligence in the United States the "Indigenous Quotient."[40]

Indigenous peoples offer possibilities for life after empire, possibilities that neither erase the crimes of colonialism nor require the disappearance of the original peoples colonized under the guise of including them as individuals. That process rightfully starts by honoring the treaties the United States made with Indigenous nations, by restoring all sacred sites, starting with the Black Hills and including most federally held parks and land and all stolen sacred items and body parts, and by payment of sufficient reparations for the reconstruction and expansion of Native nations. In the process, the continent will be radically reconfigured, physically and psychologically. For the future to be realized, it will require extensive educational programs and the full support and active participation of the descendants of settlers, enslaved Africans, and colonized Mexicans, as well as immigrant populations.

In the words of Acoma poet Simon Ortiz:

> *The future will not be mad with loss and waste though the memory will*
>
> *Be there: eyes will become kind and deep, and the bones of this nation*
>
> *Will mend after the revolution.*[41]

ACKNOWLEDGMENTS

I have dedicated this book to Vine Deloria Jr., Jack Forbes, and Howard Adams, three late Indigenous activist-scholars who pioneered the development of Native American studies programs and scholarship in universities in the 1970s.

My mentor, and a mentor and inspiration to many, Vine Deloria Jr. (1933–2005), Yankton Dakota of the Great Sioux Nation, impressed upon me the necessity for Indigenous sovereignty to be the framework and groundwork for the decolonization of Native American history. Sovereignty, he argued, is not only political but a matter of survival, and the denial of sacred lands and sites is a form of genocide. I met Vine when he recruited me to work with the Wounded Knee legal defense following the 1973 siege. I served as an expert witness at the historic federal court hearing in Lincoln, Nebraska, in 1974, when Vine and a team of lawyers initiated use of the 1868 Sioux-US treaty to validate Sioux jurisdiction over the Wounded Knee defendants being tried in federal courts. Vine also persuaded me to edit and publish the court testimony of Sioux elders and others from the two-week hearing, which would constitute an oral history of the Sioux Nation and its continuing struggle for sovereignty. The 1977 book, with Vine's introduction, *The Great Sioux Nation: An Oral History of the Sioux Nation and Its Struggle for Sovereignty,* was issued in a new edition in 2013. Vine was already a best-selling author when I met him, and he published dozens more influential books and articles. He established early Native American studies programs at the University of California at Los Angeles, University of Arizona, and University of Colorado.

Even before I met Jack Forbes (1934–2011) in 1974, his 1960 book, *Apaches, Navajos, and Spaniards,* was central to the thesis of my dissertation on the history of land tenure in New Mexico. Of Powhatan-Renapé and Lenape descent, Jack was an activist-historian who inspired me to follow that path once I received a doctorate in history. He founded the Native American Studies Department and its doctoral program at the University of California, Davis, and cofounded D-Q University. In addition to working together on developing Native American studies programs, I joined him in research with the Pit River (California) Nation's land struggle and with the Western Shoshone Nation of Battle Mountain in Nevada.

In my own political and intellectual development studying colonialism and imperialism in Africa and the Americas and supporting national liberation movements, I found a kindred soul in 1975 when I met Howard Adams (1921–2001). Howard was a Métis political leader from rural Saskatchewan, a Marxist, and professor of Native American studies at UC Davis, recruited by Jack Forbes. Howard was the first academic I had met who had grown up as poor as I had, about which we had many conversations. His heartrending and elegant 1975 memoir-history of the Métis and their great leader Louis Riel, *Prison of Grass: Canada from a Native Point of View*, now a classic, became a template for my own research and writing.

An overarching narrative of US history based on the historical experience and perspective of Indigenous peoples, which I have attempted to synthesize in this book, would not have been possible without the research, analysis, and perspectives that have emerged from several generations of Indigenous intellectuals, historians, writers, poets, filmmakers, musicians, and artists. Working singly and collectively, they contribute to decolonizing the master narratives and politics that in the past have largely covered the fingerprints of centuries of genocide and genocidal policies. Thereby, they contribute to Indigenous sovereignty, self-determination, and national liberation.

This book benefited also from conversations with Gerald Vizenor and Jean Dennison about Native constitutional developments; Andrew Curley on environmentalism and the Navajo Nation; Waziyatatawin on the catastrophe of climate change for all humanity, but especially Indigenous peoples; Nick Estes, Daphne Taylor-Garcia, Gloria Chacon, and Michael Trujillo on Indigenous identity; Susan

Miller on historical periodization and use of Indigenous sources; Elizabeth Castle about oral history; and Rachel Jackson in our decade-long and continuing discussions of settler-Indigenous relations in Oklahoma.

I want to thank my brilliant editor at Beacon Press, Gayatri Patnaik. Gayatri is a writer's dream, a hands-on editor, tough but always right. I also benefited from the careful and intelligent work of Beacon assistant editor Rachael Marks.

I appreciate that this book will take its place with other volumes in Beacon Press's ReVisioning American History series, and for that I thank and honor the memory of Howard Zinn.

Much gratitude goes to those who read parts or the whole of drafts and provided essential suggestions and much-needed support, especially Steven Baker, Steven Hiatt, Susan Miller, Aileen "Chockie" Cottier, Luke Young, Waziyatatawin, and Martin Legassick. Of course, only I am responsible for errors and interpretations in the text.

SUGGESTED READING

The essential compilation of Native historians, edited by Susan A. Miller and James Riding In, is *Native Historians Write Back: Decolonizing American Indian History* (Lubbock: Texas Tech University Press, 2011), including contributors Donna L. Akers (Choctaw), Myla Vicenti Carpio (Jicarilla Apache/Laguna/Isleta), Elizabeth Cook-Lynn (Crow Creek Sioux), Steven J. Crum (Shoshone-Paiute), Vine Deloria Jr. (Yankton Nakota), Jennifer Nez Denetdale (Diné), Lomayumtewa Ishii (Hopi), Matthew Jones (Kiowa/Otoe-Missouria), Susan A. Miller (Seminole), James Riding In (Pawnee), Leanne Betasamosake Simpson (Michi Saagnik Nishnaabeg), Winona Wheeler (Cree), and Waziyatatawin Angela Wilson (Dakota).

Joanne Barker, *Native Acts: Law, Recognition, and Cultural Authenticity* (Durham: Duke University Press, 2011).

Joanne Barker, ed., *Sovereignty Matters: Locations of Contestation and Possibility in Indigenous Struggles for Self-Determination* (Lincoln: University of Nebraska Press, 2005).

Ned Blackhawk, *Violence over the Land: Indians and Empires in the Early American West* (Cambridge, MA: Harvard University Press, 2006).

Jodi A. Byrd, *The Transit of Empire: Indigenous Critiques of Colonialism* (Minneapolis: University of Minnesota Press, 2011).

Duane Champagne, *Notes from the Center of Turtle Island* (Lanham, MD: Altamira Press, 2010).

David A. Chang, *The Color of the Land: Race, Nation, and the Politics of Landownership in Oklahoma, 1832–1929* (Chapel Hill: University of North Carolina Press, 2010).

Daniel M. Cobb, *Native Activism in Cold War America: The Struggle for Sovereignty* (Lawrence: University of Kansas Press, 2008).

Elizabeth Cook-Lynn, *A Separate Country: Postcoloniality and American Indian Nations* (Lubbock: Texas Tech University Press, 2012).

Jeff Corntassel and Richard C. Witmer, *Forced Federalism: Contemporary Challenges to Indigenous Nationhood* (Norman: University of Oklahoma Press, 2008).

James H. Cox, *The Red Land to the South: American Indian Writers and Indigenous Mexico* (Minneapolis: University of Minnesota Press, 2012).

Philip J. Deloria, *Indians in Unexpected Places* (Lawrence: University of Kansas Press, 2004).

Philip J. Deloria, *Playing Indian* (New Haven, CT: Yale University Press, 1998).

Vine Deloria Jr., *Custer Died for Your Sins: An Indian Manifesto*, new ed. (Norman: University of Oklahoma Press, 1988). First published 1969.

Vine Deloria Jr. and Clifford M. Lytle, *The Nations Within: The Past and Future of American Indian Sovereignty* (Austin: University of Texas Press, 1998).

Jennifer Nez Denetdale, *Reclaiming Diné History: The Legacies of Navajo Chief Manuelito and Juanita* (Tucson: University of Arizona Press, 2007).

Jean Dennison, *Colonial Entanglement: Constituting a Twenty-First-Century Osage Nation* (Chapel Hill: University of North Carolina Press, 2012).

Roxanne Dunbar-Ortiz, *Roots of Resistance: A History of Land Tenure in New Mexico* (Norman: University of Oklahoma Press, 2007). First published 1980.

Roxanne Dunbar-Ortiz, ed., *The Great Sioux Nation: An Oral History of the Sioux Nation and Its Struggle for Sovereignty* (Lincoln: University of Nebraska Press, 2013). First published 1977.

Walter R. Echo-Hawk, *In the Courts of the Conqueror: The 10 Worst Indian Law Cases Ever Decided* (Golden, CO: Fulcrum, 2010).

Walter R. Echo-Hawk, *In the Light of Justice: The Rise of Human Rights in Native America and the UN Declaration on the Rights of Indigenous Peoples* (Golden, CO: Fulcrum, 2013).

Jack Forbes, *Columbus and Other Cannibals* (New York: Autonomedia, 1992).

Eva Marie Garroutte, *Real Indians: Identity and the Survival of Native America* (Berkeley: University of California Press, 2003).

Juan Gómez-Quiñones, *Indigenous Quotient: Stalking Words; American Indian Heritage as Future* (San Antonio, TX: Aztlán Libre Press, 2012).

Sandy Grande, *Red Pedagogy: Native American Social and Political Thought* (Lanham, MD: Rowman & Littlefield, 2004).

Lisbeth Haas, *Saints and Citizens: Indigenous Histories of Colonial Missions and Mexican California* (Berkeley: University of California Press, 2013).

William L. Iggiagruk Hensley, *Fifty Miles from Tomorrow: A Memoir of Alaska and the Real People* (New York: Picador, 2010).

Linda Hogan, *The Woman Who Watches Over the World: A Native Memoir* (New York: W. W. Norton, 2002).

Robert H. Jackson and Edward Castillo, *Indians, Franciscans, and Spanish Colonization: The Impact of the Mission System on California Indians* (Albuquerque: University of New Mexico Press, 1995).

V. G. Kiernan, *America, the New Imperialism: From White Settlement to World Hegemony* (London: Verso, 2005). First published 1978.

Winona LaDuke with Sean Cruz, *The Militarization of Indian Country,* 2nd ed. (Minneapolis: Honor the Earth, 2012).

Brendan C. Lindsay, *Murder State: California's Native American Genocide, 1846–1873* (Lincoln: University of Nebraska Press, 2012).

Wilma Mankiller and Michael Wallis, *Mankiller: A Chief and Her People* (New York: St. Martin's, 1993).

Devon Abbott Mihesuah and Angela Cavender Wilson, eds., *Indigenizing the Academy: Transforming Scholarship and Empowering Communities* (Lincoln: University of Nebraska Press, 2004).

Peter Nabokov, *Native American Testimony: A Chronicle of Indian-*

White Relations from Prophecy to the Present, 1492–2000, revised ed. (New York: Penguin, 1999).

Peter Nabokov, *Where the Lightning Strikes: The Lives of American Indian Sacred Places* (New York: Penguin, 2006).

Jean M. O'Brien, *Firsting and Lasting: Writing Indians Out of Existence in New England* (Minneapolis: University of Minnesota Press, 2010).

Sharon O'Brien, *American Indian Tribal Governments* (Norman: University of Oklahoma Press, 1989).

Louis Owens, *Mixedblood Messages: Literature, Film, Family, Place* (Norman: University of Oklahoma Press, 1998).

Theda Perdue and Michael D. Green, *North American Indians: A Very Short Introduction* (New York: Oxford University Press, 2010).

Jacki Thompson Rand, *Kiowa Humanity and the Invasion of the State* (Lincoln: University of Nebraska Press, 2008).

Bradley G. Shreve, *Red Power Rising: The National Indian Youth Council and the Origins of Native Activism* (Norman: University of Oklahoma Press, 2011).

Andrea Smith, *Conquest: Sexual Violence and American Indian Genocide* (Boston: South End Press, 2005).

Paul Chaat Smith, *Everything You Know about Indians Is Wrong* (Minneapolis: University of Minnesota Press, 2009).

Paul Chaat Smith and Robert Allen Warrior, *Like a Hurricane: The Indian Movement from Alcatraz to Wounded Knee* (New York: New Press, 1996).

David E. Stannard, *American Holocaust: The Conquest of the New World* (New York: Oxford University Press, 1992).

David Hurst Thomas, *Skull Wars: Kennewick Man, Archaeology, and the Battle for Native American Identity* (New York: Basic Books, 2000).

Russell Thornton, *American Indian Holocaust and Survival: A Population History Since 1492* (Norman: University of Oklahoma Press, 1990). Originally published 1987.

Veronica E. Velarde Tiller, ed., *Tiller's Guide to Indian Country: Economic Profiles of American Indian Resources* (Albuquerque: BowArrow, 2006).

Haunani-Kay Trask, *From a Native Daughter: Colonialism and Sovereignty in Hawai'i* (Honolulu: University of Hawai'i Press, 1999).

Anton Treuer, *Everything You Wanted to Know About Indians But Were Afraid to Ask* (St. Paul: Borealis Books, 2012).

David Treuer, *Rez Life: An Indian's Journey through Reservation Life* (New York: Atlantic Monthly Press, 2012).

Gerald Vizenor, *Native Liberty: Natural Reason and Cultural Survivance* (Lincoln: University of Nebraska Press, 2009).

Gerald Vizenor and Jill Doerfler, *The White Earth Nation: Ratification of a Native Democratic Constitution* (Lincoln: University of Nebraska Press, 2012).

Robert Warrior, *Tribal Secrets: Recovering American Indian Intellectual Traditions* (Minneapolis: University of Minnesota Press, 1994).

Michael V. Wilcox, *The Pueblo Revolt and the Mythology of Conquest: An Indigenous Archaeology of Contact* (Berkeley: University of California Press, 2009).

Waziyatatawin Angela Wilson and Michael Yellow Bird, eds., *For Indigenous Eyes Only: A Decolonization Handbook* (Santa Fe, NM: School of American Research Press, 2005).

Laura Waterman Wittstock and Dick Bancroft, *We Are Still Here: A Photographic History of the American Indian Movement* (St. Paul: Minnesota Historical Society Press, 2013).

PERIODICALS

American Indian Culture and Research Journal
American Indian Quarterly Journal
Decolonization: Indigeneity, Education & Society
Indian Country Today
Journal of Genocide Research
Native American and Indigenous Studies Journal
Red Ink
Settler Colonial Studies Journal
Wicazo Sa Review Journal

NOTES

INTRODUCTION: THIS LAND

Epigraph: Willie Johns, "A Seminole Perspective on Ponce de León and Florida History," *Forum Magazine* (Florida Humanities Council), Fall 2012, http://indiancountrytodaymedianetwork.com/2013/04/08/seminole-perspective-ponce-de-leon-and-florida-history-148672 (accessed September 24, 2013).

1. The full refrain of Woody Guthrie's most popular song: "This land is your land / This land is my land / From California to the New York island / From the redwood forest to the Gulf Stream waters / This land was made for you and me."

2. Henry Crow Dog, testimony at the 1974 Sioux Treaty hearing, in Dunbar-Ortiz, *Great Sioux Nation*, 54.

3. Chang, *Color of the Land*, 7.

4. Wolfe, "Settler Colonialism," 387.

5. See Watson, *Buying America from the Indians*, and Robertson, *Conquest by Law*. For a list and description of each papal bull, see *The Doctrine of Discovery*, http://www.doctrineofdiscovery.org (accessed November 5, 2013).

6. Williams, *American Indian in Western Legal Thought*, 59.

7. Stewart, *Names on the Land*, 169–73, 233, 302.

8. Sheehan, "Indian-White Relations in Early America," 267–96.

9. Killsback, "Indigenous Perceptions of Time," 131.

10. Turner, *Frontier in American History*, 127.

11. "Convention on the Prevention and Punishment of the Crime of Genocide, Paris, 9 December 1948," Audiovisual Library of International Law, http://untreaty.un.org/cod/avl/ha/cppcg/cppcg.html (accessed December 6, 2012). See also Kunz, "United Nations Convention on Genocide."

12. O'Brien, *Firsting and Lasting*.

13. April 17, 1873, quoted in Marszalek, *Sherman*, 379.

14. Wolfe, "Settler Colonialism," 393.

15. 18 U.S.C.§1151 (2001).

16. Echo-Hawk, *In the Courts of the Conqueror*, 77–78.

17. "Tribes," US Department of the Interior website, http://www.doi.gov/tribes/index.cfm (accessed September 24, 2013); "Indian Reservation,"

New World Encyclopedia, http://www.newworldencyclopedia.org/entry/
Indian_reservation (accessed September 24, 2013). See also Frantz, *Indian
Reservations in the United States.*

CHAPTER ONE: FOLLOW THE CORN

Epigraph: Mann, *1491*, 252.

1. Ibid., 264.
2. Dobyns, *Native American Historical Demography*, 1; Dobyns, "Estimating Aboriginal American Population," and "Reply," 440–44. See also Thornton, *American Indian Holocaust and Survival.*
3. Quoted in Vogel, *American Indian Medicine*, 253–55. Vogel's classic text deals with every aspect of Indigenous medicine from shamanistic practices and pharmaceuticals to hygiene, surgery, and dentistry, applied to specific diseases and ailments.
4. Fiedel, *Prehistory of the Americas*, 305.
5. DiPeso, "Casas Grandes and the Gran Chichimeca," 50; Snow, "Prehistoric Southwestern Turquoise Industry," 33. DiPeso calls the area in the north "Gran Chichimeca," a term used by precolonial Mesoamericans and adopted by early Spanish explorers. Another term used in precolonial times in the south to describe the former homeland of the Aztecs is "Aztlán."
6. DiPeso, "Casas Grandes and the Gran Chichimeca," 52; Snow, "Prehistoric Southwestern Turquoise Industry," 35, 38, 43–44, 47.
7. Cox, *The Red Land to the South*, 8–12.
8. For further reading on the precolonial Southwest, see Crown and Judge, *Chaco & Hohokam.*
9. Ortiz, *Roots of Resistance*, 18–30. See also Forbes, *Apache, Navaho, and Spaniard*; Carter, *Indian Alliances and the Spanish in the Southwest.*
10. Davidson, "Black Carib Habitats in Central America."
11. Mann, *1491*, 254–57.
12. The material that follows is based on Denevan, "The Pristine Myth."
13. For the influence of the Iroquois Confederacy on the architects of the US Constitution, see Johansen, *The Forgotten Founders.*
14. Lyons, a professor at the State University of New York at Buffalo, says that when the American colonists borrowed from the Haudenosaunee system in forming the US government, they neglected to include the spirit world, and thus began the problems that beset US government today.
15. See Miller, *Coacoochee's Bones*, 1–12.
16. Mann, *1491*, 332.
17. Thomas Morton, quoted in ibid., 250.
18. Ibid., 251–52.
19. See David Wade Chambers, "Native American Road Systems and Trails," Udemy, http://www.udemy.com/lectures/unit-4-native-american-road-

systems-and-trails-76573 (accessed September 24, 2013). Graphics show locations of major roads.

20. Starr, *History of the Cherokee Indians and Their Legends and Folk Lore.*
21. Conley, *Cherokee Nation,* cited in Cox, *The Red Land to the South,* 8.

CHAPTER TWO: CULTURE OF CONQUEST

Epigraph: Marx, *Capital,* 823; http://www.marxists.org/archive/marx/works/1867-c1/ch31.htm.

1. Spicer, *Cycles of Conquest,* 283–85.
2. Linebaugh, *The Magna Carta Manifesto,* 26–27.
3. Two outstanding historical works, which have not been surpassed, probe in depth these prior colonial practices and institutions. In reference to the Iberian Peninsula and the Moors, see Kamen, *Spanish Inquisition.* For England's colonization of Ireland and the thirteen American colonies, see Jennings, *Invasion of America.*
4. Kingston-Mann, "Return of Pierre Proudhon."
5. Federici, *Caliban and the Witch,* 184.
6. Ibid., 171–72, 179–80.
7. Ibid., 237.
8. Roth, *Conversos, Inquisition, and the Expulsion of the Jews from Spain,* 229.
9. Sánchez-Albornoz, *España, un enigma histórico,* 677.
10. Stannard, *American Holocaust,* 246. For an opposing view, see Anderson, *Ethnic Cleansing and The Indian.*
11. Jennings, *Invasion of America,* 168.
12. See Curtis, *Apes and Angels.*
13. Calloway, review of *The Americas That Might Have Been,* 196.
14. Keen, "White Legend Revisited," 353.
15. Denevan, "Pristine Myth," 4–5.
16. Dobyns, *Their Number Become Thinned,* 2. See also Dobyns, *Native American Historical Demography;* and Dobyns, "Estimating Aboriginal American Population," 295–416, and "Reply," 440–44.
17. Borah, "America as Model," 381.
18. Cook, *Conflict between the California Indian and White Civilization.*
19. Wilcox, *Pueblo Revolt and the Mythology of Conquest,* 11.

CHAPTER THREE: CULT OF THE COVENANT

1. Mann, *1491,* 323.
2. Rostlund, *Myth of a Natural Prairie Belt in Alabama,* 409.
3. Mann, *1491,* 252.
4. Denevan, "Pristine Myth," 369–85.
5. Faragher, Buhle, Czitrom, and Armitage, *Out of Many,* 1–24. The title of

the textbook reflected its intent. The title of the first chapter is "A Continent of Villages, to 1500."

6. Jennings, *Invasion of America,* 15.
7. For a revealing comparative study, see Gump, "Civil Wars in South Dakota and South Africa,'" 427–44. In relying on the ancient origin story of the covenant, the modern state of Israel is also using exceptionalist ideology, refusing to acknowledge the settler-colonial nature of the state. Donald Harman Akenson, *God's Peoples: Covenant and Land in South Africa, Israel, and Ulster* (Montreal: McGill-Queen's University Press, 1991), 151–82, 227–62, 311–48.
8. Akenson, *God's Peoples,* 9.
9. Jacobson, *The Story of Stories,* 10.
10. Akenson, *God's Peoples,* 30–31, 73–74.
11. Ibid., 112.
12. See Miller, *Errand in the Wilderness;* Jennings, *Invasion of America;* Vowell, *Wordy Shipmates.*
13. Phillips, *Cousins' Wars,* 177–90.
14. Akensen, *God's Peoples,* 118.
15. See Green, *People with No Name.*
16. The presidents include Andrew Jackson, 1829–37; James K. Polk, 1845–49; James Buchanan, 1856–61; Andrew Johnson, 1865–69; Ulysses S. Grant, 1869–77; Chester A. Arthur, 1881–85; Grover Cleveland, 1885–89 and 1893–97; Benjamin Harrison, 1889–93; William McKinley, 1897–1901; Theodore Roosevelt, 1901–9; Woodrow Wilson, 1913–21; Harry S. Truman, 1949–53; Richard M. Nixon, 1969–74; Jimmy Carter, 1977–81; George H. W. Bush, 1989–93; Bill Clinton, 1993–2001; George W. Bush, 2001–2009; and Barack Obama, 2009–.
17. For a Scots-Irish family history, see James Webb, *Born Fighting.* Webb proudly served in the US Marine Corps and became navy secretary in the Reagan administration and later a Democratic Party senator from Virginia. Webb assumes that the United States is a great and powerful country and owes that position largely to Scots-Irish settlers.
18. Degler, *Out of Our Past,* 51.

CHAPTER FOUR: BLOODY FOOTPRINTS

Epigraph: John Grenier, *The First Way of War,* 5, 10. Grenier is an air force officer and associate professor of history at the US Air Force Academy.

1. LaDuke, *Militarization of Indian Country,* xv–xvii.
2. O'Brien, *American Indian Tribal Governments,* 205–6. To be recognized as "Indian Country," usually the land must either be within an Indian reservation or it must be federal trust land (land technically owned by the federal government but held in trust for a tribe or tribal member). For most purposes, the types of Indian country are as follows:

1. Reservations (18 USC 1151(a)). Historically, Indian reservations were created when particular tribes signed treaties with the United States. Among other things (treaties often included provisions for tribal members to receive law enforcement, education, health care benefits, and to retain hunting/fishing rights), the tribes typically transferred their traditional lands to the United States government but "reserved" part of their lands for tribal purposes. These "reserved" lands became known as "reservations." Later, many "reservations" were created by presidential executive orders or by congressional enactments. As defined by 18 USC 1151(a), "Indian country" consists of all land within a reservation including land that is privately owned and land that is subject to a right-of-way (for example, a publicly accessible road). However, some reservations have been "disestablished" or nullified by such things as federal court decisions or later congressional enactments.

2. Informal Reservations. If a reservation has been disestablished or if the legal existence of a reservation is not clear, remaining trust lands that have been set aside for Indian use are still Indian country (Oklahoma Tax Commission v. Chickasaw Nation, 515 US 450 and Oklahoma Tax Commission v. Sac & Fox Nation, 508 US 114).

3. Dependent Indian communities (18 USC 1151(b)). In US v. Sandoval (231 US 28) the US Supreme Court ruled that pueblo tribal lands in New Mexico are "Indian country" and in US v. McGowan (302 US 535) the Court ruled that Indian colonies in Nevada are also "Indian country." The results of these decisions were later codified at 18 USC 1151(b) as "dependent Indian communities." The Court has interpreted "dependent Indian communities" to be land that is federally supervised and which has been set aside for the use of Indians, Alaska v. Native Village of Venetie (522 US 520).

4. Allotments (18 USC 1151(c)). Primarily from 1887 until 1934, the federal government ran programs where some parcels of tribal trust land were allotted or assigned to particular Indian persons or particular Indian families (but further transfers were to be temporarily restricted by the federal government). Some of these allotments were later converted to private ownership. However, when the allotment programs were frozen by congressional enactment in 1934, many parcels of land were still in restricted or trust status; these remaining parcels are "Indian country" even if they are no longer within a reservation.

5. Special Designations. Congress can specially designate that certain lands are Indian country for jurisdictional purposes even if those lands might not fall within one of the categories mentioned above. An example of this is Santa Fe Indian School in Santa Fe, New Mexico (Public Law 106–568, section 824(c)) (O'Brien).

"What Is Indian Country?," Indian Country Criminal Jurisdiction, http://tribaljurisdiction.tripod.com/id7.html (accessed September 25, 2013).

3. Grenier, *First Way of War*, 5, 10. See also Kaplan, "Prologue: Injun Country," in *Imperial Grunts*, 3–16; and Cohen, *Conquered into Liberty*.

4. Grenier, *First Way of War*, 1.
5. Bailyn, *Barbarous Years*.
6. Grenier, *First Way of War*, 4–5, 7.
7. Ibid., 21.
8. From Samuel G. Drake, *Biography and History of the Indians of North America* (Boston, 1841), quoted in Nabokov, *Native American Testimony*, 72.
9. For the role of Pocahontas in the Powhatan resistance, see Townsend, *Pocahontas and the Powhatan Dilemma*.
10. The *Encarta World English Dictionary* defines the verb "to extirpate" as "to completely get rid of, kill off, or destroy something or somebody considered undesirable" or "to remove something surgically."
11. Grenier, *First Way of War*, 22–26.
12. Ibid., 34.
13. For a brilliant examination of this issue, see Allen, *Invention of the White Race*.
14. Zinn, *People's History of the United States*, 39–42; Washburn, *Governor and the Rebel*.
15. Foner, *Give Me Liberty!*, 100.
16. Quoted in Vowell, *Wordy Shipmates*, 31.
17. Grenier, *First Way of War*, 26–27.
18. Ibid., 27.
19. Ibid., 27–28.
20. Quoted in Zinn, *People's History of the United States*, 15.
21. "King Philip" was what the English called Wampanoag leader Metacom.
22. Colonialist recruitment of Native guides, informants, and fighters had its counterpart in the twentieth century. For example, the federally funded Guardians of the Oglala Nation (GOONs) functioned as an Indigenous paramilitary organization on the Pine Ridge Sioux Reservation in the early 1970s, attacking and murdering anyone, including old and infirm people, who supported the American Indian Movement.
23. Grenier, *First Way of War*, 29–34, 36–37, 39.
24. Taylor, *American Colonies*, 290.
25. Grenier, *First Way of War*, 39–41.
26. Ibid., 42–43.
27. Ibid., 52.
28. Ibid., 55–57.
29. Ibid., 58, 60–61.
30. See Szabo, *The Seven Years War in Europe*; and Anderson, *War That Made America*.
31. Grenier, *First Way of War*, 66, 77.
32. Ibid., 115–17.
33. Amherst quoted in Calloway, *Scratch of a Pen*, 73.

34. Quoted in Grenier, *First Way of War*, 144.

35. Ibid., 41.

36. Ibid., 141–43.

37. From *The Colonial and State Records of North Carolina* 5 (Chapel Hill: University of North Carolina), quoted in Nabokov, *Native American Testimony*, 41–42.

38. Calloway, *Scratch of a Pen*, 168–69.

39. Grenier, *First Way of War*, 148.

40. For an in-depth study of Hollywood "cowboy and Indian" movies, see Slotkin, *Gunfighter Nation*.

41. Dunmore quoted in Grenier, *First Way of War*, 150.

42. Jennings, "The Indians' Revolution," 337–38.

43. For the integral role of spiritual leaders in Indigenous resistance, see Dowd, *Spirited Resistance*.

44. Grenier, *First Way of War*, 153–54.

45. Richter, *Facing East from Indian Country*, 223.

46. Grenier, *First Way of War*, 161.

47. Richter, *Facing East from Indian Country*, 222–23.

48. Grenier, *First Way of War*, 152.

49. Calloway, *American Revolution in Indian Country*, 197–98.

50. Ibid., 197.

51. Grenier, *First Way of War*, 51–53.

52. Ibid., 17–18.

53. Ibid., 59–63.

54. Washington and Sullivan quoted in Drinnon, *Facing West*, 331.

55. Grenier, *First Way of War*, 163, 166–68.

CHAPTER FIVE: THE BIRTH OF A NATION

Epigraph: King, *Why We Can't Wait*, 41–42. Orig. published Harper and Row, 1964.

1. Richter, *Facing East From Indian Country*, 223–24.

2. See Bogus, "Hidden History of the Second Amendment"; and Hadden, *Slave Patrols*.

3. Grenier, *First Way of War*, 170–72.

4. Anderson and Cayton, *Dominion of War*, 104–59.

5. Grenier, *First Way of War*, 193–95.

6. Ibid., 195–97.

7. Ibid., 198–200.

8. Calloway, *Shawnees and the War for America*, 102–3.

9. Grenier, *First Way of War*, 201–2; Richter, *Facing East from Indian Country*, 224–25.

10. Calloway, *Shawnees and the War for America*, 137. See also Edmunds,

Tecumseh and the Quest for American Indian Leadership; and Dowd, *Spirited Resistance*.

11. Grenier, *First Way of War*, 206.
12. Ibid., 206–7.
13. Ibid., 207–8.
14. Quoted in Richter, *Facing East from Indian Country*, 231.
15. Grenier, *First Way of War*, 209–10, 213.
16. Ibid., 172.
17. Ibid., 174–75.
18. Remini, *Andrew Jackson and His Indian Wars*, 32.
19. Grenier, *First Way of War*, 176–77.
20. Ibid., 181, 184.
21. Ibid., 181–87.
22. Ibid., 187–92.
23. Ibid., 192–93.
24. Ibid., 205.
25. Ibid., 221–22.

CHAPTER SIX: THE LAST OF THE MOHICANS
AND ANDREW JACKSON'S WHITE REPUBLIC

Epigraph: Fanon, *Wretched of the Earth*, 33.
1. See Tucker and Hendrickson, *Empire of Liberty*.
2. Wilentz, *Rise of American Democracy*, 109–11; Dowd, *Spirited Resistance*, 163–64.
3. See Anderson and Cayton, *Dominion of War*.
4. Quoted in Phillips, *Cousins' Wars*, 3.
5. Grenier, *First Way of War*, 220.
6. Ibid., 214–15.
7. Remini, *Life of Andrew Jackson*, 62–69.
8. Grenier, *First Way of War*, 216–17.
9. Brinkley, *Unfinished Nation*, 85; Takaki, *Iron Cages*, 96.
10. Takaki, *Different Mirror*, 85–86.
11. Brinkley, *Unfinished Nation*, 84. On Jackson's vision to create a populist empire, see Anderson and Cayton, *Dominion of War*, 207–46.
12. Grenier, *First Way of War*, 204.
13. Ibid., 205.
14. Ibid., 218–20.
15. Ibid., 215. See also Saunt, *New Order of Things*, 236–41.
16. Miller, *Coacoochee's Bones*, xi.
17. Quoted in Rogin, *Fathers and Children*, 129.
18. Slotkin, *Fatal Environment*, 81–106.
19. In the twentieth century, during the dark days of the Depression and war, 1932–43, Laura Ingalls Wilder updated and consolidated the myth, center-

ing it on women, in her Little House on the Prairie series (with four additional books published after her death).

20. Reynolds, *Waking Giant*, 236–41.
21. Jennings, *Invasion of America*, 327–28.
22. Stegner, *Where the Bluebird Sings to the Lemonade Springs*, 71–72.
23. D. H. Lawrence, quoted in Slotkin, *Regeneration through Violence*, 466.
24. Dimock, *Empire for Liberty*, 9.
25. Slotkin, *Regeneration through Violence*, 394–95.
26. US historians see Jacksonian democracy as spanning nearly three decades, 1824 to 1852, rather than just Jackson's eight-year presidency (1828–36). There are dozens of books and articles on the era of Jacksonian democracy, as well as biographies of Andrew Jackson's life. Historian Robert V. Remini is the foremost Jacksonian scholar, with multiple books; his *Life of Andrew Jackson* (2010) is a short compilation of his previous work. A revisionist view distinguished from Remini's admiring portrayal is Michael Paul Rogin, *Fathers and Children: Andrew Jackson and the Subjugation of the American Indian* (1975). Twenty-first-century works include Brands, *Andrew Jackson*; Meacham, *American Lion*; Reynolds, *Waking Giant*; and Wilentz, *Andrew Jackson*.
27. Mankiller and Wallis, *Mankiller*, 51.
28. Rogin, *Fathers and Children*, 3–4.
29. Stannard, *American Holocaust*, 122.
30. Ibid., 122–23.
31. Prucha, *American Indian Treaties*, 184.
32. Quoted in Zinn, *People's History of the United States*, 129–30.
33. Ibid., 138.
34. Mooney, *Historical Sketch of the Cherokee*, 124.
35. Tocqueville, *Democracy in America*, 372–73.
36. Rogin, *Fathers and Children*, 3–4.
37. "Barack Obama's Inaugural Address," transcript, *New York Times*, January 20, 2009.

CHAPTER SEVEN: SEA TO SHINING SEA

1. Ford quoted in Kenner, *History of New Mexico–Plains Indian Relations*, 83; Thompson, *Recollections of Mexico*, 72.
2. Whitman quoted in McDougall, *Promised Land, Crusader State*, 11. Whitman expressed many such views during the US-Mexican War in the newspaper he edited, the *Brooklyn Daily Eagle*. For an in-depth study of the intellectual, poetic, media, and mass popularity of the war, see Johannsen, *To the Halls of the Montezumas*; also see Reynolds, *Walt Whitman's America*.
3. Whitman quoted in Reynolds, *John Brown Abolitionist*, 449.
4. Horsman, *Race and Manifest Destiny*, 185.

5. See Zacks, *Pirate Coast*; and Boot, *Savage Wars of Peace*, 3–29.

6. Blackhawk, *Violence over the Land*, 145–75.

7. Pike, *Expeditions of Zebulon Montgomery Pike*. Coues, Pike's editor, characterized the expedition's straying into Spanish territory and his arrest as "a particular accident of a general design" (499). See also Owsley and Smith, *Filibusters and Expansionists*.

8. See Unrau, *Indians, Alcohol, and the Roads to Taos and Santa Fe*.

9. Pike, *Expeditions*, 499; Blackhawk, *Violence over the Land*, 117.

10. See Weber, *Taos Trappers*.

11. Dunbar-Ortiz, *Roots of Resistance*, 80; see also Hall, *Laws of Mexico*.

12. See Sides, *Blood and Thunder*, 92–101; Chaffin, *Pathfinder*, 33–35.

13. Holton, *Unruly Americans and the Origins of the Constitution*, 14.

14. Lamar, *Far Southwest*, 7–10.

15. See Vlasich, *Pueblo Indian Agriculture*.

16. See Sando and Agoyo, *Po'Pay*; Wilcox, *Pueblo Revolt and the Mythology of Conquest*; Dunbar-Ortiz, *Roots of Resistance*, 31–45; Carter, *Indian Alliances and the Spanish in the Southwest*.

17. Anderson, *Conquest of Texas*, 4, 18–29. See also "4th Largest Tribe in US? Mexicans Who Call Themselves American Indian," *Indian Country Today*, August 5, 2013, http://indiancountrytodaymedianetwork.com/ (accessed September 27, 2013).

18. Anderson, *Conquest of Texas*, 18–29. For a fascinating and historically accurate fictional account of Texas's independence from Mexico, see Russell, *Escape from Texas*.

19. See Anderson, *Conquest of Texas*. For the Texas Rangers' continuation of their counterinsurgent role in the twentieth century, see Johnson, *Revolution in Texas*; Harris and Sadler, *Texas Rangers and the Mexican Revolution*.

20. Tinker, *Missionary Conquest*, 42.

21. For documentation of California Indian resistance, see Jackson and Castillo, *Indians, Franciscans, and Spanish Colonization*, 73–86.

22. Murguía, *Medicine of Memory*, 40–41.

23. See Heizer, *Destruction of California Indians*. See also Cook, *Population of the California Indians*.

24. See Johannsen, *To the Halls of the Montezumas*.

25. See Kiser, *Dragoons in Apacheland*.

CHAPTER EIGHT: "INDIAN COUNTRY"

Epigraph: Ortiz, *from Sand Creek*, 20.

1. "Selected Statistics on Slavery in the United States," *Causes of the Civil War*, http://www.civilwarcauses.org/stat.htm (accessed December 10, 2013).

2. Chang, *Color of the Land*, 36.

3. See Confer, *Cherokee Nation in the Civil War*; Spencer, *American Civil War in the Indian Territory*; McLoughlin, *After the Trail of Tears*.

4. See Katz, *Black Indians*; Duvall, Jacob, and Murray, *Secret History of the Cherokees*.

5. See Wilson and Schommer, *Remember This!*; Wilson, *In the Footsteps of Our Ancestors*; Anderson, *Kinsmen of Another Kind*, 261–81; Anderson, *Little Crow*.

6. From Charles Eastman, *Indian Boyhood* (1902), quoted in Nabokov, *Native American Testimony*, 22.

7. West, *Contested Plains*, 300–301.

8. Ortiz, *from Sand Creek*, 41.

9. See Kelman, *Misplaced Massacre*.

10. From A. N. Ellis, "Reflections of an Interview with Cochise," Kansas State Historical Society 13 (1913–14), quoted in Nabokov, *Native American Testimony*, 177.

11. Utley, *Indian Frontier of the American West*, 82. Also see Carleton, *Prairie Logbooks*, 3–152.

12. From *Condition of the Indian Tribes*, Senate Report no. 156, 39th Cong., 2nd sess. (Washington, DC: Government Printing Office, 1867), quoted in Nabokov, *Native American Testimony*, 197–98.

13. See Denetdale, *Long Walk*; and Denetdale, *Reclaiming Diné History*.

14. See Gates, *History of Public Land Law Development*.

15. For a booster version of the relationship between the land acts and colonization, see Hyman, *American Singularity*.

16. White, *"It's Your Misfortune and None of My Own,"* 139.

17. Westphall, *Public Domain in New Mexico*, 43.

18. See White, *Railroaded*.

19. This is the total number of treaties signed by both parties, ratified by the US Congress, and proclaimed by US presidents. Many more treaties negotiated between the United States and Indigenous nations and signed by the president were not ratified by Congress, or if ratified were not proclaimed, the California Indigenous peoples' treaties being the most numerous, so there are actually around six hundred treaties that are considered legitimate by the Indigenous nations concerned. See Deloria, *Behind the Trail of Broken Treaties*; Deloria and DeMallie, *Documents of American Indian Diplomacy*; Johansen, *Enduring Legacies*.

20. See 16 Stat. 566, Rev. Stat. Sec. 2079; 25 U.S. Code Sec. 71.

21. Hanson, *Memory and Vision*, 211.

22. From Marriott and Rachlin, *American Indian Mythology*, quoted in Nabokov, *Native American Testimony*, 174–75.

23. Parish, *Charles Ilfeld Company*, 35.

24. Sherman to Grant, May 28, 1867, quoted in Fellman, *Citizen Sherman*, 264.
25. Sherman to Herbert A. Preston, April 17, 1873, quoted in Marszalek, *Sherman*, 379.
26. See Utley, *Cavalier in Buckskin*, 57–103.
27. See Hahn, *Nation under Our Feet*.
28. See Enloe, *Ethnic Soldiers*.
29. Stanford L. Davis, "Buffalo Soldiers & Indian Wars," Buffalosoldier.net, http://www.buffalosoldier.net/index.htm (accessed September 30, 2013).
30. Jace Weaver, "A Lantern to See By," 315; see also Enloe, *Ethnic Soldiers*.
31. Bob Marley, "Buffalo Soldier," by Bob Marley and Noel G. Williams, recorded 1980, on *Confrontation*, Island Records, 90085-1, 1983.
32. See Wolfe, "Settler Colonialism and the Elimination of the Native."
33. Sandoz, *Cheyenne Autumn*.
34. See Williams, *Empire as a Way of Life*.
35. Child, *Boarding School Seasons*; also see Christine Lesiak, director, "In the White Man's Image," *The American Experience*, season four, episode twelve (PBS, 1992).
36. Deloria, *Custer Died for Your Sins*.
37. From Deloria, *Speaking of Indians*, quoted in Nabokov, *Native American Testimony*, 253–55.
38. See Brown, *Bury My Heart at Wounded Knee*; Coleman, *Voices of Wounded Knee*.
39. L. F. Baum, "Editorials on the Sioux Nation," University of Oxford History of Science, Medicine, and Technology website, http://hsmt.history.ox.ac.uk//courses_reading/undergraduate/authority_of_nature/week_7/baum.pdf.
40. Quoted in Vizenor, *Native Liberty*, 143–44.
41. Quoted in Utley, "The Ordeal of Plenty Horses," 16.
42. Deloria, *Indians in Unexpected Places*, 28.
43. Ibid., 35–36.
44. From *New Directions in Indian Purpose*, quoted in Nabokov, *Native American Testimony*, 421.
45. See Chang, *Color of the Land*. For well-documented details on widespread corruption involved in using allotment to dispose of the lands of the Native nations and individual Indian allotment holders in Oklahoma, see Debo, *And Still the Waters Run*.
46. From Deloria, *Speaking of Indians*, quoted in Nabokov, *Native American Testimony*, 249.
47. Stone, "Report on the Court of Private Land Claims."
48. "United States v. Sandoval," 28. See also Dunbar-Ortiz, *Roots of Resistance*, 114–18.

CHAPTER NINE: US TRIUMPHALISM AND PEACETIME COLONIALISM

Epigraph 1: Theodore Roosevelt, "The Expansion of the White Races," address at the Methodist Episcopal Church, Washington, DC, January 18, 1909, in "Two Essays by Theodore Roosevelt," *Modern American Poetry*, English Department, University of Illinois, http://www.english.illinois.edu/maps/poets/a_f/espada/roosevelt.htm (accessed December 10, 2013), from Roosevelt, *American Problems*. See also *The Works of Theodore Roosevelt*, memorial ed., *North American Review* 15 (1890).

Epigraph 2: Henry Crow Dog, "So That They Will Go, Your Honor, Judge," quoted in Dunbar-Ortiz, *The Great Sioux Nation*, 167.

1. Williams, *Empire as a Way of Life*, 73–76, 102–10. Marshall Islands regained full sovereignty in 1986.

2. See Kinzer, *Overthrow*.

3. For photographs and documents, see Arnaldo Dumindin, *Philippine-American War, 1899–1902*, http://philippineamericanwar.webs.com (accessed October 1, 2013).

4. Kaplan, *Imperial Grunts*, 138. On early US imperialism overseas, see Immerman, *Empire for Liberty*; Zacks, *Pirate Coast*.

5. From *Condition of the Indian Tribes*, quoted in Nabokov, *Native American Testimony*, 194–95.

6. Silbey, *War of Frontier and Empire*, 211.

7. Williams, "United States Indian Policy and the Debate over Philippine Annexation."

8. See Kuzmarov, *Modernizing Repression*.

9. See Womack and Dunbar-Ortiz, "Dreams of Revolution: Oklahoma, 1917."

10. See Eisenhower, *Intervention!*

11. Miner, *Corporation and the Indian*, xi.

12. Ibid., xiv.

13. Ibid., 10.

14. Ibid., 19.

15. From "Address of Robert Spott," *Commonwealth* 21, no. 3 (1926), quoted in Nabokov, *Native American Testimony*, 315–16.

16. See Ifill, *On the Courthouse Lawn*.

17. McGerr, *Fierce Discontent*, 305.

18. See Philip, *John Collier's Crusade for Indian Reform*; Kelly, *Assault on Assimilation*.

19. Blackman, *Oklahoma's Indian New Deal*.

20. Aberle, *Peyote Religion Among the Navaho*, 53.

21. See Lamphere, *To Run After Them*.

22. Navajo Community College, *Navajo Livestock Reduction*, 47.

23. See Drinnon, *Keeper of Concentration Camps*. Some of the Japanese concentration camps were built on Native reservations.

24. Myer quoted in ibid., 235.

25. See Cobb, *Native Activism in Cold War America*.

26. House Concurrent Resolution 108, 1953, *Digital History*, http://www.digitalhistory.uh.edu/disp_textbook.cfm?smtid=3&psid=726 (accessed October 1, 2013). See also Getches, Wilkinson, and Williams, *Cases and Materials on Federal Indian Law*; Wilkinson, *Blood Struggle*. For a survey of federal Indian policy, see O'Brien, *American Indian Tribal Governments*, 84–85.

27. See Zinn, *People's History of the United States*, 420–28.

28. Kinzer, *Overthrow*, 111–47.

CHAPTER TEN: GHOST DANCE PROPHECY

Epigraph 1: "Sioux Ghost Dance Song Lyrics," documented and translated by James Mooney in 1894, *Ghost Dance*, http://www.ghostdance.com/songs/songs-lyricssioux.html (accessed December 10, 2013).

Epigraph 2: Quoted in Zinn, *People's History of the United States*, 525.

1. Slotkin, *Gunfighter Nation*, 1–2.

2. Ibid., 3.

3. "Blue Lake," *Taos Pueblo*, http://www.taospueblo.com/blue-lake (accessed October 2, 2013).

4. From the statement of James E. Snead, president of the Santa Fe Wildlife and Conservation Association, "Taos Indians—Blue Lake," in "Hearings before the Subcommittee on Indian Affairs of the Committee on Interior and Insular Affairs, U.S. Senate, 91st Congress, 2nd Session (September 19–20, 1968)," in *Primitive Law—United States Congressional Documents*, vol. 9, pt. 1 (Washington, DC: Government Printing Office, 1968), 216.

5. For the senators' arguments against the return of Blue Lake, see "Pueblo de Taos Indians Cultural and Ceremonial Shrine Protection Act of 1970," Proceedings and Debates of the 91st Congress, 2nd Session (December 2, 1970), *Congressional Record* 116, pt. 29, 39, 587, 589–90, 594. Nielson, "American Indian Land Claims," 324. The senators on the subcommittee were concerned about the Alianza Federal de Mercedes (later renamed the Alianza Federal de Pueblos Libres), formed in 1963 to pressure the federal government for reconsideration of land-grant settlements and the loss of the commons. The organization claimed that colonialism had robbed resources, depopulated communities in northern New Mexico, and impoverished the people. The Alianza was composed of many poor land-grant heirs and was identified primarily with a Texas-born Mexican, Reies López Tijerina. In June 1967, the National Guard was dispatched with tanks, helicopters, and infantry to Rio Arriba County in search of the agrarian Mexican rebels who had participated in the "Courthouse Raid" at Tierra Amarilla.

The incident and the government's response briefly focused national and international attention on northern New Mexico, and the land-grant issue, which had been resolved in the courts over sixty years before, once again became a live issue.

Several federal Spanish and Mexican land-grant cases have been brought in federal courts, one to the Supreme Court in 1952 that was denied a hearing: Martínez v. Rivera, 196 Fed. 2nd 192 (Circuit Court of Appeals, 10th Circuit, April 16, 1952). In 2001, following more than a century of struggle by Hispanic land grantees who were deprived of most of their landholdings after the United States occupied New Mexico in 1848, the US General Accounting Office began a study of the New Mexico land grants. The GAO issued its final report in 2004, but no action has yet ensued. US General Accounting Office, *Treaty of Guadalupe Hidalgo.*

6. Cobb, *Native American Activism in Cold War America*, 58–61. For a full history of the NIYC, which still thrives, see Shreve, *Red Power Rising.*
7. Quoted in Zinn, *People's History of the United States*, 516–17.
8. Cobb, *Native American Activism in Cold War America*, 157.
9. Mantler, *Power of the Poor.*
10. Smith and Warrior, *Like a Hurricane*, 28–29.
11. Ibid., 29–30.
12. On the founding of the American Indian Movement, see ibid., 114–15, and Waterman and Bancroft, *We Are Still Here.*
13. Smith and Warrior, *Like a Hurricane*, 111.
14. "Trail of Broken Treaties 20-Point Position Paper," *American Indian Movement*, http://www.aimovement.org/ggc/trailofbrokentreaties.html (accessed December 10, 2013).
15. Robert A. Trennert, *Alternative to Extinction: Federal Indian Policy and the Beginnings of the Reservation System, 1846–51* (Philadelphia: Temple University Press, 1975), 166.
16. See testimony of Pat McLaughlin, chairman of the Standing Rock Sioux government, Fort Yates, ND (May 8, 1976), at hearings of the American Indian Policy Review Commission, established by Congress in the act of January 3, 1975.
17. See Philip, *John Collier's Crusade for Indian Reform.*
18. King quoted in Dunbar-Ortiz, *The Great Sioux Nation*, 156.
19. For a lucid discussion of neocolonialism in relation to American Indians and the reservation system, see Jorgensen, *Sun Dance Religion*, 89–146.
20. There is continuous migration from reservations to cities and border towns and back to the reservations, so that half the Indian population at any time is away from the reservation. Generally, however, relocation is not permanent and resembles migratory labor more than permanent relocation. This conclusion is based on my personal observations and on unpublished studies of the Indigenous populations in the San Francisco Bay area and Los Angeles.

21. The American Indian Movement convened a meeting in June 1974 that founded the International Indian Treaty Council (IITC), receiving consultative status in the UN Economic and Social Council (ECOSOC) in February 1977. The IITC participated in the UN Conference on Desertification in Buenos Aires, March 1977, and made presentations to the UN Human Rights Commission in August 1977 and in February and August 1978. It also led the organizing for the Non-Governmental Organizations (NGOs) Conference on Indigenous Peoples of the Americas, held at UN headquarters in Geneva, Switzerland, in September 1977; participated in the World Conference on Racism in Basel, Switzerland, in May 1978; and participated in establishing the UN Working Group on Indigenous Populations, the UN Permanent Forum on Indigenous Issues, and the 2007 UN Declaration on the Rights of Indigenous Peoples. See Echo-Hawk, *In The Light of Justice*; see also Deloria, *Behind the Trail of Broken Treaties*.

22. Herr, *Dispatches*, 45.

23. Zinn, *People's History of the United States*, 521.

24. Ellen Knickmeyer, "Troops Have Pre-Combat Meal, War Dance," Associated Press, March 19, 2003, http://www.myplainview.com/article_9c595368-42db-50b3-9647-a8d4486bff28.html.

25. Grenier, *First Way of War*, 223–24.

CHAPTER 11: THE DOCTRINE OF DISCOVERY

Epigraph 1: McNickle, *The Surrounded*, 49.

Epigraph 2: Vizenor, "Constitutional Consent," 11.

1. The author was present at the proceedings.

2. See Watson, *Buying America from the Indians*; and Robertson, *Conquest by Law*.

3. Miller, "International Law of Colonialism." See also Deloria, *Of Utmost Good Faith*, 6–39; Newcomb, *Pagans in the Promised Land*.

4. Eleventh Session, United Nations Permanent Forum on Indigenous Issues, http://social.un.org/index/IndigenousPeoples/UNPFIISessions/Eleventh.aspx (accessed October 3, 2013).

5. "International: Quakers Repudiate the Doctrine of Discovery," August 17, 2012, Indigenous Peoples Issues and Resources, http://indigenouspeoples issues.com/ (accessed October 3, 2013). See also "The Doctrine of Discovery," http://www.doctrineofdiscovery.org/ (accessed October 3, 2013).

6. "The Doctrine of Discovery: 2012 Responsive Resolution," Unitarian Universalist Association of Congregations, http://www.uua.org/statements/statements/209123.shtml (accessed October 3, 2013).

7. Vincent Warren, "Government Calls Native American Resistance of 1800s 'Much Like Modern-Day Al-Qaeda,'" *Truthout*, April 11, 2011, http://truth-out.org/news/item/330-government-calls-native-american-resis tance-of-1800s-much-like-modernday-alqaeda (accessed October 3, 2013).

8. Sharon H. Venne, "What Is the Meaning of Sovereignty," Indigenous Women's Network, June 18, 2007, http://indigenouswomen.org/ (accessed November 11, 2013).

9. Sanchez, *Treaty Council News*, 12.

10. See Dunbar-Ortiz, *Indians of the Americas*; Dunbar-Ortiz, *Roots of Resistance*, chapter 7, "Land, Indigenousness, Identity, and Self-Determination."

11. Killsback, "Indigenous Perceptions of Time," 150–51.

12. UN Commission on Human Rights, Sub-commission on Prevention of Discrimination and Protection of Minorities, 51st sess., *Human Rights of Indigenous Peoples: Study on Treaties, Agreements and Other Constructive Arrangements between States and Indigenous Populations: Final Report*, by Miguel Alfonso Martínez, special rapporteur, June 22, 1999, UN Document E/CN.4/Sub.2/1999/20. See also *Report of the Working Group on Indigenous Populations on Its Seventeenth Session, 26–30 July 1999*, UN Document E/CN.4/Sub.2/1999/20, August 12, 1999.

13. Rob Capriccioso, "*Cobell* Concludes with the Rich Getting Richer," *Indian Country Today*, June 27, 2011, http://indiancountrytodaymedianetwork.com/ (accessed October 3, 2013). See also "Indian Trust Settlement" (the *Cobell v. Salazar* settlement website), http://www.indiantrust.com/ (accessed October 3, 2013); and Jodi Rave, "Milestone in Cobell Indian Trust Case," *High Country News*, July 25, 2011, http://www.hcn.org/issues/43.12/milestone-in-cobell-indian-trust-case (accessed October 3, 2013).

14. Wilkinson, "Afterword," 468–69.

15. For the history of the establishment of Mount Rushmore as a national monument in the illegally taken Black Hills, see Larner, *Mount Rushmore*; and Taliaferro, *Great White Fathers*. For a history of the American Indian Movement, see Smith and Warrior, *Like a Hurricane*; and Wittstock and Bancroft, *We Are Still Here*. See also AIM-WEST, http://aimwest.info/ (accessed October 3, 2013). On the International Indian Treaty Council, see Dunbar-Ortiz, *Indians of the Americas*; Dunbar-Ortiz, *Blood on the Border*; and the IITC website, http://www.treatycouncil.org/ (accessed October 3, 2013).

16. "For Great Sioux Nation, Black Hills Can't Be Bought for $1.3 Billion," PBS *NewsHour*, August 24, 2011, video and transcript at http://www.pbs.org/newshour/bb/social_issues/july-dec11/blackhills_08-24.html (accessed October 3, 2013).

17. See Dunbar-Ortiz, *Economic Development in American Indian Reservations*.

18. See Harvard Project on American Indian Economic Development, *State of the Native Nations*.

19. See Light and Rand, *Indian Gaming and Tribal Sovereignty*.

20. Hedges, *Days of Destruction, Days of Revolt*, 1–58.

21. Vine Deloria Jr. speaking in PBS *Frontline* documentary *In the Spirit of Crazy Horse* (1990).

22. Lurie, "World's Oldest On-Going Protest Demonstration."

23. Poverty and class analysis can be accomplished without obliterating the particular effects of colonialism, as Alyosha Goldstein brilliantly demonstrated in *Poverty in Common*, with a chapter titled "On the Internal Border: Colonial Difference and the Locations of Underdevelopment," in which he treats Native nations and Puerto Rico with reference to sovereignty status and collective experiences of colonialism in addition to capitalism. Goldstein, *Poverty in Common*, 77–110.

24. For an excellent summary of testimonies, see Smith, "Forever Changed," 57–82.

25. From Embree, *Indians of the Americas*, quoted in Nabokov, *Native American Testimony*, 222.

26. See McBeth, *Ethnic Identity and the Boarding School Experience*, 105. See also Broker, *Night Flying Woman*, 93–94.

27. Yvonne Leif, *All Things Considered*, National Public Radio, October 14, 1991.

28. Roger Buffalohead, *All Things Considered*, National Public Radio, October 14, 1991.

29. Haig-Brown, *Resistance and Renewal*, 75.

30. Knockwood, *Out of the Depths*, 138.

31. Alfred, *Peace, Power, and Righteousness*, xii.

32. Smith, "Native American Feminism, Sovereignty and Social Change," 132; Smith, *Conquest*. See also Erdrich, *The Round House*. In this 2012 National Book Award winner for fiction, Erdrich, who is Anishinaabe from North Dakota, writes of the circumstances on reservations that allow for extreme sexual violence.

33. Amnesty International USA, *Maze of Injustice*.

34. Wilkins, "Sovereignty, Democracy, Constitution," 7.

35. Dennison, *Colonial Entanglement*, 197.

36. Vizenor and Doerfler, *White Earth Nation*, 63.

37. Ibid., 11.

CONCLUSION: THE FUTURE OF THE UNITED STATES

Epigraph: Byrd, *Transit of Empire*, 122–23.

1. For a magisterial study, see Slotkin, *Gunfighter Nation*.

2. Kaplan, *Imperial Grunts*.

3. Grenier, *First Way of War*, 10.

4. Kaplan, *Imperial Grunts*, 3–5.

5. Ibid., 6.

6. Ibid., 8, 10.

7. Ibid., 10.
8. Ibid., 7–8.
9. Hoxie, *Encyclopedia of North American Indians*, 319.
10. Byrd, *Transit of Empire*, 226–28.
11. Agamben, *Homo Sacer*.
12. Byrd, *Transit of Empire*, 226–27.
13. *The Modoc Indian Prisoners*, 14 Op. Att'y Gen. 252 (1873), quoted in John C. Yoo, *Memorandum for William J. Haynes II, General Counsel of the Department of Defense*, March 14, 2003, p. 7. Quoted in Byrd, *Transit of Empire*, 227.
14. Byrd, *Transit of Empire*, 227.
15. Vine, *Island of Shame*, 2.
16. Kissinger quoted in ibid., 15.
17. Ibid., 15–16.
18. LaDuke, *Militarization of Indian Country*, xvi.
19. Interview with Cynthia Enloe, "Militarization, Feminism, and the International Politics of Banana Boats," *Theory Talk*, no. 48, May 22, 2012, http://www.theory-talks.org/2012/05/theory-talk-48.html (accessed October 4, 2013). See also Enloe, *Bananas, Beaches and Bases*.
20. Grenier, *First Way of War*, 222.
21. Price, *Weaponizing Anthropology*, 1, 11.
22. Stone and Kuznick, *Untold History of the United States*, xii; *The Untold History of the United States*, TV series, Showtime, 2012. An interesting aside to the question of lack of national health care is that only two sectors of US society actually have national health care, with no private insurer participating: war veterans and Native Americans.
23. Byrd, *Transit of Empire*, xii–xiv.
24. Ibid., 123; Cook-Lynn, *New Indians, Old Wars*, 204.
25. Razack, *Dark Threats and White Knights*, 10.
26. For understanding the limitations of these initiatives regarding Indigenous self-determination, see Forbes, *Native Americans and Nixon*.
27. Hardt and Negri, *Commonwealth*; the first two volumes in their trilogy are *Empire* (2000) and *Multitude* (2005). Other writers calling for a "commons" include, most notably, Linebaugh, *Magna Carta Manifesto*, and theorists associated with the Midnight Notes Collective and the Retort Collective.
28. Sharma and Wright, "Decolonizing Resistance, Challenging Colonial States."
29. Lorraine Le Camp, unpublished paper, 1998, quoted in Bonita Lawrence and Enaskshi Dua, *Social Justice* 32, no. 4 (2005): 132.
30. Cook-Lynn, *Why I Can't Read Wallace Stegner and Other Essays*, 88.
31. Byrd, *Transit of Empire*, 205.
32. Johansen, *Debating Democracy*, 275.

33. See McKeown, *In the Smaller Scope of Conscience.*
34. Thomas, *Skull Wars*, 88.
35. Erik Davis, "Bodies Politic: Fetishization, Identity, and the Indigenous Dead," unpublished paper, 2010.
36. Asutru Folk Assembly statement, quoted in Downey, *Riddle of the Bones*, xxii.
37. Ibid., 11.
38. Davis, "Bodies Politic."
39. Silverberg, *Mound Builders of Ancient America*, 57.
40. Gómez-Quiñones, *Indigenous Quotient*, 13.
41. Ortiz, *from Sand Creek*, 86.

WORKS CITED

Aberle, David. *The Peyote Religion Among the Navaho.* Chicago: Aldine, 1966.

Agamben, Giorgio. *Homo Sacer: Sovereign Power and Bare Life.* Stanford, CA: Stanford University Press, 1998.

Akenson, Donald Harman. *God's Peoples: Covenant and Land in South Africa, Israel, and Ulster.* Montreal: McGill-Queen's University Press, 1991.

Alfred, Taiaiake. *Peace, Power, and Righteousness: An Indigenous Manifesto.* Don Mills, Ontario: Oxford University Press, 1999.

Allen, Theodore W. *The Invention of the White Race.* 2nd edition. 2 volumes. London: Verso, 2012.

Amnesty International USA. *Maze of Injustice: The Failure to Protect Indigenous Women from Sexual Violence in the USA.* New York: Amnesty International USA, 2007.

Anderson, Fred. *The War That Made America: A Short History of the French and Indian War.* New York: Viking, 2005.

Anderson, Fred, and Andrew Cayton. *The Dominion of War: Empire and Liberty in North America, 1500–2000.* New York: Viking, 2005.

Anderson, Gary Clayton. *The Conquest of Texas: Ethnic Cleansing in the Promised Land, 1820–1875.* Norman: University of Oklahoma Press, 2005.

———. *Ethnic Cleansing and the Indian: The Crime That Should Haunt America.* Norman: University of Oklahoma Press, 2014.

———. *Kinsmen of Another Kind: Dakota-White Relations in the Upper Mississippi Valley, 1650–1862.* Minneapolis: Minnesota Historical Society Press, 1997.

———. *Little Crow: Spokesman for the Sioux.* Minneapolis: Minnesota Historical Society Press, 1986.

Bailyn, Bernard. *The Barbarous Years: The Peopling of British North America: The Conflict of Civilizations, 1600–1675.* New York: Alfred A. Knopf, 2012.

Blackhawk, Ned. *Violence over the Land: Indians and Empires in the Early American West.* Cambridge, MA: Harvard University Press, 2006.

Blackman, Jon. *Oklahoma's Indian New Deal*. Norman: University of Oklahoma Press, 2013.

Bogus, Carl T. "The Hidden History of the Second Amendment." *University of California at Davis Law Review* 31 (1998): 309–420.

Boot, Max. *The Savage Wars of Peace: Small Wars and the Rise of American Power*. New York: Basic Books, 2002.

Borah, Woodrow Wilson. "America as Model: The Demographic Impact of European Expansion upon the Non-European World." In *Actas y Morías XXXV Congreso Internacional de Americanistas, México 1962*. 3 volumes. Mexico City: Editorial Libros de México, 1964.

Brands, H. W. *Andrew Jackson: His Life and Times*. New York: Anchor, 2005.

Brinkley, Alan. *The Unfinished Nation: A Concise History of the American People*. 3rd edition. Boston: McGraw-Hill, 2000.

Broker, Ignatia. *Night Flying Woman: An Ojiway Narrative*. St. Paul: Minnesota Historical Society Press, 1983.

Brown, Dee. *Bury My Heart at Wounded Knee: An Indian History of the American West*. New York: Owl Books, 1970.

Byrd, Jodi A. *The Transit of Empire: Indigenous Critiques of Colonialism*. Minneapolis: University of Minnesota Press, 2011.

Calloway, Colin G. *The American Revolution in Indian Country: Crisis and Diversity in Native American Communities*. Cambridge, UK: Cambridge University Press, 1995.

———. Review of *The Americas That Might Have Been: Native American Social Systems through Time*, by Julian Granberry. *Ethnohistory* 54, no. 1 (Winter 2007).

———. *The Scratch of a Pen: 1763 and the Transformation of North America*. New York: Oxford University Press, 2006.

———. *The Shawnees and the War for America*. New York: Viking, 2007.

Carleton, James Henry. *The Prairie Logbooks*. Lincoln: University of Nebraska Press, 1983.

Carter, William B. *Indian Alliances and the Spanish in the Southwest, 750–1750*. Norman: University of Oklahoma Press, 2012.

Chaffin, Tom. *Pathfinder: John Charles Frémont and the Course of American Empire*. New York: Hill and Wang, 2002.

Chang, David A. *The Color of the Land: Race, Nation, and the Politics of Landownership in Oklahoma, 1832–1929*. Chapel Hill: University of North Carolina Press, 2010.

Child, Brenda J. *Boarding School Seasons: American Indian Families, 1900–1940*. Lincoln: University of Nebraska Press, 2000.

Cobb, Daniel M. *Native Activism in Cold War America: The Struggle for Sovereignty*. Lawrence: University of Kansas Press, 2008.

Cohen, Eliot A. *Conquered into Liberty: Two Centuries of Battles along the*

Great Warpath That Made the American Way of War. New York: Free Press, 2011.

Coleman, William. *Voices of Wounded Knee.* Lincoln: University of Nebraska Press, 2000.

Condition of the Indian Tribes. Senate Report no. 156, 39th Cong., 2d sess. Washington, DC: Government Printing Office, 1867.

Confer, Clarissa W. *The Cherokee Nation in the Civil War.* Norman: University of Oklahoma Press, 2007.

Conley, Robert J. *The Cherokee Nation: A History.* Albuquerque: University of New Mexico Press, 2005.

Cook, Sherburne F. *The Conflict between the California Indian and White Civilization.* 4 volumes. Ibero-Americana nos. 21, 22, 23, 24. Berkeley: University of California Press, 1943.

———. *The Population of the California Indians, 1769–1970.* Berkeley: University of California Press, 1976.

Cook-Lynn, Elizabeth. *New Indians, Old Wars.* Urbana: University of Illinois Press, 2007.

———. *Why I Can't Read Wallace Stegner and Other Essays: A Tribal Voice.* Madison: University of Wisconsin Press, 1996.

Cox, James H. *The Red Land to the South: American Indian Writers and Indigenous Mexico.* Minneapolis: University of Minnesota Press, 2012.

Crown, Patricia L., and James W. Judge, eds. *Chaco & Hohokam: Prehistoric Regional Systems in the American Southwest.* Santa Fe: School of American Research Press, 1991.

Curtis, L. Perry, Jr. *Apes and Angels: The Irishman in Victorian Caricature.* Washington, DC: Smithsonian Institution Press, 1997.

Davidson, William V. "Black Carib Habitats in Central America." In *Frontier Adaptations in Lower Central America,* 85–94. Edited by Mary W. Helms and Franklin O. Loveland. Philadelphia: Institute for the Study of Human Issues, 1976.

Debo, Angie. *And Still the Waters Run.* Princeton, NJ: Princeton University Press, 1973.

Degler, Carl. *Out of Our Past.* New York: Harper, 1959.

Deloria, Ella. *Speaking of Indians.* New York: Friendship Press, 1944.

Deloria, Philip J. *Indians in Unexpected Places.* Lawrence: University of Kansas Press, 2004.

Deloria, Vine, Jr. *Behind the Trail of Broken Treaties: An Indian Declaration of Independence.* Austin: University of Texas Press, 1985. Originally published 1974.

———. *Custer Died for Your Sins: An Indian Manifesto.* Norman: University of Oklahoma Press, 1988. Originally published 1970.

———. *Of Utmost Good Faith.* San Francisco: Straight Arrow Books, 1971.

Deloria, Vine, Jr., and Raymond DeMallie. *Documents of American Indian Diplomacy: Treaties, Agreements, and Conventions, 1775–1979.* Norman: University of Oklahoma Press, 1999.

Denetdale, Jennifer. *The Long Walk: The Forced Navajo Exile.* New York: Chelsea House, 2007.

Denetdale, Jennifer Nez. *Reclaiming Diné History: The Legacies of Navajo Chief Manuelito and Juanita.* Tucson: University of Arizona Press, 2007.

Denevan, William M. "The Pristine Myth: The Landscape of the Americas in 1492." *Annals of the Association of America Geographers* 82, no. 3 (September 1992): 369–85.

Dennison, Jean. *Colonial Entanglement: Constituting a Twenty-First-Century Osage Nation.* Chapel Hill: University of North Carolina Press, 2012.

Dimock, Wai-chee. *Empire for Liberty: Melville and the Poetics of Individualism.* Princeton, NJ: Princeton University Press, 1989.

DiPeso, Charles. "Casas Grandes and the Gran Chichimeca." *El Palacio* 75 (Winter 1968).

Dobyns, Henry F. "Estimating Aboriginal American Population: An Appraisal of Techniques with a New Hemispheric Estimate." *Current Anthropology* 7 (1966).

———. *Native American Historical Demography: A Critical Bibliography.* Bloomington: University of Indiana Press, 1976.

———. *Their Number Become Thinned: Native American Population Dynamics in Eastern North America.* Knoxville: University of Tennessee Press/Newberry Library, 1983.

Dowd, Gregory Evans. *A Spirited Resistance: The North American Indian Struggle for Unity, 1745–1815.* Baltimore: Johns Hopkins University Press, 1993.

Downey, Roger. *Riddle of the Bones: Politics, Science, Race, and the Story of Kennewick Man.* New York: Springer, 2000.

Drinnon, Richard. *Facing West: The Metaphysics of Indian-Hating and Empire-Building.* Minneapolis: University of Minnesota Press, 1980.

———. *Keeper of Concentration Camps: Dillon S. Myer and American Racism.* Berkeley: University of California Press, 1987.

Dunbar-Ortiz, Roxanne. *Blood on the Border.* Boston: South End Press, 2006.

———. *Indians of the Americas: Human Rights and Self-Determination.* London: Zed Press, 1984.

———. *Roots of Resistance: History of Land Tenure in New Mexico.* Norman: University of Oklahoma Press, 2007.

Dunbar-Ortiz, Roxanne, ed. *Economic Development in American Indian Reservations.* Albuquerque: Native American Studies, University of New Mexico, 1979.

———. *The Great Sioux Nation: Sitting in Judgment on America.* Lincoln: University of Nebraska Press, 2013.

Duvall, Deborah L., Murv Jacob, and James Murray. *Secret History of the Cherokees: A Novel*. Tahlequah, OK: Indian Territory Press, 2012.

Echo-Hawk, Walter R. *In the Courts of the Conqueror: The 10 Worst Indian Law Cases Ever Decided*. Golden, CO: Fulcrum, 2010.

———. *In The Light of Justice: The Rise of Human Rights in Native America and the UN Declaration on the Rights of Indigenous Peoples*. Golden, CO: Fulcrum, 2013.

Edmunds, R. David. *Tecumseh and the Quest for American Indian Leadership*. Boston: Little, Brown, 1984.

Eisenhower, John S. D. *Intervention! The United States and the Mexican Revolution, 1913–1917*. New York: W. W. Norton, 1995.

Embree, Edwin R. *Indians of the Americas*. Boston: Houghton Mifflin, 1939.

Enloe, Cynthia. *Bananas, Beaches and Bases: Making Feminist Sense of International Politics*. Berkeley: University of California Press, 2000.

———. *Ethnic Soldiers: State Security in Divided Societies*. Athens: University of Georgia Press, 1982.

Erdrich, Louise. *The Round House*. New York: Harper, 2012.

Fanon, Frantz. *The Wretched of the Earth*. London: Penguin, 1967.

Faragher, John Mack, Mari Jo Buhle, Daniel Czitrom, and Susan Armitage. *Out of Many: A History of the American People*. New York: Prentice-Hall, 1994.

Federici, Silvia. *Caliban and the Witch: Women, the Body and Primitive Accumulation*. New York: Autonomedia, 2004.

Fellman, Michael. *Citizen Sherman: A Life of William Tecumseh Sherman*. Lawrence: University of Kansas Press, 1997.

Fiedel, Stuart J. *Prehistory of the Americas*, 2nd edition. New York: Cambridge University Press, 1992.

Foner, Eric. *Give Me Liberty! An American History*. New York: W. W. Norton, 2009.

Forbes, Jack D. *Apache, Navaho, and Spaniard*. Norman: University of Oklahoma, 1960.

———. *Native Americans and Nixon: Presidential Politics and Minority Self-Determination, 1960–1972*. Los Angeles: American Indian Studies Center, University of California, Los Angeles, 1981.

Frantz, Klaus. *Indian Reservations in the United States: Territory, Sovereignty, and Socioeconomic Change*. Chicago: University of Chicago Press, 1999.

Gates, Paul Wallace. *History of Public Land Law Development*. New York: Arno Press, 1979.

Getches, David H., Charles F. Wilkinson, and Robert L. Williams. *Cases and Materials on Federal Indian Law*. St. Paul, MN: West, 2006.

Goldstein, Alyosha. *Poverty in Common: The Politics of Community Action during the American Century*. Durham, NC: Duke University Press, 2012.

Gómez-Quiñones, Juan. *Indigenous Quotient: Stalking Words; American Indian Heritage as Future.* San Antonio, TX: Aztlán Libre Press, 2012.

Granberry, Julian. *The Americas That Might Have Been: Native American Social Systems through Time.* Tuscaloosa: University of Alabama Press, 2005.

Green, Patrick. *The People with No Name: Ireland's Ulster-Scots, America's Scots Irish, and the Creation of a British Atlantic World, 1689–1764.* Princeton, NJ: Princeton University Press, 2001.

Grenier, John. *The First Way of War: American War Making on the Frontier, 1607–1814.* New York: Cambridge University Press, 2005.

Gump, James O. "Civil Wars in South Dakota and South Africa: The Role of the 'Third Force.'" *Western Historical Quarterly* 34 (Winter 2003).

Hadden, Sally E. *Slave Patrols: Law and Violence in Virginia and the Carolinas.* Cambridge, MA: Harvard University Press, 2003.

Hahn, Steven. *A Nation under Our Feet: Black Political Struggles in the Rural South from Slavery to the Great Migration.* Cambridge, MA: Belknap Press of Harvard University Press, 2003.

Haig-Brown, Celia. *Resistance and Renewal.* Vancouver, British Columbia: Tillacum Library, 1988.

Hall, Frederic. *The Laws of Mexico: A Compilation and Treatise Relating to Real Property, Mines, Water Rights, Personal Rights, Contracts, and Inheritances.* San Francisco: A. L. Bancroft, 1885.

Hanson, Emma I. *Memory and Vision: Arts, Cultures, and Lives of Plains Indian People.* Cody, WY: Buffalo Bill Historical Center, 2007.

Hardt, Michael, and Antonio Negri. *Commonwealth.* Cambridge, MA: Harvard University Press, 2009.

———. *Empire.* Cambridge, MA: Harvard University Press, 2000.

———. *Multitude: War and Democracy in the Age of Empire.* New York: Penguin, 2005.

Harris, Charles H., III, and Louis R. Sadler. *The Texas Rangers and the Mexican Revolution: The Bloodiest Decade, 1910–1920.* Albuquerque: University of New Mexico Press, 2004.

Harvard Project on American Indian Economic Development. *The State of the Native Nations: Conditions under U.S. Policies of Self Determination.* New York: Oxford University Press, 2008.

Hedges, Chris. *Days of Destruction, Days of Revolt.* New York: Nation Books, 2012.

Heizer, Robert F. *The Destruction of California Indians: A Collection of Documents from the Period 1847 to 1865 in Which Are Described Some of the Things That Happened to Some of the Indians of California.* 1976; repr., Lincoln: University of Nebraska Press, 1993.

Herr, Michael. *Dispatches.* New York: Alfred A. Knopf, 1977.

Holton, Woody. *Unruly Americans and the Origins of the Constitution.* New York: Hill and Wang, 2007.

Horsman, Reginald. *Race and Manifest Destiny: The Origins of American Racial Anglo-Saxonism*. Cambridge, MA: Harvard University Press, 1981.

Hoxie, Frederick E., ed. *Encyclopedia of North American Indians: Native American History, Culture, and Life from Paleo-Indians to the Present*. Boston: Houghton Mifflin, 1996.

Hyman, Harold M. *American Singularity: The 1787 Northwest Ordinance, the 1862 Homestead and Morrill Acts, and the 1944 G.I. Bill*. Athens: University of Georgia Press, 2008.

Ifill, Sherrilyn. *On the Courthouse Lawn: Confronting the Legacy of Lynching in the 21st Century*. Boston: Beacon Press, 2007.

Immerman, Richard H. *Empire for Liberty: A History of American Imperialism from Benjamin Franklin to Paul Wolfowitz*. Princeton, NJ: Princeton University Press, 2010.

Jackson, Robert H., and Edward Castillo. *Indians, Franciscans, and Spanish Colonization: The Impact of the Mission System on California Indians*. Albuquerque: University of New México Press, 1995.

Jacobson, Dan. *The Story of Stories: The Chosen People and Its God*. New York: Harper and Row, 1982.

Jennings, Francis. "The Indians' Revolution." In *The American Revolution: Explorations in the History of American Radicalism*. Edited by Alfred F. Young. De Kalb: Northern Illinois University Press, 1976.

———. *The Invasion of America: Indians, Colonialism, and the Cant of Conquest*. New York: W. W. Norton, 1976.

Johannsen, Robert W. *To the Halls of the Montezumas: The Mexican War in the American Imagination*. New York: Oxford University Press, 1988.

Johansen, Bruce E. *Debating Democracy: Native American Legacy of Freedom*. Santa Fe, NM: Clear Light Books, 1998.

———. *The Forgotten Founders: Benjamin Franklin, the Iroquois, and the Rationale for the American Revolution*. Ipswich, MA: Gambit, 1981.

Johansen, Bruce E., ed. *Enduring Legacies: Native American Treaties and Contemporary Controversies*. Westport, CT: Praeger, 2004.

Johnson, Benjamin H. *Revolution in Texas: How a Forgotten Rebellion and Its Bloody Suppression Turned Mexicans into Americans*. New Haven, CT: Yale University Press, 2003.

Jorgensen, Joseph. *The Sun Dance Religion: Power for the Powerless*. Chicago: University of Chicago Press, 1977.

Kamen, Henry. *The Spanish Inquisition*. 2nd edition. New Haven, CT: Yale University Press, 1999.

Kaplan, Robert D. *Imperial Grunts: The American Military on the Ground*. New York: Random House, 2005.

Katz, William Loren. *Black Indians: A Hidden Heritage*. New York: Atheneum Books, 1986.

Keen, Benjamin. "The White Legend Revisited." *Hispanic American Historical Review* 51 (1971).

Kelly, Lawrence C. *The Assault on Assimilation: John Collier and the Origins of Indian Policy Reform*. Albuquerque: University of New Mexico Press, 1983.

Kelman, Ari. *A Misplaced Massacre: Struggling over the Memory of Sand Creek*. Cambridge, MA: Harvard University Press, 2013.

Kenner, Charles. *A History of New Mexico–Plains Indian Relations*. Norman: University of Oklahoma Press, 1969.

Killsback, Leo. "Indigenous Perceptions of Time: Decolonizing Theory, World History, and the Fates of Human Societies." *American Indian Culture and Research Journal* 37, no. 1 (2013).

King, Martin Luther, Jr. *Why We Can't Wait*. Boston: Beacon Press, 2011.

Kingston-Mann, Esther. "The Return of Pierre Proudhon: Privatization, Crime, and the Rules of Law." *Focaal: European Journal of Anthropology* (Fall 2006): 118–27.

Kinzer, Stephen. *Overthrow: America's Century of Regime Change from Hawaii to Iraq*. New York: Times Books, 2006.

Kiser, William S. *Dragoons in Apacheland: Conquest and Resistance in Southern New México, 1846–1861*. Norman: University of Oklahoma Press, 2013.

Knockwood, Isabelle. *Out of the Depths: The Experiences of Mi'kmaw Children at the Indian Residential School at Shubenacadie, Nova Scotia*. Lockeport, Nova Scotia: Roseway, 1992.

Kunz, Josef L. "The United Nations Convention on Genocide." *American Journal of International Law* 43, no. 4 (October 1949): 738–46.

Kuzmarov, Jeremy. *Modernizing Repression: Police Training and Nation-Building in the American Century*. Amherst: University of Massachusetts Press, 2012.

LaDuke, Winona. *The Militarization of Indian Country*. With Sean Cruz. 2nd edition. Minneapolis: Honor the Earth, 2012.

Lamar, Howard. *The Far Southwest, 1846–1912*. New Haven, CT: Yale University Press, 1966.

Lamphere, Louise. *To Run After Them: Cultural and Social Bases of Cooperation in a Navajo Community*. Tucson: University of Arizona Press, 1978.

Larner, Jess. *Mount Rushmore: An Icon Reconsidered*. New York: Nation Books, 2002.

Light, Steven Andrew, and Kathryn R. L. Rand. *Indian Gaming and Tribal Sovereignty: The Casino Compromise*. Lawrence: University Press of Kansas, 2005.

Linebaugh, Peter. *The Magna Carta Manifesto: Liberties and Commons for All*. Berkeley: University of California Press, 2008.

Lurie, Nancy Oestreich. "The World's Oldest On-Going Protest Demonstration: North American Indian Drinking Patterns." *Pacific Historical Review* 40, no. 3 (August 1971): 311–32.

Mankiller, Wilma, and Michael Wallis. *Mankiller: A Chief and Her People.* New York: St. Martin's Press, 1993.

Mann, Charles C. *1491: New Revelations of the Americas Before Columbus.* New York: Alfred A. Knopf, 2005.

Mantler, Gordon K. *Power of the Poor: Black-Brown Coalition and the Fight for Economic Justice, 1969–1974.* Chapel Hill: University of North Carolina, 2013.

Marriott, Alice, and Carol K. Rachlin. *American Indian Mythology.* New York: Thomas Y. Crowell, 1968.

Marszalek, John F. *Sherman: A Soldier's Passion for Order.* New York: Free Press, 1992.

Marx, Karl. *Capital: A Critique of Political Economy.* Volume 1. Mineola, NY: Dover, 2011. Originally published 1906.

McBeth, Sally. *Ethnic Identity and the Boarding School Experience.* Washington, DC: University Press of America, 1983.

McDougall, Walter A. *Promised Land, Crusader State: The American Encounter with the World Since 1776.* New York: Houghton Mifflin, 1997.

McGerr, Michael. *A Fierce Discontent: The Rise and Fall of the Progressive Movement in America, 1870–1920.* New York: Free Press, 2003.

McKeown, C. Timothy. *In the Smaller Scope of Conscience: The Struggle for National Repatriation.* Tucson: University of Arizona Press, 2013.

McLoughlin, William G. *After the Trail of Tears: The Cherokees' Struggle for Sovereignty, 1839–1880.* Chapel Hill: University of North Carolina Press, 1993.

McNickle, D'Arcy. *The Surrounded.* Albuquerque: University of New Mexico Press, 1978.

Meacham, Jon. *American Lion: Andrew Jackson in the White House.* New York: Random House, 2009.

Miller, Perry. *Errand in the Wilderness.* Cambridge, MA: Harvard University Press, 1956.

Miller, Robert J. "The International Law of Colonialism: A Comparative Analysis." In "Symposium of International Law in Indigenous Affairs: The Doctrine of Discovery, the United Nations, and the Organization of American States." Special issue, *Lewis and Clark Law Review* 15, no. 4 (Winter 2011): 847–922.

Miller, Susan A. *Coacoochee's Bones: A Seminole Saga.* Lawrence: University of Kansas Press, 2003.

Miller, Susan, and James Riding In. *Native Historians Write Back: Decolonizing American Indian History.* Lubbock: Texas Tech University Press, 2011.

Miner, H. Craig. *The Corporation and the Indian: Tribal Sovereignty and Industrial Civilization.* Columbia: University of Missouri Press, 1976.

Mooney, James M. *Historical Sketch of the Cherokee.* Chicago: Aldine Transacter, 1975. Originally published 1900.

Murguía, Alejandro. *The Medicine of Memory: A Mexican Clan in California.* Austin: University of Texas, 2002.

Nabokov, Peter. *Native American Testimony: A Chronicle of Indian-White Relations from Prophecy to the Present, 1492–2000.* New York: Penguin, 1999.

Navajo Community College. *Navajo Livestock Reduction: A National Disgrace.* Chinle, AZ: Navajo Community College Press, 1974.

Newcomb, Steven T. *Pagans in the Promised Land: Decoding the Doctrine of Christian Discovery.* Golden, CO: Fulcrum, 2008.

New Directions in Indian Purpose: Reflections on the American Indian Chicago Conference. Chicago: Native American Educational Services College Press, 1988.

Nielson, Richard Allen. "American Indian Land Claims." *University of Florida Law Review* 25, no. 2 (Winter 1972).

O'Brien, Jean M. *Firsting and Lasting: Writing Indians Out of Existence in New England.* Minneapolis: University of Minnesota Press, 2010.

O'Brien, Sharon. *American Indian Tribal Governments.* Norman: University of Oklahoma Press, 1989.

Ortiz, Simon J. *from Sand Creek: Rising in This Heart Which Is Our America.* Tucson: University of Arizona Press, 2000.

Owsley, Frank, Jr., and Gene A. Smith. *Filibusters and Expansionists: Jeffersonian Manifest Destiny, 1800–1821.* Tuscaloosa: University of Alabama Press, 1997.

Parish, William Jackson. *The Charles Ilfeld Company: A Study of the Rise and Decline of Mercantile Capitalism in New Mexico.* Cambridge, MA: Harvard University Press, 1961.

Phillips, Kevin. *The Cousins' Wars: Religion, Politics, and the Triumph of Anglo-America.* New York: Basic Books, 1999.

Philp, Kenneth R. *John Collier's Crusade for Indian Reform, 1920–1954.* Tucson: University of Arizona Press, 1977.

Pike, Zebulon Montgomery. *The Expeditions of Zebulon Montgomery Pike.* Edited by Elliott Coues. New York: F. P. Harper, 1895.

Price, David H. *Weaponizing Anthropology.* Oakland: AK Press, 2011.

Prucha, Francis Paul. *American Indian Treaties: The History of a Political Anomaly.* Lincoln: University of Nebraska Press, 1994.

Razack, Sherene. *Dark Threats and White Knights: The Somalia Affair, Peacekeeping, and the New Imperialism.* Toronto: University of Toronto Press, 2004.

Remini, Robert V. *Andrew Jackson and His Indian Wars.* New York: Viking, 2001.

———. *The Life of Andrew Jackson.* New York: Harper Perennial, 2010.

Reynolds, David S. *John Brown Abolitionist: The Man Who Killed Slavery, Sparked the Civil War, and Seeded Civil Rights.* New York: Alfred A. Knopf, 2005.

———. *Waking Giant: America in the Age of Jackson.* New York: Harper, 2008.

———. *Walt Whitman's America: A Cultural Biography.* New York: Vintage, 1995.

Richter, Daniel K. *Facing East from Indian Country: A Native History of Early America.* Cambridge, MA: Harvard University Press, 2001.

Robertson, Lindsey G. *Conquest by Law: How the Discovery of America Dispossessed Indigenous Peoples of Their Lands.* New York: Oxford University Press, 2005.

Rogin, Michael Paul. *Fathers and Children: Andrew Jackson and the Subjugation of the American Indian.* New Brunswick, NJ: Transaction, 1991.

Roosevelt, Theodore. *American Problems.* New York: Charles Scribner's Sons, 1926.

Rostlund, Erhard. *The Myth of a Natural Prairie Belt in Alabama: An Interpretation of Historical Records.* Washington, DC: Association of American Geographers, 1957.

Roth, Norman. *Conversos, Inquisition, and the Expulsion of the Jews from Spain.* Madison: University of Wisconsin Press, 1995.

Russell, James W. *Escape from Texas: A Novel of Slavery and the Texas War of Independence.* Cornwall-on-Hudson, NY: Sloan, 2012.

Sánchez-Albornoz, Claudio. *España, un enigma histórico*, vol. 1 Buenos Aires: Editorial Sudamericana, 1962.

Sanchez, Marie. *Treaty Council News* 1, no. 12 (October 1977).

Sando, Joe, and Herman Agoyo. *Po'Pay: Leader of the First American Revolution.* Santa Fe, NM: Clear Light, 2005.

Sandoz, Mari. *Cheyenne Autumn.* 1953; repr., Lincoln: University of Nebraska Press, 1992.

Saunt, Claudio. *A New Order of Things: Property, Power, and Transformation of the Creek Indians, 1733–1816.* New York: Cambridge University Press, 1999.

Sharma, Nandita, and Cynthia Wright. "Decolonizing Resistance, Challenging Colonial States." *Social Justice* 35, no. 3 (2009): 120–38.

Sheehan, Bernard. "Indian-White Relations in Early America." *William and Mary Quarterly* 3, no. 26 (1969).

Shreve, Bradley G. *Red Power Rising: The National Indian Youth Council and the Origins of Native Activism.* Norman: University of Oklahoma Press, 2011.

Sides, Hampton. *Blood and Thunder: An Epic of the American West.* New York: Random House, 2006.

Silbey, David J. *A War of Frontier and Empire: The Philippine-American War, 1899–1902*. New York: Hill and Wang, 2008.

Silverberg, Robert. *Mound Builders of Ancient America: The Archaeology of a Myth*. Greenwich, CT: New York Graphic Society, 1968.

Slotkin, Richard. *The Fatal Environment: The Myth of the Frontier in the Age of Industrialization, 1800–1890*. New York: Harper, 1985.

———. *Gunfighter Nation: The Myth of the Frontier in Twentieth-Century America*. New York: Atheneum, 1992.

———. *Regeneration through Violence: The Mythology of the American Frontier, 1600–1860*. Middletown, CT: Wesleyan University Press, 1973.

Smith, Andrea. *Conquest: Sexual Violence and American Indian Genocide*. Boston: South End Press, 2005.

———. "Native American Feminism, Sovereignty and Social Change." *Feminist Studies* 31, no. 1 (Spring 2005).

Smith, Maureen. "Forever Changed: Boarding School Narratives of American Indian Identity in the U.S. and Canada." *Indigenous Nations Studies Journal* 2, no. 2 (Fall 2001): 57–82.

Smith, Paul Chaat, and Robert Allen Warrior. *Like a Hurricane: The Indian Movement from Alcatraz to Wounded Knee*. New York: New Press, 1996.

Snow, David. "Prehistoric Southwestern Turquoise Industry." *El Palacio* 70 (June 1973).

Spencer, John D. *The American Civil War in the Indian Territory*. Oxford, UK: Osprey, 2006.

Spicer, Edward H. *Cycles of Conquest: The Impact of Spain, México, and the United States on the Indians of the Southwest, 1533–1960*. Tucson: University of Arizona Press, 1962.

Stannard, David E. *American Holocaust: The Conquest of the New World*. New York: Oxford University Press, 1992.

Starr, Emmet. *History of the Cherokee Indians and Their Legends and Folk Lore*. Oklahoma City: Warden, 1921.

Stegner, Wallace. *Where the Bluebird Sings to the Lemonade Springs: Living and Writing in the West*. New York: Random House, 1992.

Stewart, George R. *Names on the Land: A Historical Account of Place-Naming in the United States*. New York: New York Review Books, 2008.

Stone, Oliver, and Peter Kuznick. *The Untold History of the United States*. New York: Simon and Schuster, 2012.

Stone, William F. "Report on the Court of Private Land Claims." *Minutes of the New Mexico Bar Association Eighteenth Annual Session*. Santa Fe: New Mexico Bar Association, 1904.

Szabo, Franz A. J. *The Seven Years War in Europe: 1756–1763*. New York: Longman, 2007.

Takaki, Ronald T. *A Different Mirror: A History of Multicultural America*. New York: Little, Brown, 1993.

———. *Iron Cages: Race and Culture in 19th-Century America*. New York: Alfred A. Knopf, 1979.

Taliaferro, John. *Great White Fathers: The Story of the Obsessive Quest to Create Mount Rushmore*. New York: Public Affairs, 2002.

Taylor, Alan. *American Colonies: The Settling of North America*. New York: Viking, 2001.

Thomas, David Hurst. *Skull Wars: Kennewick Man, Archaeology, and the Battle for Native American Identity*. New York: Basic Books, 2000.

Thompson, Waddy, Jr. *Recollections of Mexico*. New York: Wiley and Putnam, 1836.

Thornton, Russell. *American Indian Holocaust and Survival: A Population History Since 1492*. Norman: University of Oklahoma Press, 1990.

Tinker, George E. *Missionary Conquest: The Gospel and Native American Cultural Genocide*. Minneapolis: Fortress Press, 1993.

Tocqueville, Alexis de. *Democracy in America*. Translated by Henry Reeve. New York: Colonial Press, 1900. Originally published 1838.

Townsend, Camilla. *Pocahontas and the Powhatan Dilemma*. New York: Hill and Wang, 2004.

Trennert, Robert A. *Alternative to Extinction: Federal Indian Policy and the Beginnings of the Reservation System, 1846–51*. Philadelphia: Temple University Press, 1975.

Tucker, Robert W., and David C. Hendrickson. *Empire of Liberty: The Statecraft of Thomas Jefferson*. New York: Oxford University Press, 1992.

Turner, Frederick Jackson. *The Frontier in American History*. New York: Henry Holt, 1920.

"United States v. Sandoval." *US Reports* 231 (1913).

Unrau, William E. *Indians, Alcohol, and the Roads to Taos and Santa Fe*. Lawrence: University Press of Kansas, 2013.

US General Accounting Office. *Treaty of Guadalupe Hidalgo: Findings and Possible Options Regarding Longstanding Community Land Grant Claims in New Mexico*, GAO-04-59. Washington, DC: Government Printing Office, 2004.

Utley, Robert M. *Cavalier in Buckskin: George Armstrong Custer and the Western Military Frontier*. Norman: University of Oklahoma Press, 2001.

———. *The Indian Frontier of the American West, 1846–1890*. Albuquerque: University of New México Press, 1984.

———. "The Ordeal of Plenty Horses." *American Heritage* 26 (December 1974).

Vine, David. *Island of Shame: The Secret History of the US Military Base on Diego Garcia*. Princeton, NJ: Princeton University Press, 2009.

Vizenor, Gerald. "Constitutional Consent: Native Traditions and Parchment Rights." In Vizenor and Doerfler, *The White Earth Nation*.

————. *Native Liberty: Natural Reason and Cultural Survivance*. Lincoln: University of Nebraska Press, 2009.

Vizenor, Gerald, and Jill Doerfler. *The White Earth Nation: Ratification of a Native Democratic Constitution*. Lincoln: University of Nebraska Press, 2012.

Vlasich, James A. *Pueblo Indian Agriculture*. Albuquerque: University of New Mexico Press, 2005.

Vogel, Virgil J. *American Indian Medicine*. Norman: University of Oklahoma Press, 1990.

Vowell, Sarah. *The Wordy Shipmates*. New York: Riverhead, 2008.

Washburn, Wilcomb E. *The Governor and the Rebel: A History of Bacon's Rebellion in Virginia*. Chapel Hill: University of North Carolina Press, 1957.

Waterman, Laura Wittstock, and Dick Bancroft. *We Are Still Here: A Photographic History of the American Indian Movement*. St. Paul: Minnesota Historical Society Press, 2013.

Watson, Blake. *Buying America from the Indians: "Johnson v. McIntosh" and the History of Native Land Rights*. Norman: University of Oklahoma Press, 2012.

Weaver, Jace. "A Lantern to See By: Survivance and a Journey into the Dark Heart of Oklahoma." In *Survivance: Narratives of Native Presence*. Edited by Gerald Vizenor. Lincoln: University of Nebraska Press, 2008.

Webb, James. *Born Fighting: How the Scots-Irish Shaped America*. New York: Broadway, 2005.

Weber, David J. *The Taos Trappers: The Fur Trade in the Far Southwest, 1540–1846*. Norman: University of Oklahoma Press, 1971.

West, Elliott. *The Contested Plains: Indians, Goldseekers, and the Rush to Colorado*. Lawrence: University Press of Kansas, 1998.

Westphall, Victor. *The Public Domain in New Mexico, 1854–1891*. Albuquerque: University of New Mexico Press, 1965.

White, Richard. *"It's Your Misfortune and None of My Own": A New History of the American West*. Norman: University of Oklahoma Press, 1991.

————. *Railroaded: The Transcontinentals and the Making of Modern America*. New York: W. W. Norton, 2011.

Wilcox, Michael V. *The Pueblo Revolt and the Mythology of Conquest: An Indigenous Archaeology of Contact*. Berkeley: University of California Press, 2009.

Wilentz, Sean. *Andrew Jackson*. New York: Henry Holt, 2005.

————. *The Rise of American Democracy: Jefferson to Lincoln*. New York: W. W. Norton, 2005.

Wilkins, David E. "Sovereignty, Democracy, Constitution: An Introduction." In Vizenor and Doerfler, *The White Earth Nation*.

Wilkinson, Charles. "Afterword." In *In the Courts of the Conqueror*. By Walter R. Echo-Hawk.

———. *Blood Struggle: The Rise of Modern Indian Nations.* New York: W. W. Norton, 2005.

Williams, Robert. *The American Indian in Western Legal Thought: The Discourses of Conquest.* New York: Oxford University Press, 1992.

Williams, Walter L. "United States Indian Policy and the Debate over Philippine Annexation: Implications for the Origins of American Imperialism." *Journal of American History* 66, no. 4 (March 1980): 810–31.

Williams, William Appleman. *Empire as a Way of Life: An Essay on the Causes and Character of America's Present Predicament along with a Few Thoughts about an Alternative.* New York: Oxford University Press, 1980.

Wilson, Waziyatawin Angela, ed. *In the Footsteps of Our Ancestors: The Dakota Commemorative Marches of the 21st Century.* St. Paul, MN: Living Justice Press, 2006.

Wilson, Waziyatawin Angela, and Wahpetunwin Carolyn Schommer. *Remember This! Dakota Decolonization and the Eli Taylor Narratives.* Lincoln: University of Nebraska Press, 2005.

Wolfe, Patrick. "Settler Colonialism and the Elimination of the Native." *Journal of Genocide Research* 8, no. 4 (December 2006): 387–409.

Womack, John, Jr., and Roxanne Dunbar-Ortiz. "Dreams of Revolution: Oklahoma, 1917." *Monthly Review* 62, no. 6 (November 2010): 41–56.

Zacks, Richard. *The Pirate Coast: Thomas Jefferson, the First Marines, and the Secret Mission of 1805.* New York: Hyperion, 2005.

Zinn, Howard. *A People's History of the United States, 1492–Present.* New York: HarperCollins, 1995.

INDEX